keyboard PRESENTS

SYNTH GODS

keyboard PRESENTS

SYNTH GODS

EDITED BY ERNIE RIDEOUT

An Imprint of Hal Leonard Corporation

Portions of this book are adapted from articles that originally appeared in *Keyboard* magazine.

Published in cooperation with Music Player Network, New Bay Media, LLC, and *Keyboard* magazines.
Keyboard magazine is a registered trademark of New Bay Media, LLC.

Published in 2011 by Backbeat Books
An Imprint of Hal Leonard Corporation
7777 West Bluemound Road
Milwaukee, WI 53213

Trade Book Division Editorial Offices
33 Plymouth St., Montclair, NJ 07042

Printed in the United States of America

Book design by Damien Casteneda

Library of Congress Cataloging-in-Publication Data
Synth gods / edited by Ernie Rideout.
p. cm.
ISBN 978-0-87930-999-2
1. Synthesizer players--Interviews. 2. Synthesizer (Musical instrument) I. Rideout, Ernie. II. Keyboard (Cupertino, Calif.)
ML1092.S96 2011
786.7'40922--dc22
[B]

2010041257

www.backbeatbooks.com

To the memory, spirit, and legacy of
Dr. Robert Moog, and to synth geeks
and synth gods everywhere

CONTENTS

INTRODUCTION

Most people get hooked on music because of a particular performer; they identify with the image the artist projects, or with the artist's style. Sometimes it's a lyric that resonates with the listener's mood. Often it's the audience that turns the newcomer into a fan; once you found a room full of others like you, wouldn't you want more of whatever it is that brought them together?

If you're the type who'll enjoy this book, though, you probably weren't attracted to music for any of those reasons. In contrast to the music fan, you probably got interested in music because of a particular sound, one that caught your ear and made you think, "What the hell is *that*?"

That sound was unique, and—depending on the decade—it sounded like nothing you had heard before. It was the sound of a synthesizer.

The next question was, of course, "*Who* is making that sound?" In most cases, that would be one of the 20 performers, composers, and designers featured in this book. These synthesizer pioneers influenced generation after generation of piano players, rock visionaries, mercurial composers, and computer geeks to get their hands on synthesizers and start figuring out how to make sounds with them. In fact, even the younger pioneers profiled in *Synth Gods* were set on their path by older trailblazers who are featured just a few pages away. As you'll see, they all influenced each other.

In addition to the mastery of musical concepts, the process of creating sounds on the synthesizers available in the 1960s and '70s also required wrestling with machine-like pieces of electronics and learning no small amount of theory behind the circuitry. This demanded considerable technical ability—an altogether different skill than the artist's musical talent.

Creating music on synthesizers also posed a public relations problem—and it does so today as it did in the early days: Many listeners believed synths and computers to be one and the same. Why were these musicians letting computers do all the work for them? they wondered. What happened to good old-fashioned musicianship?

Even if you still harbor this misapprehension, the stories in the following pages will disabuse you of it. You'll learn how these artists worked not against the technology but with it—and in many cases within it and even with the designers who invented it—to extend their musicality. The musicians you'll read about in *Synth Gods* didn't just come up with sounds that had never been heard before, they created music that had never been conceived before.

Too big a claim? Read for yourself about how Wendy Carlos created incredibly expressive melodies one note at a time, recording every other note on separate tracks, so the envelope and timbre of each note could be slightly different. The funkiest synth bass lines in pop music were played by Stevie Wonder, but you'll be amazed at the size of the instrument he played on some of his greatest hits, and you'll be surprised to learn that Malcolm Cecil and Robert Margouleff were both playing the instrument simultaneously with him. Brian Eno envisioned soundscapes that only synthesizers could realize—and he purposely never repaired his synths, so that their imperfections would always add an element of unpredictability.

The one thing that is definitely not shared among the synth gods in this book: styles of music. From Edgar Winter's ARP 2600 monster rock sound to the delicate textures of Tomita's Moog modular orchestrations, you'll find an amazing range of genres. And even within these, you'll find extremes: Jan Hammer's lightning-fast Minimoog lead lines and Joe Zawinul's vibrant multi-synth palette are both legendary in the world of jazz.

Some of our synth gods aren't known for their musical abilities, but rather for their technological vision. Arguably, Dr. Robert Moog did more than any other single instrument designer to shape the sound of modern music, inventing the parameters, features, and circuitry by which all synthesizers are judged. Dave Smith built on Bob Moog's achievements, designing synths that extended the keyboardist's arsenal and defined the sound of a generation of pop. In addition to being geniuses, Bob and Dave each reprised their roles as leaders in the world of synthesis by releasing updated designs of their classic instruments; it's the story of this renewed success that we chronicle here in *Synth Gods*.

The profiles that follow are snapshots of artists at particular points in their careers, but by no means are these from the same time period. Taken from the archives of *Keyboard* magazine, the interviews span the entire publication history of the magazine, from the mid-'70s to the present day. Since there are only 20 artists presented, there are obviously some artists not represented; look for them in one of the other books in the *Keyboard Presents* series: *The Music of the '80s* and *Classic Rock*.

There is other artistry at work here as well: The writers of the profiles in *Synth Gods* are part of an elite group, commonly known as the *Keyboard* magazine chain gang, all of them top-notch musicians and avid synthesists, as well as being hard-boiled journalists. Only talented synth geeks like Dominic Milano, Robert L. Doerschuk, Greg Rule, Ken Hughes, and Jim Aikin could provide such insightful commentary as you'll read in the following pages.

Finally, for all the varied experience and diverging fields of interest of the synth gods in this book, there is one sure thing they all have in common: they'd hardly ever use a preset sound. If this is true for you too, then you're going to have a lot of fun with *Synth Gods*.

Ernie Rideout
San Francisco, 2010

keyboard

PRESENTS

SYNTH GODS

RICHARD BARBIERI

1 MORPHING ANALOG SYNTH ARTISTRY INTO THE DIGITAL REALM

by Scott Healy and Paul Tingen

Portions of this chapter appeared in the December 1993 and June 2008 issues of Keyboard *magazine.*

"No!" exclaims Richard Barbieri, a look of horror in his eyes. Our question—"Have you ever used presets?"—seemed innocuous, but for Barbieri it stabbed into the heart of his identity as a keyboard player.

"I've never used them in my life," he insists. "And I never will. I've used sam-

Richard Barbieri onstage recently with Porcupine Tree, surrounded by his fave gear: Access Virus Indigo 2, Roland V-Synth, Ensoniq VFX, Roland JV-2080, Alesis NanoPiano, and Roland SH-201. (© Fernando Aceves/ Retna Ltd.)

ples as the basis for a sound sometimes, but that's all. I don't see the point in using presets. You'll just end up sounding like somebody else, and there is already so little individuality in electronic music today."

Barbieri's music reflects his sonic standards. He began creating his own sounds—warm, organic, dynamic, often breathy—with the band Japan in the late '70s and early '80s. Together with singer David Sylvian, he built an identity for the group based on innovative synth orchestrations. The culmination of their labor was Japan's magnum opus, *Tin Drum*, released in 1982. On those sessions, Barbieri and Sylvian drove producer/engineer Steve Nye to distraction by programming and tweaking for days on end. The results, an incredibly rich variety of synth colors, are particularly impressive because a Sequential Prophet-5, an Oberheim OB-X, and, occasionally, a Roland System 700 were the only synths they used.

"We took such care over each individual sound that we got quite paranoid about all the sounds being new and different," Barbieri recalls. "My big influence on that album was Stockhausen, especially the abstract electronic things he was doing in the late '50s. Listen to a track like 'Ghosts,' for example, and you'll hear all these metal-like sounds that hardly have a pitch yet subconsciously suggest a melody."

Since Japan's demise in 1982, Barbieri has worked on a variety of projects, often involving other former Japan members, including the group's reunion album, *Rain Tree Grow*, in 1991. His stage rig in the early '90s was characteristically sparse, in contrast to the mode of the day, in which keyboardists surrounded themselves with dozens of synths and modules. "People only have stacks of keyboards because they use the presets," he fumes. "When they run out of presets, they want something that at first sounds very different, even though it's not. With these digital keyboards, when you strip away the effects, the sounds are awful, with all kinds of digital buzzing, graininess, and glitches between the sample loops, whereas with analog synths you're working with a pure waveform. You start with a purity that you can affect as you go along. That's why I work in a very primitive way. I don't do a lot of sampling; to me, it's much more interesting to put cassettes with things like choirs or didgeridoo through my System 700, which can take outside sound sources and synthesize them. The point is, when you know a lot about the architectural process, you can program pretty much any sound you want."

In the early '90s, rather than rely on effects built into digital synth presets, Barbieri added a breathy dimension to his analog sounds with delicate touches of white and pink noise. He also enjoyed bringing modulation, stereo panning, and reverb in and out to create a sense of movement. Once he finished programming, he sweetened the results with liberal applications of effects, usually from his Roland SBF-325 stereo flanger and Roland SDE-3000 digital delay, with additional reverb from his Lexicon PCM-70, Yamaha SPX90II, and Korg SRV; distortion from Sound City pedals; and ring mod from a custom-built box.

In 2008, he released his first solo recording, *Things Buried*, a lush sonic journey whose intensity comes from Richard's craft of sound design and manipulation and draws a compelling contrast to his role as keyboardist in the rich and edgy progressive art-metal-pop band Porcupine Tree. His palette with the group varies from thick prog pads and strings to icy pianos and burning leads, an arsenal he constantly tweaks in real time onstage. In the studio, his approach is similar, but regardless of location, for Richard, the performance of the sounds is the key.

Electronic pop music was born in the world of bulky modules and messy patch cords, and soon became the realm of those who could consistently coax musically useful sounds out of some early synthesizers, most of which were underpowered, quirky, expensive, and built with obtuse interfaces. Players like Barbieri, who came up in that challenging age, have a different outlook than the archetypal modern music superstore shopper. The programming techniques that, at the time, seemed the invention of necessity (or perhaps of sonic deprivation) became valuable skills, which electronic pop and rock musicians would later turn toward. And Barbieri's work remains true to that pop-electronica lineage: You won't hear solos, or even standard song form. But what you will hear, like in good orchestral music, is the beauty in the details. Rich sound layers meld, while sonic motifs build and morph into other musical textures as the track moves through the electronic landscape.

To some digerati, the onset of digital synthesis, sampling, and now inexpensive, one-touch synths might render Barbieri's hard-won skill set quaint at best.

But the variety, depth, and the intensity of the sound design and real-time sound manipulation on *Things Buried* and *Fear of a Blank Planet* amply demonstrate how his abilities are more relevant now than ever; with so much sonic clay commercially available, it falls on artists like Barbieri to express and codify electronic music, to make it organic and real.

Who are your sonic influences?

From an experimental point, Stockhausen, and all the early electronic experimental stuff he was doing in the '50s and '60s. From an abstract sound point of view, Eno and Ryuichi Sakamoto in the early days were quite an influence on me. In terms of playing and playing sounds, Joe Zawinul. I'm not a great lover of jazz keyboards, but for me Zawinul was so different, because he used to create these sounds and then play them as the sounds should be played—he would get a beautiful flute sound, or some kind of exotic wind instrument sound, and he'd just play it right, with sensitivity. And that's really amazing programming. Early Vangelis; I was listening to the *Blade Runner* soundtrack the other day and it's just amazing. If you really want some saturated analog sounds, that's a beautiful album. And the early stuff from Tangerine Dream, Edgar Froese, the early analog sequencer music, Kraftwerk. I loved all of those sounds and approaches.

Your work with the band Japan was very influential. What synth resources did you have at your disposal?

The *Tin Drum* album was an important one in terms of synthesis, because we were working with real limitations. I had two synthesizers, an Oberheim OB-Xa and Roland System 700, and David Sylvian had a Prophet-5. That's a really valuable process for keyboardists to go through, to try to do something working with limitations, maybe working with only one synthesizer. Then you tend to find things within it. You can get very lost, because there's so much available now. In the end it's better to keep to two or three instruments and really get to the bottom of what's going on with each, and not just play a few presets.

Your first solo recording, *Things Buried*, was recorded digitally. That means nothing analog, not even synths?

Basically, it means I didn't use any analog synths, for the first time on any recording in my career. I had gotten into a real comfort zone with the old analog stuff and, as much as I love it, I thought this would be a good challenge. I want to embrace the new technology as well as the old. I thought, well, let's do the whole album with software, and see if I can get it sounding warm, if I can work with the textures the way I always used to.

What specific software instruments did you use?

A lot of it was Native Instruments software, like the Pro-53 and Absynth, but

I've also been using the synths in Reason quite a bit. I've been doing some programming for Reason, and I really got into Subtractor and Maelstrom. And to be honest, if you're working with subtractive synthesis in a software format, then I think you can more or less get what you want. I can make it sound like a Prophet-5 if I want to. If you have the sound in your head, then you can achieve that.

You obviously spend a lot time on your sounds, probably more than most keyboard players.

It's mainly because of lack of ability. I'm self-taught and I'm not a technical keyboard player. I didn't grow up knowing the scales and I didn't know how to play blues progressions, jazz progressions—all that was completely alien to me. So I just started making the sound do something, rather than my fingers. I would create sounds that evolved over ten or more seconds. I would put more features into the sound, more modulation, various kinds of effects that would come and go, filtering, panning, and LFOs. That for me was the way forward, especially hearing what Brian Eno was doing with Roxy Music in the '70s. I thought, well this is interesting, because it's quite abstract, but it's working in the context of pop music.

When your parts move and change over a few seconds, the effect is an undulating and moving part or layer. Where most keyboard players might cut and paste or loop a section, you seem to perform it.

I do. I try to avoid MIDI, to be honest. I like the performance aspect, so I don't want to get caught in that cut-and-paste kind of thing that people do sometimes when they're working with computer software. And I try not to look at the screen; people now are watching music more than actually listening, working with chunks of information and blocks and passages. I like to do most things manually, so I'll set the bpm, and I don't care if it's a half-millisecond out of time. I'll just try to get a groove going and play right through the track, but play with the synths in real time as I go. That way when I listen back to something, I'm thinking, "It's nice that changes there and this happens here." It wouldn't work in a cut-and-paste way where, well, once you've heard eight bars, you've heard it.

You seem to be discovering new aspects of a sound as you're playing it, as the sound morphs and changes. I'm thinking in particular of a sound on "Medication Time" from *Things Buried*, a warbley, lowpass filter thing with a cool envelope. It starts off as a melodic idea, then it becomes a bass. It sounds improvised.

Yes, that formed the basis of the track. It was improvised. That was on an Access Virus Indigo.

In addition to the virtual instruments, what other synths are you using for recording?

The hardware synths that I use are the Virus, the Roland V-Synth series, and the Roland SH-201. And then I use the 201 to control the computer and the software. I also use the M-Audio Radium 49.

There's tremendous layering in your music. How do you go about achieving a balance and finding a space for each sound?

It's tricky if you're just working with synths. They're not as defined as guitar, bass guitar, or drums. They have their place and their own frequency. With synths, anything goes, so it is a lot harder. In the end, unconsciously, I probably work out the frequencies and what needs to happen. I just go with whatever works, what things are working well in context with others, what creates nice combinations of sounds and textures.

> "It's tricky if you're just working with synths. They're not as defined as guitar, bass guitar, or drums."

It's interesting that you mentioned your comfort zone earlier; you and other artists in the early days of keyboards were all working outside your comfort zones.

All those keyboard players who were great in the beginning with the limited analog stuff, when digital came along, to me, their work became less what I wanted to hear. Not so many people took to the digital era, whereas now, the people pushing the envelope with digital synthesis are groups like Aphex Twin and Boards of Canada. These kinds of artists love the analog stuff, but they embrace the digital because it's what they've grown up with, in the way that Edgar Froese would have had the huge modular systems.

Regarding your own work, in writing music that doesn't have traditional song form or solos, how do you sustain interest over a long song? What do you listen for when you write?

That's the whole artistic dilemma, isn't it? Is what we think of as interesting to us, personally, interesting to people listening? I suppose when I'm writing, I just do what keeps me interested. It sounds a bit pretentious, but it's almost like going into a trance. You start something, and you take it down a certain path, and you see if that's an interesting journey, or whether there's nothing there. That's why making a solo album is always something I was a bit apprehensive about, because you're working on your own. Working with people is a lot easier, because you've got things to play off of, and you've got feedback. Whereas when you're on your own, you know what you're going to play, and you want to surprise yourself—and that's a lot harder to do.

Do you think it's ironic that some of the best music was made with some of the worst gear?

You're right. That's how I feel. I know everybody's nostalgic for the music that was there when they were growing up, but I firmly believe that the '70s were such a great time for all kinds of music—electronic, soul, heavy rock, progressive rock, dance, anything. There was such a variation of sounds and artists at that time.

It's hard to recapture that spirit because so much of that music came from artists working within strict boundaries.

Absolutely. Going back to Eno again, that was one of the things that he was interested in: using the studio as an instrument. You just kind of accepted what you were working with and that was it. That was the limit. And you just did everything you could to get every variation out of those instruments and out of those effects.

I read a quote by Steve Wilson in which he was talking about the idea behind *Fear of a Blank Planet*: "Everything has become so easily accessible that none of it means anything anymore." I imagine this might apply to you as an electronic musician. How do we find true meaning in sound among the vast amount of available sonic technology?

It comes from within yourself. I don't think the actual gear, software, and designs are the important things. The important thing is the idea that you have in your head, or the emotion that you have in your heart, and your relationship with music. I believe that the personalities of musicians are very much part of the music that they make. If you have an idea about what you want to do, then it doesn't matter what particular instrument you play. I read these synth forums and I hear kids saying, "Wow, man, I've got to have that synth because I need to make dance music!" or "No, I can't do this track until I get this new software," or "I can't write a bass line unless I have this keyboard." They get it in their minds that it's all about the gear, and that gear is going to be their answer. You get a piece of equipment, or any technology, and you think, "Right, this is going to make my life easier." But in the end it's got nothing to do with that. It's what's in your own mind and what you're going to do personally.

A SELECTED RICHARD BARBIERI DISCOGRAPHY

SOLO
Stranger Inside
Things Buried

WITH PORCUPINE TREE
In Absentia
Deadwing
Fear of a Blank Planet

WITH JAPAN
Tin Drum

FOR MORE INFORMATION ON RICHARD BARBIERI, VISIT www.richardbarbieri.net.

2 WENDY CARLOS

MUSIC FROM A MOUNTAIN OF MOOG

by Dominic Milano and Dr. Robert A. Moog

Portions of this chapter appeared in the December 1979 and November 1982 issues of Keyboard *magazine.*

The '70s have been a good decade for keyboard music, thanks in no small part to the advent of the synthesizer. It's easy to forget that this now-ubiquitous instrument was largely unknown until the release, in 1968, of a groundbreaking album called *Switched-On Bach*.

Wendy Carlos at her legendary Moog Modular, circa 1979. (Courtesy of *Keyboard* magazine)

Switched-On Bach was the creation of Walter Carlos, a young and reclusive electronic music genius who was the first to realize what potent musical resources were offered by the combination of multitrack taping techniques and the voltage-controlled modular synthesizer gear being developed by Robert Moog. Working in their home studio, Carlos and producer Rachel Elkind painstakingly assembled synthesized versions of a number of well-known Bach pieces. Columbia Records pressed and released the results, and it quickly became apparent that they had a hit on their hands. The barriers that had isolated electronic music were broken down as listeners became aware that there was something new, something musically enjoyable to be heard in Bob Moog's instrument.

For synthesists, *Switched-On Bach* continues to be perhaps the most influential album ever released. It has defined the terms by which the synthesizer is judged. The technical expertise with which it was recorded was unquestionable, the precedent it set undeniable, and the impact it had controversial. The controversy: Two people in a recording studio were creating very orchestral tone colors, and in fact putting together electronic versions of orchestral music. There were more than a few symphony musicians who feared that the next step would be an automated orchestra, that violinists and oboists would shortly find themselves unemployed. But the word "automation" is misleading, because there is nothing automatic about the way Carlos and Elkind arrive at their synthesizer realizations. The great pains Carlos takes in performing every single line, often recording only one note at a time, renders any thought of automation ludicrous. Things are done the hard way in the Carlos/Elkind studio, because there aren't any shortcuts for getting an expressive performance out of a synthesizer, any more than there are for any other instrument. In fact, the number of musicians who have followed in Carlos' footsteps has so far been disappointingly small; the time-consuming nature of the process (and the expense of the necessary equipment) have probably daunted many would-be studio synthesists.

The Carlos/Elkind output hasn't been extensive, either—five albums, one a double, in the decade since *Switched-On Bach*—but meticulous attention to expressiveness is a hallmark throughout. *The Well-Tempered Synthesizer* with its interpretations of Bach, Monteverdi, Scarlatti, and Handel; *Switched-On Bach II* with its dangerously espressivo moments; *By Request* with its variety of classical and popular selections; the score for Stanley Kubrick's film *A Clockwork Orange* with its brilliant and unnerving realization of the last movement of Beethoven's Ninth Symphony complete with a vocoder-generated chorale—five years before anyone knew what a vocoder was—and even the iconoclastic *Sonic Seasonings* with its marriage of *musique concrete* and synthesized sounds, all bear eloquent witness to this point. The understanding of orchestral nuance displayed is on a par with what is found on many orchestral recordings, and the complexity of the process by which this is made audible makes it a miraculous achievement.

Carlos and Elkind themselves have always shunned the spotlight, with no photos of them appearing on the albums and virtually no public appearances during the last seven years. The reason for this reticence finally became public knowledge with the publication of the May 1979 issue of *Playboy*, in which the former Walter Carlos revealed that she had undergone a sex-change operation and was now Wendy Carlos. Wendy Carlos' openness has made it possible for the first time to examine in depth a number of aspects of her musicmaking, not least of which is the nature of her artistic collaboration with Rachel Elkind. Elkind, it now becomes clear, is much more than a producer. Each of them provides necessary ingredients that the other lacks. Rachel provides perspective when Wendy gets so involved in the detail work of synthesis that she loses sight of the whole. Wendy is the performer, while Rachel frequently provides ideas of what to perform. When you listen to them talk, you quickly realize that they are reciprocal extensions of one another. They work together symbiotically, using their home studio with its four multitrack tape decks, mammoth Moog modular synthesizer, custom mixing deck, quad monitor system, Steinway grand, and other sundry devices to create music that has yet to be surpassed or even closely imitated.

How would you describe your style of orchestration?

One of the particularly distinctive qualities of Rachel's and my work has to do with breaking up phrases into different colors and displacing certain notes and colors spatially across a four-channel field, although most people end up hearing our work in stereo now that quad is dead. We call it pointillism or hocketing. It's this distribution of many notes and many colors between many tracks that is one of the most distinctive qualities of our orchestration style. We don't limit this distribution to just doubling notes, either. We separate single notes and groups of notes and interlocking sequences of notes. This allows you to change timbre constantly. The best example I can think of outside our work is Ravel's orchestration of Mussorgsky's *Pictures at an Exhibition*. We thought that we'd found something new with this sort of hocketing, but having looked at a Ravel score about ten years ago, we found that it was nothing new at all.

Do you think in terms of orchestral timbres rather than in terms of timbres specific to the synthesizer when you orchestrate a piece?

It depends on what we're trying to do, but I think so. We'd like to get away from the thing that we've sort of become trapped into with synthesizers. The synthesizer has to have its own literature. That takes time. Right now on our piano, and it's been there for about a year and a half, are the beginning sketches for a piece that's a homage to Ravel. I have an affinity for his head and the way he worked. There's a certain kind of pulling-a-rabbit-out-of-a-hat magic that Ravel was extraordinarily good at, and it ties in with what Rachel and I try to do. He was a very color-oriented composer, whereas many composers I know nowadays are much more harmonically or rhythmically oriented. That's secondary to us. We're much more concerned with color. Instead of thinking piano rewritten for orchestra, we're invariably thinking color first. It's not, "Here's what it would sound like on the piano," It's the other way around. Lines become linear, and harmony arises from a coincidence of several lines at one time.

Have you gotten tired of your analog synthesizer?

Rachel and I often come down into the studio and say, "Boring!" These were bells and whistles [miscellaneous gadgets] that we installed back about the time of the first and second records to control as much as we could. It hasn't changed a whole lot since. We've made a few minor shifts—we've added the new oscillators which are much more stable.

What do you do for pitch-bending?

I have a button off to the left of the keyboard by the master volume control that controls the portamento on/off. I use it to fill in the gaps when I play chromatically. That way I can control the time between bending pitches by playing on the keyboard rather than using a rotary control or a ribbon, neither of which I like. With the portamento rate set at 5, you can get all kinds of different speeds; if you look at them on a scope, they're the same, but they don't sound that way. I don't feel comfortable doing it any other way. That may be prejudice on my part. I guess the Yamaha's felt strip is the only one I think I could get to like. When I bought the synthesizer back in '65 or '66, I asked Bob if he could come up with a capacitance switch to delay the intervals between each 1/12-volt step. It seemed like a natural thing to want to do, so Bob came back with the portamento and hold switch. Before the hold switch was put on, if you took your hand off the keyboard, the frequency went to 12Hz or something. It was terrible until Bob came up with that. That was back when it really felt like you were working with an invention. I miss that time. Bob Moog has a wonderful feeling about music. It was perfect for me because it's hard for me to talk about things, and between the two of us there was a vocabulary that spoke telegraphically.

Have you been aware of the battle against the idea that the synthesizer plays itself?

In the beginning, so many people used to think of the synthesizer as being a computer. Now that they see the keyboard they think of it as an organ, which is equally fallacious. That computer idea has stuck, and I think there is an expectation that this is something that never needs to be practiced on. Somehow, the boring part, the work, is supposed to be removed by the machine. But if anything, it's as tedious and as boring as any of the other instruments that you can name. I don't think the quality of electronics has any bearing on the work that a performer needs to do. It's you arguing with your hands rather than you arguing against the device your hands control.

Do you feel people need to know more about the instruments they play in order to play them more effectively?

It's nice to realize that all of this kind of technical background is something that we need, it's part of the tools that we need so that we can function and to move forward in our own field. That way we won't perish. There's always gonna be room for people who don't know the technical side, but back in Bach's day, you had to know how to handle tunings on a pipe organ, and you'd probably have a tracker organ which had a few extra keys, because it was intended to be used with mean-tone tuning sometimes, or he'd flatten his steps a little more so that the thirds would be a little truer, and then he could play in the main keys that he was interested in; and some of the historical notes suggest that even with his traditional keyboards—clavichord, harpsichord—he tended to favor making the common keys smoother, as they say, with smaller fifths, at the expense of the further-away keys. So they had to know a lot about acoustics, too. If a string harpsichord broke a key, you had to know a little bit about wood, mechanics—it's the technology of its day, after all. And the string itself, unkinking it so it will have a purer tone. There are a lot of subtleties that go on that we take for granted, because wood, wire, mechanics, what's that? It's technology.

All of those technologies required a new set of rules to understand how to make music with them.

And so will digital. And so does an analog synthesizer. All of this stuff is so much less different than people think it is, from the past, that it scares me. I mean, how did the PR people ever convince everyone that all of this stuff is either too complicated to know, or scary in any way? How is it any different, ultimately, from what came before, from what determined the way violins got made, and brass trumpets got tuned? All of that stuff is science and technology in the service of art. And your background, as with mine, as with many people I know who practice this art, is a hybrid background, of necessity. And it's always been that way. It's not kooky, it's not strange, we're not crazy people running around kind of salivating with our pocket calculators hanging out. It's not that at all.

You were talking about *Sonic Seasonings*, saying it started off as an irreverent piece. How so?

Oh, I was the one who wasn't serious about it. We were having a little problem with Columbia, and they appeared to be disinterested in us, because of not having a real artist that they could have in pictures and stuff, and running around concertizing, which is, after all, the way most record careers are carried out. Very few people just put things down on record. So there just was not as much excitement as there had been in the beginning. And I just nastily said to Rachel, "Well, if it's not gonna sell, and it's not gonna be put in the stores, and it's not gonna be available, then it doesn't matter what we do. Let's just do any old thing, and put it on tape and release it." And we started out with, "How about something to do with the four seasons, there are four of them so we can make two records, one season per side, and we can use a lot of natural sounds. Let's see what we can do with it." Well, it turned out that once we came up with the idea of working with sounds like that, then *aha*! It doesn't have to be so simple, we can make sound collages and things that use *musique concrete* practice that both of us had been in love with for many years, things I had done back in university and pre-university days. God, this is gonna make me sound old, but I've been working with electronic music since '56 or '57. I guess my parents still have some tapes somewhere in their basement that have some of those old pieces. Of course, it was mostly *concrete* then, plus whatever you could get out of a laboratory oscillator and splice into some kind

> "There are a lot of subtleties that go on that we take for granted, because wood, wire, mechanics, what's that? It's technology."

of shape. So we applied that type of technology to things that we could record from nature. Also, Rachel has the ability to imitate many sounds with her voice, insects and frogs and birds and things, and we started using those. It grew as a tapestry. Things became woven in. We tried things and yanked them out, and tried other layers and yanked them out, and then we started to do things that had been technological ideas that I had harbored for a long while, one that it turned out Terry Riley had used, two tape machines at some distance apart being used in a tape loop, so that you get long-period delay. I had wondered what would happen if we started VFOing [variable-frequency oscillator] and ring-modulating the output before it goes back to the input, and doing other things on top of that to process it as well, crossing over, sending one cue to the echo chamber, one direct line, letting it flip-flop first and then come in later. Just hardware-oriented games, challenges. But out of such little games, not surprisingly, improvisational techniques can somehow come in, and we started to impose our own disciplines. And before you knew it, we had quite a few reels that had some very interesting things. That wetted our whistles. And then it started to take—it grew. It was—the word's been overused, but it's a valid one—it was an organic process for us.

There has been a noticeable progression in the way you use your envelopes. Early on they were almost always very plucked. Was that conscious?

Yeah, that was my decision. Tom Rhea is writing some of the notes for the *Complete Brandenburgs*, and he was very concerned about that one detail, the idea of plucked envelopes, saying somehow they work very well. And yes, I guess they did, and I had not even noticed that we had moved into more orchestral envelopes, which are never quite that plucked except when it's deliberate, when that kind of a sound is used to cut across the other types. So I guess our attack times have slipped to longer and longer values, and there are many more overlapping envelopes that occur during the durations of the sounds, so that the sound has many hard-to-hear and very subtle, yet complicated, little motions and shifts occurring in each individual note. Whereas in the old days it tended to be much more of the, well, never really three patch cord kind of sounds, but maybe no more than a half a dozen or a dozen patch cords, whereas now we seldom use less than 20 or 30 patch cords or the equivalent with switches. Yeah, our complexity has gone up. And the self-consciousness with which we look at things like super-hard attacks, high degrees of regeneration in the filter, has inhibited us from doing quite so much of it. So we've moved away from these and gone into what really is a smaller range of controls. We don't go quite so extreme, but within that range, we find now where we thought there were only three or four variations in tone color, there may be a good dozen or two.

We've heard that in a legato passage, rather than playing on a monophonic keyboard where the notes don't really overlap, you would layer each note. Do you really do that?

Not all the time. There's no one hard, fast rule. When you play a fast passage on the organ, even if you play staccato, one sound is still carrying over while the next one is attacking, so you have to have the overlap, but you can't get a group of oscillators to do that when you treat them monophonically. The only way to handle that, in the end, with this particular instrument, is to put one on one set of tracks, and one on another, and so on—a process called "sel-syncing." Of course we could discuss how overdubbing and sel-syncing practices have been tied into Rachel's and my own performances, as though they're inherent to electronic music or synthesizers, when all they are is inherent to sel-syncing. It's possible because of sel-syncing, but it's also something that one could devise a piece of hardware that would expedite, make it possible to do without recourse to this difficult method. The very first instance where we used this technique was actually on *Switched-On Bach*, in the "C Minor Prelude." There's a place where you had filled-in chords, which were done grouping several tracks together, playing the first note, then back up, yah-da, then back up, yah-da-da, collecting them in that manner. So you build your arpeggio on many tracks, and is that a hard way to work, boy! Talk about going cuckoo. But anyway, we still do things like that. We do a great many of these types of difficult animation-style ways of working instead of playing lines down in layers, and that might account greatly for the difference in sound that our records have compared to any other people's of our kind of music.

How do you arrive at a decision as to which colors go where?

Colors in general are done much in the way an orchestrator works. You make little sketches, you play the thing through on one color, you kind of hear little things, you make little notations—try triangle, try choral tone here, try a simple percussive sound here, making little sketches in pencil or just remembering it. And then as you go along and start fleshing it out, the decisions become pretty obvious to your ear. But there are a certain number of colors. I mean after all, the synthesizer doesn't have very many colors. You've got bright to dull, and if you want you can use effects, and hard to soft attacks. So there are maybe 20 basic colors, and that's it, really. You can say there are more, but really there are not. And you can do what you want to do, but you can never eliminate that inherent few colors. The orchestra just has more colors. So to get around that problem, you have to change colors quickly. You use square for a moment and then don't use it at all for quite a while, and when it comes back again it's very fresh because you've been hearing sawtooth and nasty little pulse waves, and then suddenly . . . . The square wave makes it impossible to use triangular, which is mostly also odd harmonics, because your ear has just heard that. So it's better to go to a sinusoid with a little added filtered sawtooth, which has all the harmonics in it, so then when you come to triangle, by the contrast effect it sounds like something new. I'll never forget Bob Moog's comment when he first heard the first movement of the third Brandenburg. I had given him one of the prototypes, not the final thing. He said, "My God, where did you come up with so many colors?" And he was just as amazed as we were. Theoretically there aren't that many colors there. It just sounds like it. It's magic.

Did you actually think consciously while you were doing it, "I'm not using a certain waveform now."

Yes. Like any magic trick, as the magician you're aware how to—the word isn't manipulate, I'm not manipulating the audience, we are not that way, that is not Rachel's and my goal; maybe we're manipulating ourselves, since we want to be pleased by the final tape. No, I think what you do is manipulate the ear. The ear fatigues quickly, and since the waveforms here were rather paltry, rather thin, thin in a very special way, you give it enough of other things so that it is never too conscious of what it's missing. And that part is rather deliberate, although coming up with the sounds themselves is much more spontaneous. But we never take notes. There's no diagram, no nothing. We'll go back and say, "We want a wave like that;' and we listen to it, and usually you can come very close, because after you've done this sort of thing often enough, your analysis-to-synthesis loop is pretty refined, and there's really no need to write things down. Even when they're fairly esoteric, you can come up with something that has the same aural impact, and that's the point. A bright wave tends to be a bright wave, whether it's really a group of pulses or has some sawtooths in there. That doesn't much matter. These names are much more vivid as names and as patterns on an oscilloscope than they are vivid to the ear. The ear hears on a much simpler level. If you compare each little note, there will be a slight difference between pulse and sawtooth. I'm not pretending that there's not a reason to juxtapose one after the other, because it makes them both sound a little fresher to keep doing that, but functionally it gets to be almost an arbitrary decision when to use one and when to use the other.

What led you to pick the modules in your Moog?

Well, I don't want to pull the game of "I was one of Bob Moog's first customers." I was a very early customer, certainly, and obviously without him I would never have had the engineering ideas and feedback on what I wanted in a touch-sensitive device, which is very critical to my system. By the same token, he adopted some of my ideas. I had thought of using three oscillators with one controller, and that became standard. I wasn't quite sure how helpful the highpass filter would be, but the voltage-controlled lowpass was clearly good. I really wanted to upgrade the envelopers. The keyboard came with its own envelopers. You had a choice of hard and soft attack, and that was it. You couldn't run the 911 envelope generator from the keyboard at all. Bob added a switch for that, the trigger relay that runs those envelopes. During the first year I used the instrument, I collected a few more modules. I added a lot more envelopes and got a dual trigger delay. That was back when delays were handled separately; of course now they have envelopes with built-in initial delay. But my instrument was different from any of his suggested stock systems. I was immediately more interested in the custom things. Okay, we could add these other things, but what about this keyboard? It's like an organ. Touch sensitivity was an important thing, and Rachel's disenchantment, if I can understate it, with the earlier stuff, was mainly because there was no performance value. It was as all of the synthesizer music tends to be right now. I probably sound like Stravinsky saying, "After *Rite of Spring*, I've heard nothing new in the way of meter and rhythm." Well, after the touch sensitivity of our 1968–'69 record, I've heard nothing more in the way of performance value on synthesizer. That's a bitter-sounding statement. I don't mean it that literally. The important thing in that first instrument was to add something like touch sensitivity. And then came the idea of that portamento device, because when you start glissing notes it seemed like a natural. All the other ways of glissing notes I loathe when I try doing them.

What brought you together with Bob Moog?

I met him for the first time when I was a student at Columbia, in fall of '63 or '64. It was the first year he exhibited at the AES [Audio Engineering Society convention]. He really didn't remember me as well as I remembered him because I came to him with Ussachevsky, who brought me with him to the AES. It was the first time I was ever at the AES. The next year, I was still a student and went to see him when he was explaining the voltage-controlled filter at the show. Bob was a nice guy. I ended up waking him up at the show. There was no one else around and he was asleep. It was a cockamamie hour and no one was up but me. I wished I had money on the spot to buy something, but I didn't have any money at that time. And we started corresponding and I started collecting money and acquired some of the first modules, which was a long time ago. We became friends at the same time that system was being put together. Then I did the demo record for Moog.

You have an interest in tunings that go beyond equal temperament.

That's one reason that digital oscillators are nice. For somebody, me, who's been obsessed with tuning, it's nice to see digital oscillators starting to happen. They make it much easier to get into a number of different tunings. I built my first prototype of a keyboard that wasn't equal-tempered in about 1954. I have a passionate desire to see equal temperament used only where it is effective. That is, in allegro things with harmonics that die off quickly so you don't hear all that awful beating unless you want it. The dangerous effect equal temperament has is not unlike the effect of a ring modulator. That cacophony of partials that produce the wrong difference tones. The nastiness you get in a Hammond organ is due to equal temperament. The 31 and the 53 equal-spaced scales are two obvious scales we'd like to start using.

There's a very characteristic shimmery sound which comes up a lot in your music.

That's what we call our Christmas sound. There's a way of tuning white noise by feeding it through a high- and lowpass filter. You know, you set it with high regeneration, you tie the two together so there's very little above and below a particular bandpass, and you voltage-control the filter. Another thing I've been doing lately is taking white noise and pre-filtering it to a band. It works rather differently, using that as a modulation on a sine. You get a different kind of feel. It's no big deal, but it's one of those ways of getting magic.

In doing the music for *Tron*, you were under some deadline pressure.

Often I look back after finishing a project and wonder, "Where did that come from?" And I start to be afraid that I'll never be able to do it again. It's a scary feeling that you probably never totally lose. But some part of it went away after *Tron*. That was the most concentrated, tightly packed amount of work, from both a technical and an artistic viewpoint, that I had ever done in my life. I had never been this forced to plan out and produce in so little time. So I had to run more by the seat of my pants and hope that I was really as professional as people were telling me I was. And yet I didn't feel that I ever resorted to formulas or compromises. Somehow I feel that my experiences over the past 20 years have made me a composer now

A SELECTED WENDY CARLOS DISCOGRAPHY

Rediscovering Lost Scores, Vols. 1 and 2

Switched-On Bach 2000

By Request

Secrets of Synthesis

Tron (soundtrack)

Switched-On Bach II

Switched-On Brandenburgs

Switched-On Bach

The Well-Tempered Synthesizer

Beauty in the Beast

Digital Moonscapes

Sonic Seasonings / Land of the Midnight Sun

A Clockwork Orange (soundtrack)

Tales of Heaven and Hell

FOR MORE INFORMATION ON WENDY CARLOS, VISIT www.wendycarlos.com.

in a way that I never felt I was before. I'm not afraid to say that, yes, I can compose to order. I'm not afraid that I will lack inspiration, or that my output will be just plain lousy. At the same time, I feel much less that I am actually the personal author of the work. I feel that I'm part of a process. I watch from afar, as it were, and see something like the satellite phone system, where I'm not originating a transmission, but it's passing through me and I'm responsible for keeping its coherence and its intelligibility. At the same time, I know that something is part of me when it's all finished. Clearly it reflects some of the things I like to hear. These are my feelings. I'm not trying to put a value on these feelings, just to observe that they exist.

MALCOLM CECIL

3 PUTTING SOUL INTO SYNTHS WITH STEVIE WONDER AND TONTO

by John Diliberto

Portions of this chapter originally appeared in the January 1984 issue of Keyboard *magazine.*

Synthesizers are so pervasive an element in popular music today that it's easy to forget what a novelty they were a few years ago, and how difficult it was at first for musicians to find valid uses for them. When they were employed at all, it was likely to be for novelties like Gershon Kingsley's hit "Popcorn." But while Keith

Malcolm in the middle: The resurrected and modernized TONTO surrounds Malcolm Cecil in the current TONTO Studio in upstate New York. (Courtesy of *Keyboard* magazine)

Emerson was still pitch-bending his way through "Lucky Man," another synthesizer record was released that was influential in a more subversive fashion. This was *Zero Time*, a minor classic of electronic music by the psychedelically named group Tonto's Expanding Head Band.

Robert Margouleff and Malcolm Cecil, who were the Expanding Head Band, made music that was warm and human, that evoked but did not imitate, and that was surprisingly free of self-consciousness and restraints. *Zero Time* was arguably the first purely electronic album to take the synthesizer to the limits of its liberating capabilities while still making music that average people could enjoy listening to. TONTO—an acronym for The Original New Timbral Orchestra—was their synthesizer rig. It produced synthesized voices, instruments, and sequencer rhythms that still sound fresh today. It would be several more years before people like Tangerine Dream, Vangelis, and Jean Michel Jarre would make music as sophisticated and multi-layered with electronics.

While *Zero Time* was embraced by audiophiles (it was great for showing off your speaker system), it quickly faded into obscurity. Its composers also disappeared, unless you were inclined to squint at the small type of album credits. Cecil and Margouleff were still active behind the scenes, quietly influencing the shape of progressive funk and R&B. A year after *Zero Time* came *Music of My Mind*, the album on which Stevie Wonder came of age musically. And Cecil and Margouleff were acknowledged as associate producers, engineers, and Moog programmers. The classic Stevie Wonder albums that followed—*Talking Book*, *Innervisions*, and *Fulfillingness' First Finale*—were all a result of this collaboration, and they changed the perspectives of black pop music as much as the Beatles' *Sgt. Pepper's Lonely*

Hearts Club Band altered the concepts of white rock. More than a little credit for Stevie Wonder's breakthrough sound belongs to the artists who introduced him to the possibilities of the synthesizer.

When other artists heard Wonder's new direction, they came to Cecil and Margouleff to make use of their production skills and the sounds of TONTO. The roster of acts they produced includes the Isley Brothers, Minnie Riperton, Steve Stills, Steve Hillage, and the Jackson Five. After *Fulfillingness'*, Margouleff and Cecil parted ways. Malcolm Cecil retained ownership of the amazing (and still growing) TONTO.

What equipment is in TONTO?

There's an enormous number of individual synthesizer modules. There's the equivalent of two complete Moog IIIs, four of the old Oberheim Xpander Modules, two complete ARP 2600s, an enormous amount of EMS equipment, and in excess of 70 modules by Serge Modular. Serge Tcherepnin has built some special oscillators for me, some special filters, gobs and gobs of VCAs that I use all over as CV (control voltage) controllers, and about 30 voltage-controlled envelope generators. There are several envelope generators that are specially built to provide very, very long envelopes, in excess of ten minutes if required. I use these over the length of an entire piece, to control dynamics. I have a heavily modified EMS 256 sequencer, and a couple of keyboards from the EMS AKS which are integrated into TONTO as part of the control system. Then there are between 20 and 30 special modules that I designed and built myself over the years. And of course all of this equipment has been modified so that it's totally interfaced. All the control voltages have been standardized at one volt per octave, and I can go either positive trigger, grounding trigger, or negative trigger.

How did the concept of TONTO originate?

I was working as a maintenance engineer for Media Sound in New York in 1969, and Bob Margouleff was the Moogist in residence. He had made a film called *Ciao Manhattan*, and he couldn't afford to get a film score done, so he figured he'd get a synthesizer and do the score on that. He learned to play it just by experimenting with it; his main musical training was as a singer. He was coming from a musical point of view, and technically he had very little knowledge. But he had a knack, as he put it, to hear sonorities. So I was in the studio late at night, working on clearing all the problems that had shown up the previous day, and Bob would come in to mess around and experiment with this instrument. One evening he approached me and asked if I could help him. He was having a problem with the mixing board in Studio A, because none of the engineers would show him how to run the board. I said, "Sure, I'll show you how to run the board, but if I do, will you show me how to run that thing?" He said, "Well, I'll let you stand and watch. You'll have to pick it up. That's how I picked it up." There was no vocabulary at that time for passing information on.

What was the first piece of music you worked on together?

That was "Aurora," one of the tracks that appeared on the first TONTO album, *It's About Time* [available on *Tonto Rides Again*]. It was a 27-minute-long drony sort of piece, and we weren't even sure at first that it was music. But I finally said, "Well, of course it's music. What else could it be? There's no other definition for it. If we treat it as music, it'll be music." So we proceeded to work on it and refine it and put more and more lines on it, engineering and producing one another. I was sort of awed by the finished track. Media Sound was in a church, and when we played it back in the church I got a chilly feeling up and down my spine. So then it was my turn to start a piece, and being a bass player, I started off with the bass line for what became "Cybernaut." We had three sequencers, and I managed to hook them up together to produce a bass line which was longer than the normal sequence. Getting it to do that was quite a technical trip.

How did the first album come to be released?

We got to the point where we had three or four finished pieces, but we weren't working for anything other than our own enjoyment. Then one day I bumped into Herbie Mann, the flute player, who was an old friend of mine from my days at Ronnie Scott's in England. Herbie wanted to know what I was doing now, if I was playing any music. At that time I was subbing for [bassist] Ron Carter on duo dates with [guitarist] Jim Hall, but I told Herbie I was mostly playing synthesizer. He didn't like the idea, but I said, "Maybe you should listen to it before you pass judgment." He said, "Well, since it's you, all right." So he came and listened to "Aurora," and he was totally transfixed. He asked what record label we were on, and we said, "Record label? We're just doing this for fun." He said, "I'm with Atlantic Records. They've given me a label, and I'm looking for acts. I have carte blanche to put out anything I want. Do you want to be on my label?" We thought he must be crazy, but we let him play it out. We had to do three or four more pieces to finish the album, and then when it was all finished we thought about what we were going to call the group. We decided we wanted to have an expanding band. The original idea was to contact people like the two Walters—Carlos and Sears—and we would put down a track and send them the tape and have them put down a track and send it along to the next person, so it would be an expanding band. And since it was the '60s, the idea of a "head" band came into it. Then we came up with the phrase "The Original New Timbral Orchestra" as an alternative title, which gave us Tonto's Head Band—it was all too punny to be true. I wasn't sure it was a good idea, but Bob convinced me it was the right move.

How did TONTO come to assume its somewhat unusual shape?

It was originally a two-keyboard Moog III. Then we got our hands on another Moog that had been involved in a fire. It came our way with the case all burnt up. So we got into the idea of building a new case for it. The man who was responsible for that is John Storyk, who designed Electric Ladyland studios. He's a Buckminster Fuller student. When TONTO got to be nine feet long and we were running from one end of the instrument to the other towing a trolley behind us with the keyboards on it, we decided there had to be a better way to lay the instrument out. We had already moved from Media Sound to Electric Lady to record with Stevie Wonder, and they were going to build a special room for TONTO. But John decided that the first thing to do was build a new case. He said, "Ergonomically speaking, we should make it so that everything is within reach, so you guys don't have to move around." He measured our arms and the size of the unit and drew up the plans. So now it looks like the inside of a spaceship, which of course is an ergonomic design. You don't want to be doing a lot of running around inside a spaceship either. We had lots of control panels, so the thing to do was to angle them upwards. The vertical and horizontal surfaces turn out to form the inside of a sphere. Of course, spherical geometry is one of Buckminster Fuller's strong points, with his geodesic domes and so on.

Can you tell us more about your work with Stevie Wonder?

Stevie showed up with the TONTO LP under his arm. He said, "I don't believe all this was done on one instrument. Show me the instrument." He was always talking about seeing. So we dragged his hands all over the instrument, and he thought he'd never be able to play it. But we told him we'd get it together for him. And we ended up doing four albums with him. Stevie, Bob, and I made *Music of My Mind*, *Talking Book*, *Innervisions*, which we all got Grammys for, and *Fulfillingness' First Finale*. We also left 240 songs in various stages of development, 40 of them finished and mixed.

Why did the collaboration come to an end?

For business reasons. Bob and I split up, and we both split up with Stevie at the same time, all because of business. There are two aspects to music. There's the music business, and then there's making music. Frankly, I'm more interested in the latter than in the former. I'd rather be a starving artist in a garrett expressing myself than a rich, frustrated musician or producer.

Since working with Stevie, you've produced a variety of other people, like the Isley Brothers, Steve Hillage, and Gil Scott-Heron. How did that come about?

It's all an offshoot of the Stevie thing. Nobody was quite sure what we were doing, because it was only Bob, Stevie, and me in the room, with maybe a tape operator. Later, towards the end, there were the nameless 10,000 who would file through and disrupt the work. But in the beginning it was just the three of us, and those were the best times. The influx of external business came through the success of *Talking Book*. People would look at the credits and say, "Hey, Stevie's last album didn't sound like this. It must be because of these guys." They would get hold of Bob and me and say, "We don't know which one of you it is, but we want you to work with us." The Isleys called and said, "We want to get sounds like Stevie's. Whatever you do for Stevie, we want you to do for us."

What exactly did you do for them?

We did everything to do with the production that they didn't do. They wrote the songs, they rehearsed them. When they came into the studio, we recorded them, we coached them, and we gave them comments wherever we felt it was necessary. We created the musical sounds on TONTO that we were asked for. I got Ernie Isley's guitar fixed up. He was looking for a Hendrixy sound so I got him hooked up with Roger Meyer in New York, who made all of Hendrix's boxes. But I never felt the same rapport with them as with Stevie, because the creative involvement was not as great. With Stevie, we would help with lyrics here and there, work on songs, select songs for albums, create the sounds, and sometimes I'd play the synthesizer parts myself and Stevie would like them, so they'd stay on the record.

You've been associated with a number of R&B artists. Yet your own 1981 LP, *Radiance*, has a very different sound.

Radiance was done as a recreational thing because the R&B stuff was driving me crazy. It was all just boom-boom, boom-boom, boom-boom. I wanted something a little more relaxing. Having gone into Tai Chi, which is a Chinese art of longevity and health, I was into gentle, slowing-down rhythms. The reality of that became very important to me, and I needed to do the music just for my own sake. It was originally done for no record company at all, and I don't anticipate it being an easy job to pick up any royalties on it. That's not why I made it. But I do keep up my work with Gil Scott-Heron and several other artists. I'll produce records and engineer for other people and play synthesizer as an adjunct to their music, because it pays well enough to leave me free to do what I want to do. That was the falling-out point for Bob and me. He no longer felt that TONTO was an asset. He felt it was a millstone around his neck. It was costing us a fortune. We had spent $22,000 on getting a polyphonic keyboard together, and it still wasn't working. It was draining resources, when what he wanted to do, as he expressed it to me at the time, was to produce records and make money. He has since gone on to do just that. He's done very well as a producer, working with some fairly high sellers like Devo. But for me, while I'm happy to produce records, I couldn't possibly let TONTO die. For me, that's my expressive tool, my musical instrument. It's part of my life.

Let's talk a bit more about TONTO. How did you first acquire a working polyphonic keyboard for it?

The keyboards were made by Armand Pascetta. He's the man who first invented the polyphonic keyboard. When we were working with Stevie Wonder at the Record Plant, Armand showed up one day and asked if I could help him by defining the parameters and tolerances that were needed for voltage control, because he was thinking of making a digitally controlled polyphonic keyboard. How close his D-to-A converters would have to be to get the voltages for tuning, and so on. I thought nothing more of it at that point; he was just one of many people who had come up to me and asked questions. Well, about a year and a half after that first meeting, I had a knock at the door of my house. It was Armand, and he had a prototype in his car and wanted to test it, because he didn't have any synthesizers. So he brought the keyboard in and we spent the next day and a half sitting on the floor soldering and pushing and poking and thumping and banging. We got the thing up and running, and it worked pretty well, but there were a few little problems. So over the next year we worked with Armand with prototype after prototype, until eventually we had a really fine working system, which we demonstrated to a group of synthesists in L.A. One of the people that we invited to that demonstration was Tom Oberheim, and after Tom had seen it, he said, "I don't want to know how it works. Don't tell me. I want to develop one of my own." Which of course is what he did.

> "Just because something is new doesn't necessarily mean it's better."

Initially the keyboard wasn't touch-sensitive, was it?

No. But another person who was at the demonstration was poor Paul Beaver, who passed away shortly afterward. Paul said, "Well, that's all very well, but when are you going to have a touch-sensitive polyphonic keyboard?" Of course, EMS had velocity sensitivity for attack on their 256. But my idea was to have velocity for release also, so that you could make the tail of a note either short or long, depending on how quickly you lift your finger. And I couldn't interest any synthesizer manufacturer in making this keyboard at the time.

The new Prophet-T8 has release velocity sensing.

Ten years later. I spoke to the guys at Sequential Circuits at a trade show three or four years ago, when they were showing a prototype of the T8. I went up and messed around with it. I don't think they knew who I was. I asked them if they couldn't put release sensing on it, and they thought it was quite a good idea. But Armand and I came up with a way of doing attack and release velocity sensing, as well as pressure sensitivity—which of course requires an entirely different keyboard technique than either piano or organ, so we're talking about a whole new animal now. I think that's the main reason a lot of the manufacturers were not interested.

In spite of the amount of computerization you've done, TONTO still uses patch cords, doesn't it?

It works both ways. The original modules were all patched. What we have done is put little hardware devices behind the panels which are then switchable by computer, so that we can connect anything to anything through the computer. But that aspect of it is by no means a 100 percent thing. We don't have every control available to go to every other. The amount of point-to-point wiring that would be required for that would be just beyond my scope to contemplate. There are probably 25 miles of wire in TONTO—nothing to do with the modules, this is just for the cases. I've had to go to all sorts of trouble to insure that I don't have RF [radio frequency interference] problems, but my systems engineering background stood me in good stead there. It's been very carefully thought out, and of course it's a hand-built instrument.

Can you sit down and play full-sounding music on TONTO? Or do you have to stop and plug things in and switch things around and do overdubs?

It really works both ways. I think of TONTO mainly as a recording instrument rather than a live performance instrument. But the more we get the computer systems together, the more live performance oriented it gets. I have done live performances with it; it's just a pain to get everything set up and tuned, and you really do have to have your program together. But then, that's true of anything. If you're going to go out and perform a classical piano piece, you have to have it together. It's nothing new, it's just that here the technical complexities can overshadow the musical. That's the thing I wanted to get away from. I wanted to get to a point where, for example, you can get a really good bass sound and then, without disturbing that, go on and get some other sound and play the two at the same time. That's how I came up with the idea of The Original New Timbral Orchestra, the idea of an orchestra of synthesizers. What I've found is that for recording purposes, I usually have certain favorite sections of the instrument that perform specific tasks well. I particularly like the bass sound that I get from the Moog III equipment, so I tend to gravitate toward it when I want bass. That doesn't mean there are no other ways of creating bass sounds, it's just that that's the one I usually go for. But once it's set up, there's no need to go back and overdub. You can sit down and play all the sounds at once with the polyphonic keyboard.

You're using digital technology extensively for control functions. But there are people who would consider your analog oscillators and other modules obsolete. Have you looked into using digital synthesis in TONTO?

I do have some digital synthesis modules that are hand-built. But I don't believe in throwing out the baby with the bathwater. Just because something is new doesn't necessarily mean it's better. I haven't gone over to 100 percent digital synthesis because there are certain things that, in my opinion, analog is better at. Bass sounds, for a start. Digital is tremendously good in upper-range sounds, but it's very difficult in digital to get good bass sounds. So I think that a hybrid instrument is the correct course for me. It gives me the ability to draw on both worlds. A lot of the recent digital stuff—like the devices where you can sample a real live sound and then modify it—that's very nice, but the thing I like about synthesis is the ability to do things which cannot be done any other way. I've gone away from the idea of imitative synthesis, and a lot of digital synthesis is still in the imitative era, so to speak. And that's normal. Any child, as he grows up, the first thing he does is imitate. So imitation is the first way you find out how to do things. Later, you innovate. My feeling is that the stage to reach is innovation, where you're creating things with the synthesizer that can't be done on other instruments. That's why, when musicians ask me, "Don't you think you're putting guys out of work with these synthesizers?" I say, "No, quite the contrary. I'm giving musicians an opportunity to create things that have never been possible before." We've never been at this type of crossroads. That's one of the reasons why I've thrown myself so heavily into the technical arena. Unless musicians get into that area, we are not going to be able to control the kind of instruments that are going to come out. We are going to have engineers giving us the instruments, and I don't think that's correct.

What were some of the concepts you were working with at the time of the first TONTO album, *Zero Time*? Especially on the second side, it's very different from any kind of music that was happening at the time.

Well, "Aurora" just grew out of an experiment. We were playing monophonically, layering things, and experimenting with space.

A SELECTED MALCOLM CECIL (WITH TONTO) DISCOGRAPHY

WITH TONTO'S EXPANDING HEAD BAND
TONTO Rides Again

WITH STEVIE WONDER
Music of My Mind
Talking Book
Innervisions
Fulfillingness' First Finale

FOR MORE INFORMATION ON MALCOLM CECIL AND TONTO, VISIT www.tontostudio.com.

There are three glide tones that go up an octave in "Aurora." They came about because we were talking about intervals. Why should there be only twelve tones to the scale? With the synthesizer we're not limited to twelve tones. We can change the tuning and put 17, 19, 25—pick a number! We wondered how many intervals there were in an octave and decided to check it out with these glide tones. They're spread over a long time because we were trying to pick out individual notes. When we came to an interesting interval we'd look at one another and say, "Hey, listen to that one!"

The first side of *Zero Time* is much more rhythmic. The album defined the nature of sequencer rhythms for the next ten years.

Well, I'm a bass player, so rhythms are part of my stock in trade. Many a time I had stood in the back of the stage in a jazz club after 27 choruses of the blues, thinking that I might as well be a machine. To be creative night after night when all you've got is the same 12 measures, no break and no bridge, you get into finding all sorts of patterns that will break up the monotony. Sequences get very monotonous if you're not careful with them. So when we were doing these sequences, one of the things that I already knew, even though I knew nothing about the synthesizer before meeting Bob, was that rhythmic patterns get very boring unless you very subtly make changes. We figured out a way to hook up the keyboard so that we could move the sequence around musically. Also, there were two of us, and since I was controlling the keyboard there was nothing for Bob to do except turn the knobs. So he was changing the filters and the envelopes to make the accents come in different places, which made it very alive and interesting. Bob is a vocalist and I'm a bass player, so consequently we didn't approach the music pianistically.

One of the advantages of the synthesizer is that it eliminates the need for virtuosity in finger technique. It allows people who have music in their heads to get it out without having to study the piano for twenty years.

I agree. But it still takes musicality to approach the instrument and come out with something that is interesting to the ears. I still think it takes schooling on some instrument. It doesn't have to be keyboards, but I think it is useful to have mastered at least one instrument before taking up the synthesizer. It's a second instrument, an advanced instrument. It's not a beginner's instrument.

Letting it be: Brian Eno with his organically decaying yet artistically improving Minimoog and EMS Synthi AKS.
(© Ebet Roberts)

4 BRIAN ENO

THE POWER OF THE OBLIQUE

by Jim Aikin

Portions of this chapter appeared in the July 1981 issue of Keyboard *magazine.*

In an era whose artistic expression has come to be dominated by the stultifying forces of financial and ideological conservatism, Brian Eno reminds us to keep our options open. Eno is a visionary—perhaps the leading visionary of rock music. In the last eight years his solo albums and collaborations have provided a continuing stream of exciting new music, and his influence is clearly evident in the work of a number of experimental musicians who are exploring the rich vein of sound materials he has discovered. But Eno is far more than a creator of intriguing music, just as he is far more than a synthesizer player. He is an articulate spokesman for a philosophy of discovery, of intuition and transcendence, that, although it would seem vital to the creative process, is seldom encountered in either popular or "serious" art. The real rewards of Eno's influence are bound to go not to those who ape his innovations in composition and sound design, but to those who are willing to apply his insights so as to discover the sources of their own creativity—to those who are willing, as Eno is willing, to take chances.

Of course there's more to it than that. The secret is to develop your feeling for which chances to take at which times, for which unorthodox procedures are likely to yield the most interesting results. And Eno's unorthodox background gave him the best possible training in this neglected artistic process.

Born in East Anglia, England, in May 1948, Brian Eno managed to struggle through his early years without any piano lessons, or even any desire for any. Which is not to say that there weren't hints of what was to come. When he first discovered what a tape recorder was, he was fascinated by the possibilities he saw in it, and began pestering his parents to buy him one. At the age of 16, Eno went off to the Ipswich Art School, intending to become a painter. But it wasn't long before he found that the school had sound taping facilities. His first piece was constructed by banging on a big metal lampshade and recording the bell-like sound at various speeds to create beating between the tones.

By the time he got his degree in fine arts from the Winchester School of Art in 1969, Eno had already been involved in a couple of local experimental bands. His first large-scale public exposure came a couple of years later, when he became one of the founding members of the British rock band Roxy Music. He first met the other members of the band not as a musician at an audition but when he was brought in to engineer some demo tapes. Fortunately, there was a synthesizer at the session, and Eno, who had never seen a synthesizer before, started toying with it as well. Unlike many people trained in the arts, he was even then quite comfortable around machinery, and he had no trouble seeing the possibilities of the synthesizer.

He continued to think of himself more as a technician than a performer even after he joined the band. At Roxy's early gigs, Eno wasn't even onstage—he was in the back of the hall mixing the sound. But record company representatives suggested that it was odd to have somebody at the back of the hall singing occasional vocals, so Eno moved up onto the stage. Once he was in the spotlight, however, he showed little reticence about playing the rock star game. During his two years with Roxy Music he became the epitome of glitter rock, appearing onstage in lipstick, mascara, and ostrich plumes. But even this wasn't done solely in order to be shocking. He has since remarked that during this period he objected to masculine clothing because it reflected a rationalistic, goal-oriented approach. He contrasted "rational man" with "intuitive woman," and having been through Ipswich Art School, he was in no doubt that the side of himself he wanted to express was his intuitive side. In the last five or six years, however, he has gone to the other extreme, sartorially; his appearance is almost monkishly severe.

When he left Roxy Music in 1973, Eno started off along the conventional route laid out for ex-band members: a solo performing career. But he quickly found that fronting a band wasn't to his liking, so he abandoned the idea and started looking around for more stimulating projects. Some of his comments about the rock star syndrome have been quite critical. He has pointed out how the star becomes the prisoner of his or her own image, and is expected to keep putting out an identifiable sort of product, plodding down a well-trodden path rather than going off on tangents and experimenting with new directions and ideas.

The tangents, of course, are what interests Eno. No one could accuse him of plodding down any well-trodden paths. Since leaving Roxy, he has engaged in a bewildering variety of projects, most of them strikingly original in content. He put out four solo albums of rock songs, *Here Come the Warm Jets*, *Taking Tiger Mountain (By Strategy)*, *Another Green World*, and *Before and After Science*, the most recent (*Science*) in 1978. The arrangements on these albums are often raucously strident, though the quiet tunes become eerily luminous. Two elements in particular set the albums apart from the mainstream: the unusual tone colors given familiar instruments by means of elaborate electronic processing, and the enigmatic lyrics. As he explains briefly in the following interview, the lyrics are intended not so much to make sense as to almost make sense, forcing the listener to create his or her own interpretation of them. Encouraging the listener to become involved in the music in this way is another important aspect of Eno's work.

More recently, he has been concentrating on instrumental music to the exclusion of lyrics. As far back as 1972, he and guitarist Robert Fripp were experimenting with hypnotic extended compositions using tape loops; their collaboration appeared in 1974 on the album *No Pussyfooting*. This was followed in 1975 by Eno's *Discreet Music*, an extremely quiet, placid album of extended instrumentals. But the idea of ethereally peaceful music began to take off in 1978 with the release of *Ambient 1: Music for Airports*. The term "ambient music" has begun to gain some currency; it describes music that can function as background music but that offers a profound alternative to conventional Muzak-type sound environments. Since the sound environment we all live in consists mostly of machine hum occasionally blanketed by bland pop arrangements, it's hard to escape the feeling that ambient music would be a welcome change.

Eno's current interests are not, however, limited to background music. His fascination with exotic music is seen in *Fourth World, Vol. 1: Possible Musics*, on which he teamed up with trumpeter Jon Hassell to create some intensely evocative and thoroughly alien pieces, and in his most recent work, *My Life in the Bush of Ghosts*, a collaboration with guitarist David Byrne of Talking Heads. *Bush of Ghosts* utilizes fairly conventional funky rhythm tracks—at least they're conventional by Eno's standards. But above these, in place of lyrics, are "found vocals," including the voices of radio evangelists and Arabian singers, which are intended to affect the listener more because of their rhythm, tone, and inflection than as a result of what the words are.

When not occupied with his own projects, Eno has found time to produce albums by a number of new wave bands, including Ultravox, Devo, and Talking Heads. He also co-produced and helped compose three David Bowie albums. Nor are his interests confined strictly to music. He has recently begun experimenting with video, and has had several shows of his videotape productions.

What Eno is doing with his music, more than anything else, is introducing us to the world. It's a world of sound and other subtler resonances that surrounds us, whether we're aware of it or not. But in addition to being a philosopher, a composer, and a producer, he is, after all, a synthesizer player. He has been working actively with electronic musical equipment for many years, and he has some strong opinions about synthesizers that haven't been brought out in any of his previous interviews. We talked to Eno by phone at his apartment in New York, and since we knew the conversation was going to head for outer space as it went along, we thought it would be best to start by asking about his experiences with and attitudes toward the hardware.

Could you tell us what kind of synthesizers you own?

They're all very commonplace and not very exciting. One is a Minimoog. It's a very old one—one of the first ones they made, I suspect. The second is the EMS. It was made by EMS, and the model is called an AKS. It's a briefcase model. It's a very nice little thing. It has a routing matrix. You just put a little plug in and route one thing to another by doing that. I also have a Korg Micropreset. The Minimoog and the AKS I've had for years, actually. The Korg is quite new. And I have a lot of auxiliary equipment as well that I use with these. I use all the things a guitar player might have: phase pedals, fuzz boxes, echo units. The echo unit is particularly important.

Your music seems to rely pretty heavily on echo.

It really does. The important thing about using effects in connection with synthesizers is that they mess the sound up a little bit. My problem with synthesizers has always been that the sound is so inorganic of itself that it sticks out too much. It's far too obvious and high-definition in a track. So one of the main points of the echo unit is not just for the sake of echo, but also to knock off a few of the high frequencies of the synthesizer, and introduce some distortion as well. It's actually being used rather like a graphic equalizer. I do have two graphics as well, which I use. Those I should have mentioned first, because they are really the most important.

For your purposes, what features would you like to see in a synthesizer?

Well, the development of synthesizers so far has all been predicated on a particular assumption that I feel I no longer agree with. That assumption is that the best synthesizer is the one that gives you the largest number of possibilities. Clearly this is what's been happening with the big digital synthesizers. Now, the effect of this on the players—or at least the conspicuous effect, as far as I can see—is that the players move very quickly from sound to sound, so that for any new situation there would be a novel sound for it, because there's such a wide palette to choose from. This seems to me to produce a compositional weakness. These players are working in terms of sounds they don't really understand yet, you know—the sound is too novel for them to have actually understood its strengths and weaknesses, and to have made something on that basis. It's like continually being given a new instrument. Well, that's exciting for the player. Every ten minutes somebody says, "Hey, here's another instrument. Now try this one." But from the point of view of the music, it seems to produce a rather shallow compositional approach. Frequently in the studios, you see synthesizer players fiddling for six hours getting this sound and then that sound and so on, in a kind of almost random search.

What's clear, if you're watching this process, is that what they're in search of is not a new sound but a new idea. The synthesizer gives them the illusion that they'll find it somewhere in there. Really, it would make more sense to sit down and say, "Hey, look, what am I doing? Why don't I just think for a minute, and then go and do it?" Rather than this scramble through the electrons. You could contrast this approach to that taken by Glenn Gould, for instance. In the article in *Keyboard* [August '80] he mentions the fact that he has been working with the same piano for years and years. Clearly he understands that piano in a way that no synthesizer player alive understands his instrument. You see, there are really distinct advantages to working within a quite restricted range of possibilities, and getting a deeper and deeper understanding of those.

What other musicians can you think of who have taken this approach?

It's true of most of the great musicians I can think of. Jimi Hendrix, for instance, always worked with a Stratocaster and a particular type of amp. If I think of singers I like, clearly they're working with a limited palette, that being their voice. They don't have the option of infinitely extending that. Jon Hassell, the trumpet player I worked with—what makes his work so lovely is that he really understands the sound he makes. He understands it in a way I've never heard a synthesizer player understand his sound. So, to answer your question about what features I would like to see in a synthesizer, I think it might be interesting if people now started making electronic instruments that were deliberately limited, that had maybe four or five great sounds on them. Well, a Minimoog is rather like that, actually. Within a few months you know pretty well what its limits are, so you don't waste a lot of time trying to program novelties into it. You know what the instrument can do, and you choose from among its possibilities. So this becomes a musical choice, not just a sound choice. Of course I'm not suggesting that people stop developing big synthesizers. What I'm suggesting is that big synthesizers aren't necessarily going to produce the most interesting music, which has been the tacit assumption, I think, that the bigger the synthesizer, the more interesting the music would be. That isn't going to be the case. My recommendation, which might come as a relief to people who can't afford big synthesizers, is that the quality of the music has nothing to do with that anyway.

Does the evenness of a synthesizer's tone cause problems for you?

There are two things that the synthesizer lacks. One is that it lacks a sound that is idiosyncratic enough to be interesting. By that I mean that all natural instruments respond naturally, which is to say they respond unevenly, and somewhat unpredictably. You know, a guitar sounds slightly different at each fret, and it has oddities, which are undoubtedly a large part of the interest of the instrument. A good player will understand and make use of those oddities. But synthesizers in general don't have that. The aspiration of synthesizer designers is to produce maximum evenness. And that was actually the aspiration of traditional instrument designers—violin makers, for instance. They wanted to produce an instrument that was completely even in timbre at every pitch. Of course they failed, because they were working with materials that wouldn't permit that, and their failure is what makes those instruments interesting.

Some non-European instruments embody these imperfections to an even greater degree.

And that accounts for a good part of their interest. Look at the shakuhachi, the Japanese flute. The intention in its development, in contrast to what we've been talking about, was to produce a quite different timbre at each pitch, and for each individual sound to have its own distinct character. What I'm saying is that as far as I'm concerned it would be much nicer if synthesizers began moving away from their perfection and through the violin stage of imperfection towards the shakuhachi stage. Now, in doing this you can move in one of two directions. In the direction of very high technology you can do that—with instruments like the Synclavier and the Fairlight you can program each note to have its own special idiosyncrasies. Or you can move in the direction of very low technology, which is the direction I'm much more likely to take. If I built a synthesizer, it would be fairly unpredictable. In fact, the synthesizers I own have already become fairly unpredictable because I've had them a long time and haven't had them serviced very much. I know a lot of people are into the inhuman cleanness of a synthesizer, but I don't like that, and I subvert it number one by laziness: I never get my instruments serviced, so they start to become a little bit more idiosyncratic, and I also use a lot of auxiliary equipment, which I also don't get serviced. Now this sounds flippant, this not getting things serviced. I actually do get things serviced sometimes, but a lot of the faults that develop are rather interesting, so I leave those alone.

> "You see, there are really distinct advantages to working within a quite restricted range of possibilities, and getting a deeper and deeper understanding of those."

What kind of faults?

Well, for instance on my little EMS a fault has developed whereby if I feed a loud input signal into the ring modulator it will trigger the envelope. This isn't supposed to happen, but of course it's very useful, because then you can use the envelope to trigger any other function in the synthesizer, so I can follow the input sound with another sound if I like, or feed the input sound through a filter, that's controlled by the envelope—that kind of thing. Now this is distinctly a fault of the synthesizer, and when I do get it serviced I have to put little notes all over the thing saying, "Don't service this part. Don't change this."

At one time or another we've all played on instruments that weren't behaving the way they were supposed to. It can be frustrating, but rather than being frustrated, you seem to turn it to your advantage.

I don't mind it at all. I'm very familiar with these synthesizers. I know all the things they do incorrectly, and I've turned those things into strengths now rather than weaknesses.

But it's important that you're familiar with the instruments, so that their unpredictabilities are in some sense predictable to you.

That's right. They're within a range. So I've allowed the things to become unique; actually. Rather than servicing them regularly so that my Minimoog is like everybody else's Minimoog, I now have a Minimoog that isn't like anybody else's, and that has certain features that I find very attractive.

Instead of having a technician modify your instruments, you've let the process of aging modify them.

Exactly. In much the way I think happens with traditional instruments. So that's one of the things I feel is missing with synthesizers—a personality. I find them instruments without personality. The other thing I find missing is the sense of a real contact between me as the player and it as the instrument. Again, in some of the more expensive synthesizers, people have tried to design in touch sensitivity, finger velocity sensors, and things like that. But I think some of the greatest inventions in this direction have gone unnoticed. For instance, there's a Yamaha synthesizer [Yamaha YC-4SD organ] whose keyboard wobbles from side to side to make a vibrato effect. I don't own one of those, but I'm always hiring one in the studio just because I love that effect. When I go back to a normal keyboard, I find myself shaking my fingers in that same way, expecting to get vibrato. Now, I looked at the circuit for that, and it's so incredibly simple! I can't understand why it has never been used on any other keyboard instrument. Maybe they patented it, but even if they did, I can think of six other ways to do that. That's such a simple thing, but most synthesizer designers have overlooked it. They won't deal with something that's as mechanical, rather than electronic, as that. But that's the kind of thing I really would appreciate in a synthesizer: some sense of physical activity making a difference to how the thing responded. That happens with every other instrument, after all. The piano less than most, I suppose, but with most instruments your physical stance does make a difference in how the thing sounds. The whole point of using effects devices is to try to reintroduce those idiosyncrasies into the sound, to take the sound out of the realm of the perfect and into the realm of the real. I'll put any amount of junk in a long line after any synthesizer to see what will happen to it.

Do you work with foot pedals to give you that physical control?

Yeah, because the foot pedal is a very physical device, and I tend to go for anything that has a quality that I can control in a real physical way.

What would a normal foot pedal setup be for you as you're playing something?

It changes all the time. I don't have a constant set of things. The things I always have are first of all the graphic equalizer, which is totally essential as far as I'm concerned. And almost equally essential is the echo unit. Since I'm normally working in studios I'm liable to use two or three echoes at once. For instance, the Roland Space Echo RE-201, and then a Lexicon Prime Time, and then maybe a long digital reverb as well, a Lexicon 224 or something like that, or the plate reverb or whatever they have in the studio. Quite often I get a sound by mixing three different echoes together. The echo unit nearly always comes last in the chain, by the way, so anything else I mention will come before that. I use a fuzz box quite a lot. I've never heard of another synthesizer player using a fuzz box.

What kind of fuzz box do you have?

I have a great one. It's very old. It's called a Project WEM. I've never seen another one. But it's a lovely fuzz box. It's been used by many famous guitar players, because they say it's got a unique sound. People have actually tried to make copies of it. They took down all the components and tried to build other ones, but they never really got quite the same thing. I've used it on all my records, actually, from the first record I made. Whenever you hear my particular fuzz guitar sound, that's the fuzz box. Sometimes· what sounds like guitar is really synthesizer or vice versa. Then the less essential things, things that aren't always there: I sometimes use phasers, though I'm pretty uninterested in them. They work with certain types of sounds, but I dislike the regularity of the sweep. I might be more interested in one that switched between different phase angles, for instance, rather than sweeping between them. I use a pitch-to-voltage converter sometimes.

Do you ever hook up other instruments and process them through the EMS?

Oh, very much. That's almost more important to me than playing the thing. The EMS has two main uses for me: Either I use it for animal and insect noises, at which I'm now, I'm sure, the world specialist, or I process other instruments with it. It's not much good as a keyboard instrument. It's incredibly hard to tune. When I'm processing something, it will go through the synthesizer and then through the chain of effects devices I just spoke about. But the great thing about processing is that what you do is create a new instrument. You create an instrument that has all of the interesting idiosyncrasies of a natural instrument, but also some of the special features of a synthesizer, so you're really dealing with a powerful new instrument. Very often when I'm mixing I have the synthesizer set up in the same way you would set up an echo or any other treatment, so I can send any instrument or set of instruments to the EMS from a send on the mixing desk. When I'm recording I nearly always have something going through the EMS. It's a way of giving a character to the track, from a very early stage, that takes it away from being just another bass and drums and blah, blah, blah. Though I must say I don't work with any of those conventional instruments very much at the moment.

What does the EMS have on it?

It's got two oscillators—well, it has three, but one is a low-frequency oscillator that one usually uses as a control oscillator. It has a ring modulator; an envelope shaper; a filter; a reverb; two little output tone controllers; a white noise generator, a joystick; which is very nice; and four inputs for other instruments. That's about it. The thing that makes this a great machine is that, whereas nearly all other synthesizers are set up so that you have a fixed signal path—you have to go from the oscillator to the filter to the envelope shaper, and out—with the EMS you can go from the oscillator to the filter, and then use the filter output to control the same oscillator again. This is how you get your bird sounds and things like that. You get a kind of squagging effect. It feeds back on itself in interesting ways, because you can make very complicated drones through the synthesizer. Also, on the EMS every single function is on a potentiometer. There are no switched functions, which is to say that you can infinitely adjust every single control. Even the waveform is adjustable, as opposed to the Moog, where you switch from one waveform to another. With the EMS you can make a mixture of waveforms, which has certain distinct advantages.

The ARP 2600 is another small synthesizer that has that capability.

That's a very nice synthesizer as well. I've worked with one of those. I've never owned one, but I do like them. Actually, the second piece on the second side of *Music for Airports* was done with an ARP 2600. It's a beautiful sound, I think, and one that I couldn't have got from any other synthesizer that I know of. The thing that makes it so luscious is that it's slowed down, and it has three kinds of echo on it.

What about research in psychoacoustics? How heavily have you gone into that?

Most of my research in that area has been fairly intuitive, or based on a study of my own reaction to things. I don't compulsively listen to music. I don't con-

A SELECTED BRIAN ENO DISCOGRAPHY

Brian Eno's discography is as broad as it is deep, and though the discs selected below contain synth work contemporary with the interview in this chapter, there are many other collaborations worth exploring, such as his work with David Bowie, Robert Fripp, King Crimson, Talking Heads, David Byrne, and Devo.

SOLO

Another Day on Earth

Drawn from Life

I Dormienti

Neroli

Wrong Way Up

Ambient 1: Music for Airports

Music for Films

Before and After Science

Discreet Music

Another Green World

Here Come the Warm Jets

WITH ROXY MUSIC

Siren

Country Life

Stranded

For Your Pleasure

FOR MORE INFORMATION ON BRIAN ENO, VISIT www.enoshop.co.uk.

stantly have the radio or records on, so when I do listen to things I'm quite aware of how they affect me, of what kind of imagery is being evoked by them. I sort of file that away, and it definitely becomes useful to me. For instance, one of the things that has interested me a lot is dealing with echo. Now, people think, "Echo? What's the big deal about echo?" What echo does is give you some information about the location of the piece of music. It tells you where this piece of music is happening. Consequently, if used properly, it can evoke a whole geography. It's a very potent tool if you're working in a recording studio the way I do. Generally I'm putting thing directly onto tape, so I have to manufacture the psychoacoustic space that I want the music to be heard in. Echo is one of the primary techniques for doing that. And of course, normally when one is manufacturing something like this, one is working on the edges of reality. You're working with things that are slightly familiar, but that are not real. They evoke, but they don't depict, exactly. So I think that would come under what you mean by psychoacoustics. Another psychoacoustic area that I've been extremely interested in, as is probably evident, is repetition and the effect of repetition. One of the Oblique Strategies that I wrote actually says, "Repetition is a form of change." The point of that comment was to make it clear that repetition doesn't really exist. As far as your mind is concerned, nothing happens the same twice, even if, in every technical sense, the thing is identical. Your perception is constantly shifting. It doesn't stay in one place. So a lot of the work I've done has involved repetition or drones, which are another form of repetition. It has relied on some kind of perceptual modification as being the composer of the piece, really. What you do is, you offer something that allows the listener's perception to become a composer.

Jan Hammer with his famous Probe (circa 1976), with which he coaxed screaming leads from his Oberheim Xpander. (Courtesy of *Keyboard* magazine)

5 JAN HAMMER

MAKING THE SYNTH SCREAM

by Dominic Milano and John Stix

Portions of this chapter appeared in the August 1976, October 1978, and September 1985 issues of Keyboard *magazine.*

His haunts have ranged from strip joints to Avery Fisher Hall. His keyboard playing has enhanced the music of Jeremy Steig, Sarah Vaughan, Stanley Clarke, John Abercrombie, Elvin Jones, and most recently, Jeff Beck. His guitar-like synthesizer playing with the Mahavishnu Orchestra set a precedent that has been followed by practically every jazz/rock synthesist. His name is Jan Hammer.

Born in Czechoslovakia, Hammer credits his parents for starting him in music. "When I was four, I remember all kinds of jazz going on around the house," he reminisces. "My mother sang, and my father had put himself through school playing bass and vibes." So Jan (pronounced like "yawn") found himself with no choice in the matter. His parents started him on the only instrument in their house that wasn't in constant use: the piano.

His formal training began when he was six with "straight ahead" classical lessons. His teacher was very strict, and Hammer learned by the book. But as Jan puts it, "There was always an unspoken assumption between my parents and myself that I was going to be a jazz musician." Thus his conservative training couldn't keep Jan from being interested in the music of Oscar Peterson, Erroll Garner, and Bill Evans. It was Paul Bley, however, who opened the door to improvisation for Jan. "Bley reached me like no other player," he reports. "Before I discovered Bley, I thought music had been all laid out. There was a narrow path to travel on. Paul Bley opened it much wider. Suddenly, I realized that you can go anywhere you choose. Since then I've been disregarding assumptions as to how things should be done."

Upon entering high school in Prague in 1962, Jan formed the Junior Trio with bassist Miroslav Vitous and Miroslav's brother [drummer] Alan Vitous. The trio appeared on a few *Jazz in Czechoslovakia* anthology albums in 1964 and 1965. With Jan's ever-growing appetite for musical knowledge, he entered the Academy of Musical Arts at Prague University. In 1966, Jan and Miroslav topped an international musical competition of young jazz talent held in Vienna, and were awarded scholarships to Boston's Berklee College of Music. Hammer was quick to take advantage of the opportunity to visit the States, and attended Berklee for a short while. "I thought Berklee was great," he recalls. "But I left because I wasn't into going to school anymore. I would do anything to play. And I did—the Playboy Clubs, strip joints, you name it."

Early in 1970, Jan met Gene Perla, bassist with the Sarah Vaughan Trio. Perla, upon hearing Jan's abilities, enlisted him in the group, which then included drummer Jimmy Cobb. Without any rehearsal, Jan began playing for them. His stay lasted 13 months.

"Sarah was fantastic," states Hammer. "She performed the magical feat of lifting me from below the ground. When I arrived here I was in a hole looking up with awe at these legendary players. Suddenly, playing with Sarah, I was on an eye-to-eye level with people that I thought of as semi-gods. I was one of them. Not one of the gods, but one of these people—I learned that they were human—just like me."

During this period Hammer was living in the legendary artists' loft at 76 Jefferson Street in New York's Lower East Side. Needless to say, Jan played New York extensively. He recorded an album with Jeremy Steig called *Energy*, and later recorded with drummer Elvin Jones for Blue Note (*Mr. Jones and Merry Go Round*).

His home became school every night, as musicians such as the Brecker brothers, Dave Liebman, Steve Grossman, and many others got together, teaching each other their art. The music they played was free-form, and in Hammer's words, "it was a Cecil Taylor kind of thing. I'm glad I did it. I got it out of my system and realized I didn't want to play it any more."

Jan's next major step was to help break down the barriers between jazz and rock as part of the original Mahavishnu Orchestra, a band that from its inception at the Gaslight Au Go Go in New York left its audiences in stunned silence. Of the Mahavishnu Orchestra, Jan relates, "My memories of it are all great. The music was fresh and powerful. It started as a collective situation. John [McLaughlin] would have a sketch, and everybody contributed. I added much of the band's harmonies while [drummer] Billy Cobham gave us many of our rhythmic elements. Though the credit usually ended up with John, it was the band that converged on his ideas and made them into pieces of music. A lot of people say that things I do now sound like the Mahavishnu Orchestra. That's why. It was me then, and it's me now."

Jan feels that *Birds of Fire* was the best album he did with the Orchestra, and it represents the first time he recorded on a synthesizer. Having played a lot of organ while in Europe, he didn't start playing electric piano until he arrived in the States in 1968. At first, the electric was used because it could stand up to the volume of the drums. Soon, however, Jan found he could alter his sound as well as get volume with the instrument. Then came his discovery of the synthesizer. "I was searching for an expressive melodic instrument," he explains, "and the synthesizer was perfect. I played one on and off for a while, mostly fooling around with the bigger units. That is how I learned about the instrument: by fooling around. I used my ears and trial and error.

"Synthesizers gave me a new lease on musical life," he continues. "I felt a void in playing the piano. As a solo voice it does not come up to the level of expression that a synthesizer can give you. Keith Jarrett's playing will totally dispel anything I've said about the piano being limited, but it all depends on the music you want to play. Once you get down to serious business with the synthesizer, you realize that the possibilities are endless. Yet only a few will lend themselves to your music."

Hammer's trademarks in terms of synthesizer sounds are his flute and guitar-like timbres. When asked about their patch settings he replies, "I don't actually have standard arrangements for them, It's a funny thing, and may sound like I don't want to give them out, but I've gotten the flute sound with three different waveforms: pulse, square, and sawtooth. Something that people don't realize is that it's not how you set the instrument, but what you play on it, how you bend the notes.

"It's all a matter of deciding in your head what you want to do and throwing out all that's unnecessary to doing it. Sounds will start coming out because you know what you're looking for. That's why the synthesizer is an amazing instrument. It works not by itself, but by the human ear. The settings change from day to day, but when I start playing, the chemistry happens. For a synthesizer to tick, it takes a receptive human ear on the other end."

Jan uses a variety of keyboard instruments to express his musical ideas. Each instrument is treated in a different manner, depending upon its function in his music. For a single-voice statement he would use a synthesizer. To create textures Jan turns to electric piano, whereas the acoustic piano is reserved for the quiet, introspective moments. "My taste runs to Moog and Tom Oberheim's gear for synthesizers. I'm concerned with size, versatility, and how quickly I can get from one sound to another." He goes on, "I use two Minimoogs and one Oberheim Xpander Module/Digital Sequencer." He also uses a Fender Rhodes 88 and a rebuilt Freeman String Symphonizer—Bob Moog put a newly designed resonant filter network in it to give it a more "wooden, resonant sound."

Over the past two years, Jan Hammer has been busy recording three very diverse albums: *The First Seven Days*, *Elvin Jones on the Mountain*, and *Oh Yeah?* He believes that [*Seven Days*] is his most refined work to date. It was produced, recorded, and engineered by Hammer himself in his home studio, Red Gate, which he helped build with his friend and electronics advisor Andy Topeka. With the exception of some percussion by David Johnson and violin by Steve Kindler, Hammer played all the music. Those looking for the high-energy electric jazz he dispensed on Billy Cobham's *Spectrum* album will no doubt be disappointed. This is a composer's recording, and is closer to a form of contemporary classical music than jazz. Jan adds, "It is communication that uses simple elements. I'm not trying to complicate things. The point of the music is to communicate, not stun or leave people breathless."

On the Mountain, on the other hand, is more of a view of Jan's past, having featured Gene Perla on bass and Elvin Jones on drums. And the newly released *Oh Yeah?* includes the work of Steve Kindler (violin), Fernando Saunders (bass), and Tony Smith (drums), and is an exploration of what Hammer calls "progressive R&B." On his latest tour, Jan joined forces with guitar legend Jeff Beck to delve into the realm of jazz, rock, and funk. Why this wide-ranging interest in styles? Hammer explains, "I don't have to go to any lengths to disown jazz or rock. I enjoy going back to my roots, because I have my new music, my soul food. What I play speaks for itself."

More recently, Jan's changes in style have led him to move away from the traditional sit-down-at-the-keyboard approach to playing toward the use of a custom-built portable keyboard controller, complete with Minimoog pitch and modulation wheels. This instrument interfaces with his Minimoog and Oberheim Xpander Module outfit.

Your keyboard setup is currently in a state of change.

Right. I'm having an updated version of Roger Powell's Probe built for me by Royalex. The electronics will be about the same as Roger's, but the left-hand control section will be revised. It will be sort of custom-fitted to my hand. That's what's taking the most time, finding the correct angles. It's going to have the pitch and modulation wheels of a Minimoog.

Instead of the smaller cylindrical wheels Roger used?

Yeah. I couldn't use those things at all. They're nice in theory, but when it comes right down to playing the instrument, it's not there. Their position inside of the little hand grip puts your left hand out of commission as far as playing the keyboard goes. What I like to do is use my left hand to complement what my right hand is doing, going back and forth between the wheels and the keyboard. I do that on the Minimoog monophonically, and now on the Probe, which is hooked up to an Oberheim Xpander Module system, I'm going to need my left hand as near as possible to the keyboard. At this point, we've got a wooden model put together. The final version is in fiberglass. I should be seeing it very shortly. It's an incredible system—all multiplexed into just 19 leads between the instrument and the synthesizer electronics, controlling 40 to 50 functions.

Is your Probe going to be controlling just the Oberheim Six-Voice system?

No. I'm going to be playing the Oberheim and my Minis. I could never leave those behind. Are you kidding? That's my sound, really. I consider the Minimoog my main instrument.

Are you going to drop your Rhodes and Freeman String Symphonizer?

The Rhodes won't take as dominant a role as it used to, just because I like to move around now. The Rhodes is a bit heavy to carry around onstage. Now that we're a power trio in the tradition of Cream and Jimi Hendrix, I really have to stand up when I'm playing. I'm fulfilling the role of the guitar player, and to do that you can't just sit in the background. In fact, it's quite stark, you know? I really enjoy being able to move around and play in different directions physically. You can actually point the music with your body the way you want it to go.

Do you find that having the keyboard vertical to your body makes you develop different muscles and playing techniques?

Very much so. I've learned things. I've been using this keyboard for about a year and a half now, and I've found altogether new techniques of playing the keyboard that I was never able to do when I was using a horizontal keyboard. There are different muscle groups at work. Your wrists take on a different role. You can use straight-ahead keyboard technique, but you can enhance it just by slight wrist motion, like rotating wrist motion which will enable you to play something you could never do on an ordinary horizontal keyboard. It's hard to describe; it's a very subtle thing, but once you get used to it, it's amazing what you can do.

Initially, what made you gravitate to the Minimoog?

Money [*laughs*]. I couldn't afford anything bigger. But at the same time it was a blessing, because none of the other bigger synthesizers had the wheel assembly. And to me, that is the most important feature, in addition to the Minimoog being so versatile, of course. I cannot get by without the wheel.

What made you begin—and this is a bad way to put it—imitating the guitar?

You're right, it's probably not the right way to put it, simply because it's not just imitating the guitar with the synthesizer. It's more freeing yourself from the fixed keyboard, which sits on those 12 notes and never moves. Horns move in pitch but they aren't imitating the guitar; Indian instruments like the sitar and vina don't imitate the guitar, but they use the same inflections; bagpipes and horns used in Eastern European music use that same inflection, but they don't imitate the guitar. And I'm from Eastern Europe, so I've been exposed to this. This thing is planet-wide. It's a certain approach to monophonic playing that has been popularized in the United States by the guitar. But I think it's open to anyone who can find the means to do it. And I have found the means through the Minimoog.

> "I mean, I've played for musicians all of my life, but it's time I played for people. That's where I stand now."

How much do the syncable oscillators on the Oberheim Xpander Module have to do with your "guitar" sound?

A lot. That's exactly why I use the Oberheim. I've heard that Moog is coming out with a new small synthesizer with that feature on it. I've been talking their ears off about that for years. Now they're finally going to put it in.

Are you talking about the Multimoog?

I think that's the name of it. I get them confused. Dave Luce [Moog's director of engineering] mentioned it to me.

Do you use any external effects devices with your synthesizers?

Yes, a little bit of flanging. The one I use is made by MXR.

Don't you also use some type of compressor/limiter arrangement?

Yes, made by DBX. I use them mostly for the Rhodes. One is to take the bark off and the other is just a spare. Sometimes I'll use it to compress my Echoplex. It does all kinds of things to the return—the way the echoes return. It can stretch them out; it does crazy things like that. It's hard to describe. You have to experiment with it.

Was that used at all on the beginning of "The First Seven Days'?

No. That was all done in the studio. The big deep sound was fed direct into the board; the lead sound in the solo was recorded, believe it or not, through a Pignose amp. An original Pignose, miked with a Neumann mike. It was smoking, melting the speaker.

What other types of studio effects like that have you done?

That's pretty much it. You go back and forth, depending on what you're looking for, between the very clear full frequency range studio direct input and the completely distorted speaker sound. I've used all kinds of speakers and amps ranging from Fender to Marshall to Hiwatt and all of those things. You get different sets of harmonics and harmonic distortion and intermodulation distortion between those two signals, the clean and the distorted; then you blend them according to your taste. That's pretty much how these sounds are achieved. That's how everyone does it, I guess.

You used to have some kind of device lying on the floor between your Rhodes and your Freeman String Symphonizer. What did it do?

I haven't been using that lately because that was before I started using polyphonic synthesizers. It was a Bode frequency shifter. It was used to shift the frequency of the Rhodes up and down. I had it connected to a control-voltage pedal. People would come up to me and say, "What happened? That can't be done!" It was amazing. Since I haven't been playing the Rhodes much and I've gotten both the Polymoog and the Oberheim Four-Voice in the stage setup now, I don't need the frequency shifter. The polyphonic bending on the synthesizers is much more pronounced. I do still use the Bode in the studio, though. It's a fantastic tool. You can get tubular bells, giant chimes, or resonating rail sounds—all very metallic. On *The First Seven Days* the melodies were done through that.

What kinds of things do you use the Polymoog for?

I guess it really depends on the piece of music. It's very hard to describe. The Polymoog strings are fantastic. I really love them. The harpsichords are incredible; clavinet, too. It's useful for things like that—imitating something that already exists. But that really understates the instrument's potential.

What about the Oberheim?

The Oberheim is completely from Neptune. It's unlike anything that's ever been here before. You just don't attempt to imitate anything with it, you go for brand-new sounds. I think you need both instruments to create the full spectrum of sound.

Which of the two did you use for that flanged sounding instrument on "Hyperspace" from the *Melodies* album?

"Hyperspace" was done mostly with the Oberheim.

Do you find monophonic playing is becoming more of a limitation for you within a three-piece band because you're having to fill more space?

That's not really what's happening. The violin didn't really fill too much space because it was not an accompanying instrument. It was another solo voice. So all this format provides is more solo space, which I choose not to fill because I'd much rather play more pieces of music. I'm tired of playing pieces that stretch on for half an hour. I don't feel any mid-range texture lacking within the three-piece format. If I need it, I go and play piano or polyphonic synthesizer. I don't think it would sound exactly the same if I were working with another bass player. Fernando [Saunders] has a way of complementing the lead instrument. Between the two of us it sometimes sounds like there is somebody comping in the middle, but it's just our combined playing forming a kind of implied polyphony. It's a concept. When you study music you talk about Bach being a polyphonic composer, but also writing for single-note instruments like the violin. You'll have a violin piece where he'll imply polyphony, but the fact that it's not happening simultaneously doesn't distract you. It still sounds polyphonic. That's the effect we're shooting for between the bass and the lead instrument.

How did the Mahavishnu Orchestra work out tunes?

It was usually by singing; word of mouth. There was very little written out. There were some super-complex passages that had to be written out and rehearsed, but those were usually only short segments of pieces. Overall it was pretty much either played or hummed. In the case of that band, it was more playing, because you couldn't really sing most of the things [*laughs*]. You'd tie your vocal chords in knots.

Has any of your interest in exploring odd meters carried over from the Orchestra?

Well, I don't know. I can say with a straight face that I have played just about every conceivable odd time signature without putting them in chains like having 5 followed by 7 followed by 3, because then the combinations become endless. But as far as straightforward time signatures and different time signatures are concerned, I've played them all, and it's become very easy for me. The challenge sort of went out of it. You get to a point where you don't enjoy listening to what you played anymore. But within the music we do now, which is pretty much basic 4/4, there are implied polyrhythms. The experience of playing complex rhythms isn't going to evaporate overnight, and it has stuck around. Anyway, the secret to playing complicated time signatures is not to play them as

A SELECTED JAN HAMMER DISCOGRAPHY

AS A LEADER
Miami Vice: The Complete Collection
Drive
Beyond the Mind's Eye
Untold Passion
Hammer
Black Sheep
Melodies
Jeff Beck with the Jan Hammer Group Live
Oh, Yeah?
The First Seven Days
Like Children

WITH THE MAHAVISHNU ORCHESTRA
Birds of Fire
Inner Mounting Flame

WITH JEFF BECK
Wired

FOR MORE INFORMATION ON JAN HAMMER, VISIT www.janhammer.com.

if they were cockeyed or turned upside-down or inside-out, but to find a common pulse within the time signature that will relate to a basic regular pulse like 4/4. All those time signatures have it going through them. That's the reason some people can sound totally smooth and unaffected while playing in 19 or 21. It's because they've found the pulse that will relate to the human heart, a pulse that anyone can relate to. That's what makes it smooth.

What about something with a lot of layers happening, something like "Darkness/Earth in Search of a Sun," the beginning of *The First Seven Days*? How was that conceived?

Most of that whole record was done instantaneously using an 8-track recorder. I would do one track spontaneously, and then respond to it on another track, and then respond to those two tracks on another track, and so on. That was a matter of writing music on tape.

A lot of people probably wonder if we'll ever see the Mahavishnu Orchestra get back together.

It almost happened when John did his new album, *Johnny McLaughlin Electric Guitarist.* I couldn't really agree to do it. I was asked to several times, but it's just not where I'm at now. I'm in a totally different place now, and I can't go back. It feels too soon. If it's going to happen, it will happen in another four or five years. You know, with all those bands copying the Mahavishnu Orchestra trip, who needs the Mahavishnu Orchestra? We would just sound like a good copy of ourselves anyway. I'm tired of listening to all the copies. I can't bring myself to play that way. I couldn't do it with a straight face. I would crack up; I would feel like I was copying myself. It's crazy. I'm glad I found a way out at this point. About two years ago I started to feel closed in by that approach to music, and by the number of people copying us. It was all just a drop in the bucket, it didn't mean anything, because people couldn't tell the difference between, say, John McLaughlin and Al Di Meola. To them it's just fast guitar leads. You and I as musicians can tell the difference, but that's neither here nor there, because we're playing for people, we're not playing for us. I mean, I've played for musicians all of my life, but it's time I played for people. That's where I stand now.

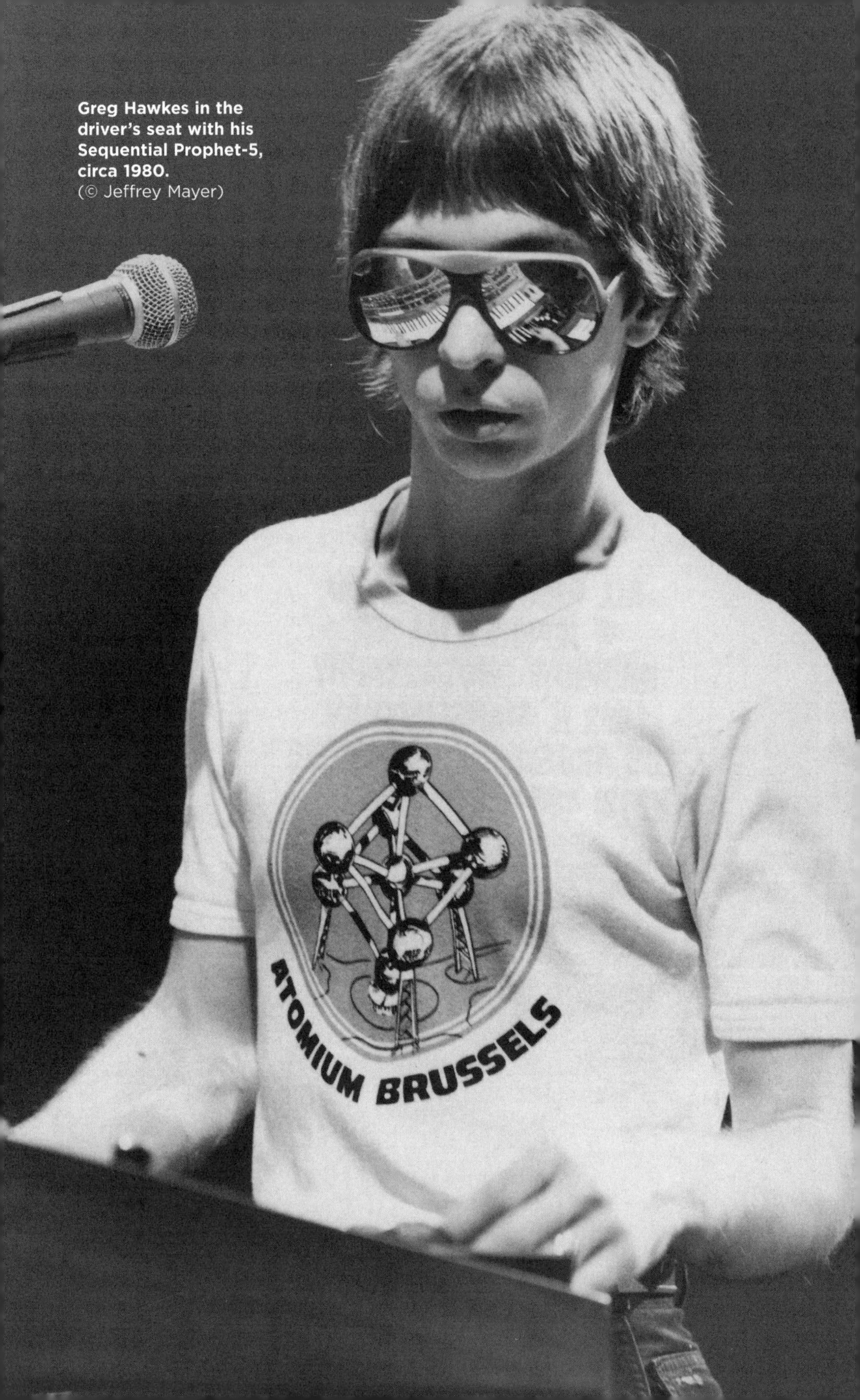

Greg Hawkes in the driver's seat with his Sequential Prophet-5, circa 1980.
(© Jeffrey Mayer)

GREG HAWKES

SYNTHS DRIVE THE CARS

by Jim Aikin, Robert L. Doerschuk, and Russ Summers

Portions of this chapter appeared in the April 1980 and December 1983 of Keyboard *magazine.*

From out of Boston, a city known to visitors and natives alike for its bewildering maze of wrong-way streets, came, fittingly, the Cars. Unlike the Beantown roadway system, however, this rock quintet drove straight toward its goal of winning critical and popular acclaim, while earning recognition along the way from *Rolling Stone*, *Creem*, *Circus*, and *Crawdaddy* as Best New Artists of 1978, not to mention a Grammy nomination.

One major reason for their success as exponents of the new wave is the keyboard work of Greg Hawkes. His sense of musical texture, his ability to play a solid role in the rhythm section, and his knack for coming up with memorable hooks in tunes like "Just What I Needed" [from *The Cars*] and "Let's Go" [from *Candy-o*] were also factors in his finish in a tie for second place in the 1979 Keyboard Poll balloting for Best New Talent.

Hawkes had only limited training on the piano, taking lessons for about three years beginning in third grade. He lost interest in the instrument for a number of years after that, and didn't go back to the keyboard until he was 15 or 16, a year or two after he had started playing guitar. The Beatles, and later the Mothers of Invention and various English bands, had moved him back to the keyboard in an attempt to play along with the new records, but even then he deigned not to practice in the technical sense.

"The first band I ever played keyboards in full-time was a band called Richard and the Rabbits," he continues, "and they also had Rick [Ocasek, guitarist] and Ben [Orr, bassist], who are now with the Cars. That was the first band I was ever in with anybody from the Cars. We just played locally around Boston."

Hawkes didn't have a keyboard of his own, despite his busy performing schedule, until 1973 or '74, when he bought a Sound City electric piano, which he still owns. Aside from the piano at his parents' house, he had done most of his playing on a friend's Hohner Clavinet C, which he borrowed regularly from job to job.

Luckily, Times have changed since then, and now Greg uses a Yamaha CP-30 electric piano ("which I like because it sounds electronic"), a Vox Continental organ, and three synthesizers, namely an ARP Omni, a Mini-Korg, and a Sequential Circuits Prophet-5. They are funneled into Yamaha power amps and out of a couple of JBL cabinets, each of which has a horn and a 15" speaker.

As its road-worn appearance testifies, the Mini-Korg is a longtime favorite of Greg's. "I must have had it for four or five years," he estimates. "It's holding up great. I've never had any problems with it. In fact, for the first two or three years I owned it, I didn't even have a case for it. I used to wrap it up in a blanket and carry it around in my car, and it's never messed up. It's worked perfectly. It's also fun to play. I like the sound of it because it doesn't sound like a Minimoog or some other familiar model. It's just a nice little melody synthesizer. That's about all there is to it."

The Prophet became a part of the Hawkes setup after the group had released its first recording, *The Cars*. In concert he uses one bank of eight programs, some of which are factory presets, either untouched or with slight alterations such as a modified envelope filter, and others of which are his own. Greg is particularly careful about finding the right combination of subtle nuances on a Prophet program when getting ready to record in the studio, since "you're going to pick up little things there that you wouldn't notice if we were playing in a hockey rink."

"I think a lot of the factory presets sound real good as they are," he states. "Anybody who's actually familiar with them will probably notice that the little synthesizer part on 'Let's Go' is not very much different in tone than what you hear with factory preset number 22. On 'Dangerous Type' it's pretty similar to the first preset, number 11. I would usually start with one of the presets and just keep messing around with it until I found another sound that I liked. A lot of times I didn't even have the foresight to record it in one of the banks."

Greg relies on his other polyphonic synth, the Omni, for string sounds, which he considers the instrument's strongest feature. When playing them, he generally uses the viola setting. "But I'm not even looking for an accurate string sound," he points out. "Again, I like the fact that it sounds somewhat electronic. To me, it sounds like an even more electronic version of the Mellotron sound. If I was looking for an accurate string sound, I would write out string parts and record them that way, using real string players." On *The Cars*, before the arrival of the Prophet, the Omni and the Mini-Korg were the backbone of the keyboard tracks. In fact, all of the keyboard parts to "Moving in Stereo" were done with the Omni.

The synthesizer is the ideal instrument for Hawkes when it comes to playing the repetitive sequencer-like lines that color much of his work. On "Shoo Be Doo," from *Candy-o*, he used a Sequential Circuits sequencer to lay down the pattern over a multi-layered texture of keyboard overdubs; in fact, Dave Robinson's Syndrums and Elliot Easton's guitar were the only non-keyboard instruments on that track. But often Greg plays sequencer-like parts by hand, as in the songs "Candy-o" and "Nightspots:' both from *Candy-o*, with a touch of either an Echoplex or a Roland Space Echo on the former tune. Hawkes acknowledges that the music of Kraftwerk and other German electronic artists has affected this side of his performance.

"It's bound to rub off," he admits. "Everything that you listen to is bound to rub off to a certain degree, but I think that at this time I'm probably influenced more by the other four people in the Cars than by anything else!"

> "I think there's a lot to be said for simplicity. You could say there is real complexity in simplicity."

Like many new wave keyboardists, Hawkes has looked back to the electronic organs of the '60s for musical inspiration. But unlike Blondie's Jimmy Destri or Steve Nieve of Elvis Costello's band, Greg prefers the Vox Continental to the Farfisa organ. In fact, he owns two Continentals to be sure that there is always at least one within reach that works. Both of them have been slightly modified by Skip Sweeney, a Boston-based technician. Greg's favorite setting on the Vox is to have the low-mid and high-mid drawbars pulled out, and he seldom experiments with new tone combinations onstage, because "the drawbars on my Vox are pretty noisy. If I move them around too much, you can really hear them."

On rare occasions Hawkes has used an acoustic piano or a Hammond organ in the studio. The piano sound, however, has never been an important element in his approach to keyboards, and Greg feels that the material performed by the Cars doesn't generally lend itself well to either an acoustic or electric grand onstage. Besides, he adds, "I'd never be interested in traveling with an electric piano. They're just too much trouble!"

When it comes to the electric and/or acoustic piano family, Hawkes vouches for the Yamaha CP-30. "The Rhodes, to me, is just a little too overused:' he explains, "a little too familiar-sounding. The same goes for the Wurlitzer, in a way, although if I owned either one of the two I would probably prefer the Wurlitzer. But the Yamaha touch sensitivity is great. I also love the stereo output, and I like the sound. You can make it sound like a Rhodes too, if you want. It can get close enough to a Rhodes for anything I'd need it for!"

The Cars record with one of the more popular producers in rock, Roy Thomas Baker, whose myriad credits include Journey, Foreigner, and Pink Floyd.

Hawkes is happy with their working relationship. "Roy's real good," he states. "He knows the studio inside and out, for sure, and he's got a pretty identifiable sound, especially with drums. You can hear his touch on the vocal sounds too. We get along with him real well personally. He lets us do whatever we want; he's not at all dictatorial. He just tries to keep everybody from taking the thing too seriously. If he likes something, he never says, 'You're doing great!' He'll just say it's okay. He's also got a Stevens 40-track board that he carries around with him from studio to studio; it's his own personal machine."

In recording with Baker, Greg plays his keyboards direct into the board, usually starting with a basic electric piano track, then overdubbing the synthesizers and/or acoustic piano over the next two or three days. He deviated from this formula only on "Shoo Be Doo," in which the basic track was the sequencer, followed by the electronic drums and the rest of the keyboard parts.

The concept of simplicity is at the core of the Cars and their music. "When the Cars first got together," Hawkes relates, "I think there was a fairly conscious effort to keep things on a simple and to-the-point basis. We didn't want to get in each other's way. We just wanted to play as a unit, so we all sort of realized that the songs were really the main focal point, rather than any particular musicianship behind them."

This approach made for some tight performances and for a direct and clean musical co-existence between the guitar and keyboard parts. It also provoked some critics to dismiss the Cars, and the other bands at the forefront of the new wave that also subscribe to this formula, as being too basic, not ambitious or complex enough. This kind of analysis leaves Hawkes shaking his head.

"It's just a shame," he shrugs. "I'm not going to try to defend what we play, because I think the music has to speak for itself. If you don't like it, I'm not going to try to convince you that you should. But I like stuff that's even more minimalistic than the Cars, like Suicide. They've opened several concerts for us, and I think they're doing amazing things, especially since they are only two guys, and one of them is the front man. They do things like just repeat one riff over and over. I love that type of stuff, drone music; that's what I listen to at home. I'm not bored if I hear Brian Eno's *Music for Airports* or stuff like Phil Glass things that just stay on one chord. I also like the Normal, whose music is really simplistic, and I'm a Devo fan too."

What, then, does leave Greg cold when it comes to music? "I do get bored by endless soloing," he notes. "I don't really listen to keyboard players, so I don't have favorite soloists, in the Minimoog sort of tradition of fake guitar-style playing. That doesn't interest me. The stuff I listen to, like Kraftwerk, doesn't have much of that going on. It creates a mood more than anything by its total effect; the overall sound gets me more than any person's particular style of playing. I think there's a lot to be said for simplicity. You could say there is real complexity in simplicity."

There was a good deal of anticipation and speculation earlier this year when Hawkes became the first of the Cars to step out from Ric Ocasek's shadow, releasing a solo album called *Niagara Falls*. Would Hawkes' solo vehicle stay in the Cars' fast lane, or would it take a detour into the dark regions of the cutout bins?

Well, *Niagara Falls* didn't exactly break any sales records after its release earlier this year, but it did indicate that, artistically, Hawkes is his own man. The drum parts, the lead lines, the backup parts, all emanated from Hawkes' various synthesizers and drum machines and evoked the mechanistic repetitions of Kraftwerk and other techno-pop groups. Since Hawkes contributes a very different kind of color to the tight, high-strung feeling rampant in the Cars' recordings, *Niagara Falls* is an indicator both of his ability to adapt to the musical requirements of other artists with whom he plays, and of his individual expressive style.

His musical tastes and recreational diversions, with their built-in electronic sounds, ring true on *Niagara Falls*, and on the last Cars LP, *Shake It Up*, as well. Though the drummer David Robinson and guitarist/ bandleader Ric Ocasek are the key elements in the group's pumping beat, it is Hawkes' spare fills that have established the Cars' distinctive sound since their debut release, *The Cars*, broke onto the charts five years ago. As for their band's next album, due out in January '84, we could only conjecture, based on the fact that the quintet had flown to London to do the project with Mutt Lange, the English producer behind Def Leppard's heavy-metal clangor.

"The guy is really a perfectionist," Hawkes tells us, "a perfectionist like I've never seen before. Often I ended up playing maybe five different sounds on one part before he got what worked best. I've always gone for the idea of using just one sound per part, or possibly a stereo setup with an effect or two added, so this kind of orchestral sound, this layering process, is new for me. I can't really say which I like better."

At the time of our interview, Hawkes had finished with, he estimated, about half of the keyboard parts for the new recording, *Heatbeat City*. Much of the keyboard playing on it was done on Greg's Roland Jupiter-8, with additional parts from the PPG Wave 2 and the Fairlight CMI. Hawkes played the PPG because "it was lying around the studio," using it mainly for metallic sounds. "So far I haven't been able to sync it up with my MicroComposer," he confesses. "I'm having a little trouble with that. For the sounds I've used from it so far, I've just been playing it by hand."

On all the songs they finished by the time we spoke, as well as on the projected cuts for this album, Hawkes had used the Fairlight to lay down a sync track, with elaborated rhythm sounds following on the MicroComposer, Linn drum machine, or Fairlight. Though the Cars had done similar work in the past off of sync tracks, this marks the first time they have done so on every song of an LP. The decision to work off a reference track was made by Lange, but Greg has embraced the idea with enthusiasm. He had used that approach on his solo album, and felt at home doing it with the band as well.

"I actually used the LinnDrum as part of the writing process on *Niagara Falls*," he recalls. "I had gotten my Linn—the newer, compact version—around the time that I was writing most of those tunes. I'd often start with a rhythm pattern and a bass line, then work up little melodies on top of them. I also have two Roland rhythm machines, an 808 and a CR-78, and they show up on the record, often synced together."

When asked specifically what he likes about the rhythm machines he uses, Hawkes explains, "The CR-78 has some funny sounds that neither of the other two have, like this neat white-noise tambourine; I used it on 'Ants in Your Pants' and flanged it a little. I almost always used the Linn at least for bass drum and snare drum sounds, but I did use the 808 for some handclaps and some of their tom sounds, which really don't sound as much like toms as the Linn, although you can still use them to good effect. Once I got into the MicroComposer, I started using it as sort of a master clock, because I didn't have any trouble with its sync time, but I only used it on three or four songs, because the others had a different kind of sync tone and I didn't want too much of a change. So what I usually did on *Niagara Falls* was start by recording the sync tone, then lay down the basic rhythm track with the Linn, some sort of bass sequencer, and the MC-4 MicroComposer."

The steady sequential rhythms and metallic tones prevalent on *Niagara Falls* bring to mind Hawkes' admiration for artists like Philip Glass, Steve Reich, Brian Eno, and especially Kraftwerk. He acknowledged Kraftwerk as a primary influence, and some of the pieces on his solo album were written around that time, like "Ants in Your Pants." However, he also discarded a number of

A SELECTED GREG HAWKES DISCOGRAPHY

WITH THE NEW CARS
It's Alive

WITH PAUL MCCARTNEY
Flowers in the Dirt

WITH THE CARS
Door to Door
Heartbeat City
Shake It Up
Panorama
Candy-o
The Cars

FOR MORE INFORMATION ON GREG HAWKES, VISIT www.greghawkesmusic.com.

tunes he had composed several years ago in favor of newer material, which, he believes, reflects an important change in his style. "There's more structure in what I'm doing now," he says. "The old stuff was a little more drony, with fewer chord changes; it would stay in one mode for three or four minutes. The things on my album turned out to be a little more pop."

Most of the synthesizer parts on *Niagara Falls* were done on a Roland Jupiter-8 and Sequential Circuits Prophet-5, with some bass lines laid down on the Roland TB-303; a bit of judicious effects applications with his Roland 555 tape delay and Boss flanger; distortion, phase shift, and chorus pedals; and miscellaneous effects from various other synthesizers. He cites the arpeggiator and split keyboard feature on the Jupiter-8 as major reasons why he likes to use that instrument, and adds, "I found that if I had been working with the Jupiter-8 all day, and then plugged in the Prophet, it sounded just a little bit duller, a little more muted. The Jupiter seems to have more high brightness; that's the range where I really notice the difference in their sounds." In addition to these, Hawkes has a Roland Vocoder Plus, a Yamaha CP-30 electric piano, an ARP Omni, a Roland Jupiter-4, and his first synthesizer, a Mini-Korg, at home.

For their projected tour, Hawkes hopes to streamline his keyboard setup as much as possible. The Prophet-5 and Jupiter-8 would almost certainly be taken along, but he hadn't made up his mind about whether to travel with the vocoder. "I've used it onstage," he recalls. "A couple of tours ago, we used it to play vocoded vocals on 'Shoo Be Doo' [from *Candy-o*] live. We probably won't play that on this tour, but I might still want to use the vocoder to thicken up background vocals."

Greg is not the only member of the Cars with a few keyboards stashed away. Ric Ocasek, the group's leader, owns a Prophet and a Jupiter as well, along with a Korg string synthesizer and some Yamaha and Casio portable keyboards, all of which he uses to lay down 8-track demos of original tunes for the rest of the band to learn. "Most of the time the parts that Ric plays sound fine," Hawkes says, "so I end up playing them, maybe just changing the sound a little, or doing a couple of things of my own. I'd like to encourage him to play some of the parts on the records himself, if he wants to."

Though there may be other solo endeavors down the road, Hawkes believes that most of his musical work in the foreseeable future will involve the Cars. "I could never imagine doing anything else," he states. "I mean, I've tried having normal jobs, but I could never keep 'em. Even doing my own album was a little strange, taking on more responsibility than I'm used to. I still like to hear even the old Cars' songs—they hold up pretty well—but I wonder what I'll think of them 25 years from now."

The sounds behind the sculptor: Jean Michel Jarre with his Moog III, one of his many sound sources. (Courtesy of *Keyboard* magazine)

7 JEAN MICHEL JARRE

SYNTHESIS AS LIBERATION

by Jim Aikin

Portions of this chapter appeared in the April 1978 issue of Keyboard *magazine.*

European audiences were treated last summer to a concentrated dose of pop-oriented synthesizer music in the form of *Oxygene*, an album that spent months at the top of the charts in France and the Netherlands. *Oxygene* was the creation of 29-year-old Frenchman Jean Michel Jarre, a native of Lyon whose preparations for eventual success included study of classical piano and classical synthesizer techniques as well as playing in rock groups in Paris and composing advertising jingles for radio and TV. In person, Jarre proves to have an excellent command of English, which he uses to tell us about his equipment and recording techniques, and also to articulate some fascinating insights into the role of music, and specifically the synthesizer, in today's popular culture. If the sound of his music and the clarity of his ideas are reliable indicators, Jarre is a young man on the way up.

Was your first instrument the piano?

Yes. I studied classical piano at the Paris Conservatory, and I must say that the way we are taught music, both in America and in Europe, is quite old-fashioned, because we learn from books that were written at the beginning of the 19th century. At the same time I was studying there, I was playing in local pop groups in France, playing both piano and electric guitar. I also began working at the Electronic Music Center [Groupe de Recherches Musicales], which is directed by Pierre Henry and Pierre Schaeffer. Pierre Schaeffer is really the man who invented electro-acoustic music. He is the father of *musique concrete.* They started the Center in 1945 or so, long before electronics became the fashion in pop music, and composers such as John Cage, Stockhausen, and Xenakis came there to study. I worked with them for three years, which gave me the opportunity to work with what was at that time one of the biggest synthesizers in the world.

And yet your music is quite different from classical electronic music.

I realized that the people in contemporary classical music have a very intellectual approach to their music. They deal with the mathematics of music, the philosophy of music, even the sociology of music, rather than just with music. And because I'm mainly a composer and not a scientist, I decided to put together my own studio, little by little, in my flat. At the same time, I was quite involved in working with the music of Japan and other kinds of non-European music.

What kind of influence did that have on you?

I discovered that we in Western music are the only artists who work with a written system of notation, a written code. It doesn't exist in painting, it doesn't exist in choreography, and even in music it doesn't exist in the same way in Oriental music or African music. It has only existed in Occidental music during the last few hundred years; before that it wasn't the case here either. And because we have this written notation, we have a tendency to consider music an abstract art, something very intellectual. At the beginning of the 20th century, Schoenberg, Webern, and Berg realized that they needed something more than traditional music. But what did they do? They just made another intellectual system, a system so complex that after a while you are obliged to be a doctor of philosophy and mathematics in order to understand the music, in order to read the 200-page book that explains the concepts. It became more and more for the head and less and less for the sensitivity.

But when I make this point, some people think it's ironic that I'm trying to communicate this sensitivity using electronic instruments. There is some confusion about electronic music, because it is not the music that is electronic, but the instruments. If the music is robotized or mechanical or without any heart, it's not because of the machine, but because of the human being in front of the machine. The difference between a machine and a musical instrument lies in the way you use it. If you have an emotion to communicate, you can communicate through a tom-tom, through a sitar, through a piano, or through a synthesizer or computer. It's a question of approach, that's all.

You use the instrument to communicate.

That's right. And because we live in the electronic age, I use the instruments of my generation. Electronic devices are really the best adapted to communication, because 95 percent of the public listens to music using electronics. Even Beethoven has become an electronic experience. The acoustic instruments that we know so well, like the violin and the harp, and the piano somewhat later, they were all created by the craftsmen of the time working closely with the composers of the time. The composers said, "Try to make me an instrument like a violin, because I need this type of sound." Now, I have nothing against acoustic instruments, obviously. But if we want a new music adapted to our time, and we do not work with our own craftsmen to make new instruments, it means only that we are less clever than the composers of three centuries ago.

Speaking of Beethoven becoming an electronic experience, what do you think of electronic symphonists like Walter Carlos and Isao Tomita?

I have a lot of respect for them, because they're doing interesting things, but I don't agree that that's the best use for synthesizers. I think it's a narrow use of electronic devices to use them just for imitating classical instruments or to make electronic versions of classical scores. I think we have to consider that this instrument is an original instrument on the highest possible level. Obviously I'm interested in Tomita's work, because he's a fine musician, but I think we have to consider that here for the first time we have before us the opportunity to be exactly like a sculptor standing in front of his stone. All the acoustic instruments have a sound that is determined from the beginning. When you build a piano, you determine its sound forever, and everybody knows the sound of the piano. But nobody knows the sound of the synthesizer. You have to invent it. You have to work on the sound with your hands the way a sculptor does with his stone. We need to refine the natural attitude that musical instruments are extensions of the hands before being extensions of the brain. Maybe it's because of the written system of notation that we forget. We're always thinking about the music before doing the music. It's so sad that many people say, "I should like very much to make music, but I never learned how to read it or write it." That's not the only approach. Children get discouraged because in school they must learn do, re, mi, fa, so, la, si, do before ever touching the instrument.

How did you go about sculpting *Oxygene*? Did you compose it before you recorded it, or did it evolve as you recorded it?

Rather than using sculpture as an analogy, let's use painting. I think I have the same attitude as a painter. At the beginning I have a rough idea, and after that it's a dialog with the instrument. A painter can say, "Yes, I want to draw some birds on a branch," and as he is working on his canvas he has further ideas about what they will look like. It's an evolution. But it's not really improvisation. I try to be quite structured in my work. When I have a rough idea, I find something and try to integrate it into the whole structure of the music.

How do you intend to go about doing your own live performances?

I'm trying to have an ecological attitude vis-à-vis the music and the technology. Use the technology because it's here, but don't be trapped by it. That's why there are places in *Oxygene* where there are only two or three tracks. I have ten fingers, so I won't need to use tapes or anything like that. I am thinking about having a computer to help change settings while I'm playing.

What's your current equipment lineup?

I use both the ARP 2600 and the ARP 2500, and sometimes the Moog III, but that not so much. I use a VCS-3 synthesizer, which is very interesting, mainly because of the matrix board. It's the only [modular] synthesizer that doesn't use patch cords. Wires are not so easy to use, because after about 20 wires you are a bit lost, but with the matrix board you have just pins, and it's very clear. And I use a Mellotron, and a Farfisa organ that has been totally modified, and another organ that isn't so well known in the U.S. called Eminent. And the RMI Keyboard Computer, the one that uses punch cards, and also the RMI Harmonic Synthesizer. It has 16 harmonics, and you can build your tone with them. And a Korg polyphonic. I've been working with a very fine French electronic engineer named Michel Geiss. Electronic engineers are the modern versions of violin makers. They're the craftsmen of today, or perhaps I should say of tomorrow. Geiss is making a 1,000-note sequencer for me, with pins mainly, and I'll be able to program the length of each note, and a lot of other parameters. It's very interesting, because I'll be able to change the sequence during the sequence, which will eliminate the mechanical sound of the sequencer. Another thing he's devising is a way of programming some delay, or some slight variations in the filter, on some of the notes. It will make it possible for me to add the human aspects of interpretation to the sequence.

Is there a particular reason why you prefer the Mellotron to a string synthesizer?

It was really by chance, because I have this Mellotron. I use it mainly with a flanger. I find the Mellotron very interesting because it's not a very good instrument. The time that it takes for the tape to start moving makes it sound like old movie soundtracks from the '30s. I like electronic deformations of sounds, and I use the Mellotron in that way.

What about reverb?

I used several different units on the album, two Revox magnetic echoes, an Echoplex, and a reverb made by EMS. In my opinion, the Revox is the best one, because they have a very good frequency response and a good signal-to-noise ratio. And I used an AKG stereo reverb, and an EMT plate reverb that's five meters long. I had eight different stereo echoes for the mixing.

Was the echo done in the mixing, or did you put some on the initial tracks?

Some at the beginning, but mainly in the mixing. You add the echo in the mix to create depth.

How long did it take to record *Oxygene*?

Four months of solid work. But the conception took me many years to arrive at. Before I left the Center, I made electronic music for the Opera of Paris. It was the first time that electronic music had entered this bastion of tradition. They made me paint the loudspeakers gold to match the decor, which should tell you something. The music I did then was quite different from *Oxygene*, but that was maybe the beginning for me, because the occasion was quite important in France. I came into contact with the media, and I realized how isolated we are as composers. A century ago there were no such barriers. Tchaikovsky, for instance, conducted his orchestra in front of his public. Now, you have recording studios, you have record companies, you have TV, radio, the press, hi-fi, loudspeakers, and then the public. If you don't know how to go through these channels, you are losing your function as an artist, which is communication.

The relationship in popular music is more direct, because we have more composer/performers.

Yes, but you have to go through other media anyway. And the performance itself, the tour, the concert stage, has become only an extension of the record. The record is an original expression by itself. We can make a comparison with film: Would you ask Stanley Kubrick to mount a stage version of *2001*? But records are stacked in the stores like bottles of whiskey—which means that the record is considered a consumer product. And that's not right. The record is the modern version of the novel; it's like the film. We have to consider two ways of using the record. It can be a documentation of a live performance, as it has been from the beginning, for Beethoven, or Kiss, or Elvis Presley, or Frank Sinatra. It's a kind of souvenir. Or, on the other hand, we can consider the record as an original expression, in its own terms as a medium, with music that has been conceived especially for the record. That's the way that *Oxygene* was conceived. Then, on top of that, you can consider doing a live performance of the material—but I hope that the version of *Oxygene* that I do onstage will be different from the version on record, because if all I do is duplicate the record, you would be much better off staying at home and listening to my music on your stereo.

> "If the music is robotized or mechanical or without any heart, it's not because of the machine, but because of the human being in front of the machine."

Some of the melody lines on *Oxygene* seemed reminiscent of Bach. Has he been an important influence on you?

Not consciously. I love Bach, and I love Mahler and Wagner, but if we talk about influence, I must say that I am much more influenced by cinema than by music, on an emotional level. I mean, so many composers during the 19th century were influenced by literature, by novels: Wagner was, Liszt was. And I should say that the masterpieces of our time are to be found not in literature but in the cinema. Cinema is really the main expression of our time. *2001* was a masterpiece because it was the first film to describe our electronic age in a romantic sense.

The six movements of *Oxygene* flow into one another without any sharp breaks. Why did you choose that kind of structure?

I think maybe we tend to think that the only possible music is a song that's three minutes long. Just as, on the other hand, we forget that Mozart wrote some pop songs for the society of his time, and even made some pieces for dancing, for balls, which were the discos of that time. And besides that he also made symphonies, just pure music. When I left the Center, I realized that the musician was quite isolated, and I decided to try other ways of getting music to the public, making music for movies, for TV, even jingles. It scandalized a part of the French intelligentsia, the fact that I was making music for the opera, and also music for jingles. But they're both legitimate fields of music.

It's unusual for a musician to do a promotional tour that involves only interviews rather than concerts.

I view what we are doing today as part of my job as a composer. It's part of the music, if I may say that, because if the music is to be communicated, it's the composer who has to communicate. His or her work is not finished at the door of the recording studio. We are making perhaps a kind of concerto for media and orchestra. There is quite a new wave in France, of philosophers who refuse to make philosophy just inside the walls of the university, of painters who refuse to stay in the garret. They want to touch the public where it lives, even if that's in the midst of the naked women of *Playboy* magazine, or on TV, or whatever. They're criticized as pop philosophers—but I think we are living in a pop culture, and I consider myself and my generation as pop musicians: If a painter does an image for the TV screen, or the cover of a magazine, he or she will touch the public more in one week than they would in their whole life if they stayed in the garret. I recently did a TV show in France, and I began the show by moving up to the camera and knocking on the lens and saying to my guests, "You are not to be frightened by this machine. It's a part of us. It's not a barrier, it's a help." This is the kind of attitude I think we must have in our generation.

A SELECTED JEAN MICHEL JARRE DISCOGRAPHY

Teo and Tea

Metamorphoses

Zoolook

Les Chants Magnetiques

Equinoxe

Oxygene

FOR MORE INFORMATION ON JEAN MICHEL JARRE, VISIT www.jeanmicheljarre.com.

Do you think you could have got to where you are now if you hadn't studied music in an isolated academic environment?

Obviously my music would be different, but that doesn't mean that academic training is necessary. Nobody should have a complex because of an academic musical training, because it's nothing; it's just a way to make music, not the only way to make music. When I work with electronic instruments, I am not using my classical background. Why? Because electronic instruments are totally new, and so I have a totally spontaneous approach to them. I couldn't approach acoustic instruments so spontaneously, because I learned them. When I ask a craftsman to make me an electronic device, I am at the beginning again in front of it. I don't know how to play it, and I have to find my own way. I agree that you are always a product of your background, but maybe I'm using electronic instruments to go faster, to forget, no, not to forget my background, because it's not bad, but only to take the music to more of a sensitive level than an intellectual level. In our world, which is harder and harder, the function of an artist becomes more and more important. When you are listening to the music, or standing in front of the painting, or watching the cinema, that is the only moment that you can use your sensitivity, because in our world we are using our sensitivity less and less, and it is atrophying. So when you are in front of the music, you are refining your individuality. It doesn't matter whether you have a broad musical background or none at all, you are right to like or dislike this piece of music. It's not wrong to like or dislike a certain piece. You are right for yourself. We have to be very careful, if we have a background in music, not to use it to decide what's good and what's bad and to tell people that they are right or wrong to like certain things. The main result of that kind of criticism is that people become totally intimidated when they listen to music. Of course, it's because I have the classical background that I can make the statement that the classical way is not the only way to go, and expect to be taken seriously. If I didn't have the classical background and said the same thing, nobody would pay any attention to me. So in that sense, it has a positive value to have the background.

What is your feeling about Kraftwerk?

I like some of their music, but not all of it. I don't feel very close to them, because they approach music very intellectually; and they say that, that's not just my opinion. They kind of glorify the machine. Maybe it's in the German mind to do that. And I don't agree with the way they leave the stage and let the machines play, because we must not forget that music is the human treatment or organization of sounds. They have a very clinical approach. They approach the music with white coats, like doctors. I don't agree with that use of the machine. I think it's superficial.

There's a sound on *Oxygene* that sounds very much like an acoustic hi-hat. Was it?

No, that was an electronic rhythm box, but with special phasing on it. It's funny. I didn't set out to make it sound like a hi-hat, but after the mixing and the echoes it came out like that. This is an interesting thing about the synthesizer: It's maybe the first impressionist instrument. I mean, when you look at a Van Gogh painting from a distance of three meters you see, let's say, red flowers. You are sure they're red flowers. But from 30 centimeters they're not red flowers at all, just a piece of red painting. You can't paint a flower, but only the idea of a flower. On *Oxygene,* in the last part where you have these sort of waves of the sea, obviously when you take this sound out of the context and listen closely to it, it's not the sound of the sea. But integrated into the arrangement, it is in fact the idea of the sea. What is quite new about electronic instruments is that you can integrate into your music the idea of the wind, the idea of the rain, the idea of the sea; the idea of life, in fact.

A genius at his day job: Bob Moog representing Norlin at a trade show in the late '70s, a transitional time for Moog synthesizers. (Courtesy of *Keyboard* magazine)

DR. ROBERT A. MOOG

8 THE MAKING OF A MINIMOOG FOR THE MILLENNIUM

by Ernie Rideout

The valley that sits at the confluence of the Blue Ridge, Appalachian, and Smoky Mountains is well known as a center for traditional arts. Collectors with an eye for fine needlework, hand sewing, and quilting make it a routine stop on their whirlwind shopping tours. The cabinetry and fine furniture of the area is no less sought after. You'd also expect to find musical instrument makers here, and you wouldn't be disappointed.

You might, however, possibly be surprised to find one of the biggest names in synthesizers plying their high-tech trade in complete harmony with the decidedly hand-hewn traditions of the region. Moog Music sits near the river in Asheville, North Carolina, occupying its share of an unremarkable commercial space among auto body shops and woodworkers. The paint on the shingle that says Moog Music isn't exactly still wet, but it wasn't that long ago that the sign said Big Briar, under which name synthesizer pioneer Bob Moog produced his line of theremins and Moogerfooger analog effects pedals.

Inside or out, the casual observer would be hard pressed to articulate the difference between Moog Music and Big Briar. The loading dock has piles of instrument boxes waiting to ship. The small but devoted staff moves through the amicable disarray of a small business. Bob Moog's tools occupy a large portion of a parts room, and evidence of his brainstorms clutters his own cubicle space. Look at the business plan, though, and it's obvious Moog Music is not only a different animal from Big Briar, it's a different breed.

A MOOG BY ANY OTHER NAME . . .

First, a little history. Bob Moog is happy to be an ex-member of an exclusive music-industry club called the Dead President's Society. Well, it wasn't really a club, but one could indeed be a member simply by losing the right to use one's own name for one's business. Other unwitting members have included Ray Kurzweil and Tom Oberheim. The process of regaining his trademarks has been arduous and expensive, and he's got a ways to go before he has worldwide rights. A business in the U.K. refuses to give up the rights to the name, so every Voyager shipped there has to have every mention of Moog removed from every possible part, from circuit boards to chassis, even the manual and shipping carton—not exactly how Bob wants to spend his money. But the story of how he got his name back is best told in his own words.

"I was 19 in 1954," he says. "I wanted to make theremins. I formed a sole proprietorship called R. A. Moog, Co. I kept that going all through college. When I started making synthesizers in 1964, it was still R. A. Moog, Co. I didn't know much about business at all. By 1967, we were doing well, so I followed the advice that was given to me, and I incorporated. At that point, the company was R. A. Moog, Inc. All the modular systems from the '60s were built under that name. I sold the controlling interest in my company to a guy who had a company called Musonics, in 1971. He changed the name to Moog/Musonics, then later that same year, changed it to Moog Music. Then he sold it to Norlin Music, which was the largest musical instrument manufacturer at the time. They owned Gibson, Lowrey Organs, Maestro Effects, Epiphone, and Pearl Drums. They were so big, they were listed on the N.Y. Stock Exchange. Moog Music became a division of Norlin, and remained that way until the mid-'80s, when Norlin fell on hard times, and basically fell apart. In the early '80s, a couple of executives of Moog Music staged a leveraged buyout and made it a freestanding company. They kept up until 1986 or so.

The synth mentioned so frequently in other chapters in this book is here on the top: the original Minimoog, Model D. On the bottom, the Mini reborn as the Voyager in 2003.

"This was the time when digital synthesizers had buried analog completely. Moog Music languished and became inactive. By 1994, the trademark office declared that the Moog Music trademark had been abandoned. According to trademark law, if a trademark isn't used for a specified period of time, it is declared abandoned, and other people can apply for the right to own the registration of the name. Several people applied, without my knowledge—I was occupied with things in my personal life. By the time it was brought to my attention, there was this whole brawl going on over the rights to use the name.

"One by one, most of them dropped out of the contest. I thought

I'd join in, since because of my name and reputation, I had as much right to the name as anyone else. To make a long story short, a year or two ago, we acquired the registration of the Moog, Minimoog, and Moog Music trademarks. We own them in the U.S., Germany, France, Italy, Japan, and we have the rights to use the name in other countries. At this point, there is a company in Wales, U.K., calling itself Moog Music, Ltd., who at one time produced fake Minimoogs, five of them in all. Under British law, they were able to acquire the registration in the U.K. We're contesting it on the grounds that it is misleading. The company that had been doing business as Moog Music in Cincinnati, Ohio, is no longer in existence."

THE SPIRIT IN THE MACHINE

Bob Moog is the first to acknowledge that, historically, he hasn't exactly been on the cutting edge of solid business practices. His humility being legendary, you wouldn't expect him to swagger down the aisles at trade shows now that Moog Music has a better foundation than ever. But he is decidedly happy about what's going on with his business.

"The complexity of the hardware in the Voyager is just one type of complexity," he says. "There's a lot of shit in this thing! I'm serious! Most of our suppliers are used to circuit boards with a couple of relays and resistors and industrial controls. Here we have a circuit board with over 800 parts on it: That's state of the art! It takes some real manufacturing expertise to do.

"But the interaction between the hardware requirements and the people dealing with the money—that's really complicated, too! The money management skills we have here exceeds that of much bigger companies. Everyone here loves doing what we do, and they love serving our customers. We're incredibly lucky to have a guy like Mike Adams running the company."

The Voyager itself didn't exactly come together in a day. Some serious analog genius brain cells worked overtime to come up with this reborn Minimoog. "The Voyager has been kicking around in my head for a long time," says Bob, "way before the time when we started working on it, which was in the fall of 2000. At the 2001 winter NAMM show, we showed a mock-up of it, not even a prototype. That had a different concept: It had a fixed front panel, instead of the hinged one the Voyager has. We got a lot of interest in it, even though we didn't quote prices, take orders, or make any delivery promises. We talked to a lot of musicians about what they liked about it and what they didn't, and from that input, we came up with the design.

"The main design goal that I had was to make sure we could get the Minimoog sound. That was the number one request from musicians. Whatever else we did, people wanted the Minimoog sound. We were already in production with the Moogerfooger MF-101 lowpass filter, and that's the so-called Moog filter, using new parts. So that served as the basis for the filters in the Voyager.

"But the oscillators were somewhat special. One part of the Voyager's oscillator design that's extremely advanced is that you have voltage control of everything. Not only do you have voltage control over a very wide pitch range—wider than the original Minimoog—but now you have voltage control of the waveforms, which you can change continuously, from triangle to sawtooth, and through every width of rectangular, with just one voltage. And you can do that with all three oscillators. The more things that are voltage controlled and that you can play with your hand, the more alive the sound is going to be.

"All the waveforms are made up of straight lines that go in various directions. The triangle has a straight line up, and one down. The sawtooth is a straight line up, then it snaps back. All the rectangular waves are straight lines at one voltage that jump up to another voltage, then jump back. These lines represent changes in voltage. Once you know that, you've described something a circuit designer would understand how to control with a varying voltage.

"But it's tricky. You can always design circuits that will change a waveform in response to a changing voltage with diodes. But to do it precisely so that each instrument is the same, and when you turn the knob, the waveform changes smoothly through all these different shapes, that takes a little craft. Just like someone making a fine piece of furniture.

"To stabilize the oscillators in the later Minimoogs, we used a heated-chip technology. That means that the transistor that actually determines the frequency by setting the current has to be kept at an absolute, constant temperature. A change in temperature would change the current. So in the Voyager, we used a chip with several transistors on it. One transistor is used as the current source for the oscillator, and all the other transistors are used to keep the temperature constant. It's the same technology that we used in the Micromoog, but the chip we use now is of much higher quality. It's very stable.

"This is tricky stuff, even for trained engineers. If you're designing digital circuits, you have to worry about things other than temperature stability. Even if you're designing audio components, you might be interested in the effect of temperature, but you don't need the kind of stability in your circuit that you do with a musical oscillator, which if it goes out one part in a thousand, you can hear it.

FOR MORE INFORMATION ON MOOG MUSIC AND THEIR AMAZING INSTRUMENTS, VISIT www.moogmusic.com.

TO LEARN ABOUT BOB MOOG'S ARCHIVES, EDUCATIONAL OUTREACH USING MOOG SYNTHESIZERS, AND THE COMMUNITY THAT HONORS BOB'S LEGACY, VISIT www.moogfoundation.org.

"Another design goal was to make everything on the front panel part of the presets. That means all those knobs have to be controllable, which means the circuit has to be completely voltage controlled. Every single thing that gets varied by a knob is a voltage-controlled parameter. Back in the Minimoog days, you had three or four things that were voltage controlled, now there are thirty. There was a lot of engineering involved there, to come up with all new circuits that could do that. I don't think I could've done this thirty years ago. There are things that have come out since then that make this possible.

"I call it the Cosmic Network, the source of creativity. It's really out there."

"The filter spacing is new, too; it opens up a new window in sound design. What's in the Voyager now are two identical lowpass filters. I noticed in my experiments with the old modular equipment that if you put two completely separate lowpass filters together and separate their cutoff frequencies, you get sounds that have more vocal qualities than when you just have one lowpass filter. It's possible to get a single bandpass filter when you hook them up.

"What happens with any of these features is that you begin with an idea of what they might sound like, then you put the circuitry together, and it usually sounds different than what you thought it would. Then you play with it, you try changing it one way or another, and you get a sense of what a really interesting and musically useful configuration would be. It's the same way a musician tries out a melody, and changes a note here and there until they like it.

"But musicians always come up with stuff I couldn't imagine, using my instruments. I can get a sense of whether something would be a good musical resource, but I don't do music. I'm a toolmaker. It's always amazing what someone like Herbie Hancock, Wendy Carlos, or Stevie Wonder can come up with. What they'll do when you put something new in front of them is they'll turn a couple knobs and listen, and immediately get a sense of where to go. The muse talks to them."

The "muse" plays a big part in Bob Moog's own work, though he maintains that he's anything but a musician. "I call it the Cosmic Network, the source of creativity. It's really out there. It's not just for music, it's for writing, and for designing hardware. I think different people experience it in different ways. Sometimes an idea will come to me as I'm waking up. Sometimes it will come to me here in the office, with the phones ringing all around.

"There's no way to do this just by opening up an engineering book and finding the formula," he says. "It's a matter of judgment and intuition. That's what I've been doing all my life." He smiles, "I'm pretty good at it now."

9 GARY NUMAN

SYNTHS, SIMPLICITY, AND SUCCESS

by Bruce Dancis

Portions of this chapter originally appeared in the August 1980 issue of Keyboard *magazine.*

First comes the catchy synthesizer riff. Once the hook is implanted in the listener's brain, a crunching rhythm pickup and carries it along, usually at mid-tempo until joined by sweeping layers of synthesized harmonies. When these striking chords swoop down upon a rhythm, they suggest Rodan, the giant movie ptero-

With a few synths, some backlight, and a ton of attitude, Gary Numan takes the States by storm, circa 1980. (Courtesy of *Keyboard* magazine)

dactyl, plunging toward Tokyo.

Sound familiar? A number of artists have followed this formula over the past few year to establish themselves as techno-rock cult figures—Kraftwerk and, on occasion, Briar Eno come to mind—but none with as much visibility or instant commercial impact as Gary Numan, whose simple hypnotic style of synthesis has combined with his android-like stage image and pessimistic science fiction-inspired vision of the future to make him the most popular British rock star of the past year. In 1979 the 22-year-old from just outside London racked up two number one singles there, along with two number one LPs and the BBC's annual Pop and Rock Award as Best Male Singer.

He is making himself known in the States as well. His first American tour, buoyed by an appearance on NBC's *Saturday Night Live*, was quite successful. Numan's first album, *Replicas*, sold well here, and by mid-April 1980 his second LP, *The Pleasure Principle* and his single, "Cars," from the same album, were both riding high in the U.S. charts.

Numan is the first to admit that he isn't a proficient keyboard player; in fact, he was introduced to synthesizers only a short while ago. But by merging a carefully crafted public persona with an expert ear for sound and melody, he has developed a distinct musical personality through his various electronic keyboards and brought heavily synthesized rock to a new group of listeners.

The dense sound of Numan's records is reproduced effectively onstage by the young artist and his band. Altogether the group uses six Minimoogs, five Polymoogs, and two electric pianos, not to mention guitar, bass, drums, percussion, assorted other synths, and viola. Numan himself plays two Minimoogs and a six-channel Roland SH-2000 synthesizer, and doubles up on guitarist Russell

Bell's Polymoog. He also uses a Yamaha analog delay echo with the Roland, going through three MXR digital delays and an MXR flanger/doubler.

Most of the live keyboard work is handled by Denis Haines and Christopher Payne. Haines plays five different axes: a Yamaha CP-30 electronic piano, a Polymoog, a Minimoog, an ARP Odyssey, and an ARP Pro Soloist. They all run through an MXR flanger/doubler, an MXR digital delay, a Yamaha analog delay, and a Yamaha six-channel mixer. Payne works with two regular Polymoogs, one modified Polymoog, two Minimoogs, and a Yamaha CP-70 electric grand. These, in turn, are sent through an MXR phaser, three MXR noise gates, two MXR digital delays, two Yamaha delay echo units, and a Yamaha 12-channel mixer. Each of the three keyboardists has two Yamaha bass cabinets, including horns, with 12" speakers.

In his search for a live experience that could encompass his multi-level sensory approach, Numan has produced visuals that dazzle as much as the aurals. Onstage his band and all its gear are displayed in a set that resembles a scene from *Darth Vader Meets the Hollywood Squares*. Numan stands with his synthesizers at center stage, flanked by bassist Paul Gardiner and guitarist Russell Bell. The drummer, Cedric Sharpley, sits behind him on a platform ten feet off the ground. Haines and Payne are perched on platforms 15 feet high, on both sides of Sharpley and directly behind Gardiner and Bell.

What makes all this even more spectacular are the rows of horizontal rectangular lights that provide a backdrop for the two keyboardists in the upper platforms. These lights shine alternately in white, gray, black, red, green, and blue, and can create an elevator effect by shimmering in rising or falling patterns. When the lights are white, the black-clad musicians appear as silhouettes against them, and when they flash or move upwards, they function as visual percussion, pulsating along with and enriching the musical rhythm.

Numan evidently remains unaware of, or at least unaffected by, the current energy crisis, but his ostentatious live show has made a lot of keyboard equipment manufacturers and electricians, not to mention fans, happy. His performing stance as the alienated outsider contemplating a cold, machine-dominated environment provides a contrast to his shy offstage personality.

When did you get interested in music?

I started when I was four. I was interested in the guitar. When I was 11, I found a cousin who had an electric guitar, and I used it. The first group I liked was the Monkees. Then there was a gap. And then T. Rex guitarist Marc Bolan.

When did you first get into keyboards?

Just over a year ago.

When did you decide to become a professional musician?

I decided when I was 11, when I first started to learn the guitar. I wasn't interested in the music. I was interested in the glamour and the atmosphere that was around it. I first started writing songs when I was about 15 or 16, but I didn't start writing and playing songs for anyone else until I was 18.

How did your current band come into existence?

I joined a band called the Lasers—it must have been mid-'77. I joined as a guitarist. This group had Paul [Gardiner] in it, who was doing the singing and playing the bass. They did all the old '60s songs with punk style. Just terrible, but I thought, "You've got to start somewhere." I told them I didn't like the songs much, and I played them some of the stuff I wrote in "Mean Street." About a week later they dropped their set and were doing this stuff of mine, so I became the singer. Then I said I didn't like the name 'cause it was dumb, and everything was called "The Something," anyway. And they said, "What did you have in mind?" I said, "Anything, as long as it doesn't start with 'The'." *Tubeway Army* was a chapter title from a book I was writing, which ended up being the *Replicas* album 'cause I'm not very good at writing books, so that's what we wound up calling ourselves.

***Replicas* is quite different from the first album that came out in England [*Tubeway Army*, Beggars Banquet]. You were moving away from guitars at that point. And *The Pleasure Principle* doesn't have any guitars on it. Why have you moved in this direction?**

It's just a personal experiment to see if rock could be played as effectively without guitars, guitars supposedly being the main or only instrument of rock. I didn't think that was so, especially after I started messing around with synthesizers a bit and heard what they could do.

Were you influenced by any people who were playing synthesizer then?

Not when I got into them. I was influenced afterwards, about how to use them. What happened was I got fed up with guitars. I couldn't write anything on them; every time I tried to write something on guitar, it sounded the way everyone else did. In a song like "Down in the Park" [*Replicas*], about machines in a park, I just couldn't play it on a guitar. It's probably my fault, 'cause I'm not a very good guitar player. I couldn't get anything out of it other than the same predictable chord changes every time.

And then I found the synthesizer, and it opened up a whole new field. That's why I went into it. After, I found out what they could do. Basically, I listened to a few other people that were using them, to see what had been done up to then, and then went on from there. Ultravox's Billy Currie was the main one.

Did Brian Eno have any impact on you?

No [*disdainfully*]. I didn't listen to Brian Eno until somebody said I sounded like him, that I had ripped him off. So I thought I'd better listen to him to see what I supposedly ripped off. I think Eno verges from brilliant to shit to nice. He goes from one extreme to the other. I did like him until he came out with a few stupid comments. He sounds like he's getting a bit stuck up. He seems to think too highly of himself at the moment. I'd have to meet him to know what he's like, I suppose.

Did you have any nonmusical influences?

Well, I'm not really much of a musician anyway. I approach the piano or the keyboard as a guitar player. My brother took piano lessons, and he said that all my fingers are wrong. Apparently you have to use certain fingers for certain notes. Well, I don't know none of that [*laughs*]. I'm very much limited to a one-finger motion, two at the most. To be honest, I'm not that good a player at all. I can get quite nice sounds. I know what the dials do on a Minimoog. I know what the gadgets are and can work them quite well. Now Denis [Haines] can really play. He's the newest member and a piano teacher.

What was the first synthesizer you used?

A Minimoog.

Why did you choose it?

It was the first one I found. I only got into them because one was in the studio that had been left behind from the session before. So when nobody was looking I played it. I just happened to play it when it was lined up to a 32' stop, and it just went bang! This big, deep rumble. I had never heard anything like it in me life. And I thought, "Christ, I've been messing around with guitars, but it's all here. Just press a button and off it goes." Fascinating, it really was. And that was why I went to Minimoog—it was the first one I had ever seen. It's like sticking to what you know, really. Now I've got six Minimoogs, five or six Polymoogs. I'm starting to get into ARPs. I've got an Odyssey, a Pro Soloist. I'm getting a Prophet and the Roland G-54. I've got the Roland SH-2000, a Yamaha CP-30, the grand [Yamaha CP-70].

How have you been learning about synthesizers? Are you just teaching yourself or is anyone helping you?

Nobody that I know seems to know much about it. Denis can play them really well, but he still hasn't quite got an edge when it comes to the sounds. I still have to say to him, "No, it's too thick," or whatever.

Are you able to create the sounds you want?

Yeah. I feel that just comes with time. I suppose if Denis had had a Minimoog for a year, then he would know it as well as I did or probably better. Then you have to have the money to buy them in the first place.

Has it been a process where you've continued to add on new keyboards all the time?

No. What happened was I didn't actually own one until around June last year. I didn't have one when we did the *Replicas* album. They were all hired. When we did *The Pleasure Principle*, I had a Polymoog and one Minimoog and one MXR digital delay.

In making *The Pleasure Principle*, how did you and Christopher Payne divide the keyboard playing?

It was mainly me. In the studio I did most of the overdub electronic stuff, all the synthesizer stuff. From now on, Denis will do the bulk of the piano playing, the straight keyboard playing. If it's a Polymoog on its 6 preset or the Yamahas, then Denis will do that as well. I will do the Minimoogs, the first preset Polymoogs, and the effects.

How have you been dividing up the keyboard work in live performances? Do you have to de-emphasize your role on keyboards because you have to sing?

I don't have much to do with the keyboards at all. I walk around. All I do is the noises that are on the records. I do all of them. And the others spend most of their time doing the actual playing itself. So they can have both their hands working, playing all the overdubs and things. Everything we do in the studio, we can do live. If it comes to noises and things, we can do all those as well. If it comes to a point where they can't actually do all the noises, then I step back. On "Praying to the Aliens" [*Replicas*] I do the little squeaky noises. I've got two mic stands around where my keyboards are.

> "Well, I'm not really much of a musician anyway. I approach the piano or the keyboard as a guitar player."

In your own setup you had two Minimoogs and a Roland. Will you be playing the Minimoogs simultaneously?

No. I play the left-hand one during "Cars" and another song and the right-hand one when I feel like it, really [*laughs*]. It's just a matter of pressing it and up it goes [*makes a soaring sound*]. The left-hand one is set up for a siren effect. And I use a pitch-bender to take it down. That's preset. The other one is set up for white noise. We just use a filter to change that around.

What about when you walk over to the Roland? What are you playing on that?

That's just for the little noises on "Praying to the Aliens." I do it in other numbers also. It's just for an effect like a pulse.

A lot of your songs have a riff that gets played in the beginning, with some layers added to it later. Who plays which part live?

It varies. On "Cars," Russell [Bell], the guitarist, plays the Minimoog rhythm line. For the very high part, Denis plays that bit. And the harmony line at the end, that's Chris. So they're chopping and changing all the time, doing other effects and overdubs. Chris also does the white noise crashes in "Cars" on the album, when normally Russell does them on the Synare 3 onstage. We're constantly changing. That's why we need so many keyboards. I can't possibly play five Polymoogs at once. I need that many to keep going.

Do you think you're able to duplicate your studio sound live?

Exactly. The only thing that affects it is the fact that you're in a hall, so the acoustics are different. You get that extra ambience. But apart from that, a lot of the stuff we did [live] from *Pleasure Principle* was so accurate we couldn't release any of it, 'cause it was just like the records. There was no point in releasing it. Identical. It was quite nice, really. The *Replicas* stuff we have added to because obviously I've learned a lot more since then about synthesizers. I could find a lot more things to put on to them—extra harmonies and noises. And so they sound better than the record. I think so, anyway. "Down in the Park" onstage has ten times the power it has on record. The whole place shakes at the end of it.

You've produced all of your albums. Are you self-taught as a producer as well?

All it was, was that I didn't have anyone come to produce it. The very first album, before *Replicas*, was just demos. Well, *Replicas* was demos, actually, in 16-track. You see, you don't take a producer for demos. So in I went and just thought, well, there's a gap there, and that's a bit too bass-heavy, so I'll stick on some middle or some top or whatever. I always work it down as bass, mid, and top, and then go through it like a jigsaw puzzle. If it's bass-heavy there, then I stick some midrange on it. It's a very, very simple way of looking at it. It seems to work quite well.

How long did it take you to make *Replicas*?

Replicas was five days. The one before that was four days. *The Pleasure Principle* took 11 days in 24-track, but we had a really awkward engineer and it would have taken me a lot less.

Eleven days is very fast. Does that mean you and the band were very tightly rehearsed before you went in?

Not really. When we did the last demos, the band had never heard the songs until we went into the studio. I put the piano part down along with a drum machine and said, "Well, that's how it goes." Then I did some overdubs. Then we put the drums on. I went in with the drummer and gave him cues where to start. They didn't know the songs till they actually got the tapes.

How do you write songs?

Normally, I come up with the title first, and then I work on music, if it's a riff or just one run. I tend to get about 20 to 30 different little pictures, some five seconds long, some a minute long. It may be a riff or a run or anything. Then I think about what the song needs to be about, or a riff that would suit it. Then I tape about 30 various ones and piece them together. I pick out the one I want to be the riff and I play that and get the phrasing for the lyrics. Then I think, "That's enough for eight bars; now it's about time we had a chorus." And I get off with the others and think what will fit it. It's a lot like putting a jigsaw together. And then I do the lyrics afterwards.

On *The Pleasure Principle* all of the songs have one-word titles, and they seem to be expressions of your thoughts on the particular subject. Did you have an overall conception worked out when you started to plan the album?

I knew it was all going to be one-word songs and I knew what the title of the album was long before *Replicas* was released. Not an overall concept as such, but I had guidelines for it. It just worked out that three of the songs were futurist and the rest quite personal.

Were you trying to fit the songs together in a thematic framework?

That's why the predominance is in Polymoog and Minimoog. Each song has a similar sound, without being different from the next song. So anytime you listen to any song from that album, you know it's from that album. I think that's important, to get each album to have its own sound.

Were you surprised at the success you had in Great Britain? You sort of came out of nowhere, it seemed, and very quickly had number one albums and singles.

I wasn't surprised I made it. I was surprised I made it with that song, "Are 'Friends' Electric?" [*Replicas*]. I didn't think that song had a chance in hell of getting in the charts. I thought "Cars" had a pretty good shot at the charts. It seemed just right: hook lines, catchy, fast, current subject, not too heavy, nice and short for the DJs, good intro, nice fadeout. Everything was suitable for radio airplay and for the mass market. But "Are 'Friends' Electric?" was a real surprise.

What do you think pushed you beyond cult status? Was it your ability to write a riff that people could instantly catch onto, or do you think it was your image?

I think it was everything. I think it was the song, what we looked like, the image. We presented ourselves on *Top of the Pops* like nobody had ever done before. We used all white light, wore black, and the makeup—we just stood out like a sore thumb. You could hate it or love it; you couldn't ignore it. I said to the band, "Just stand there. Don't smile or nothing. Look at the camera and just stare at it." We tried to be very, very static. And I was at the front. All I did was just move my head from side to side a bit, with if-looks-could-kill stares at the camera. And it all went down a storm.

Why do you think some groups that are quite successful in England fail to make any impact in America?

I think England is always into new things, and America tends to have what it's got and stick with it for years and years. That's why the English always think of the Americans as being incredibly boring when it comes to music taste, 'cause they're so reluctant to accept anything new. We've been doing quite well up to now. We've sold out everywhere except for a few places.

Do you see anything in any American groups that you respect?

I like the Cars. I think they're really good.

If you were looking back at the songs you've recorded, which ones do you think represent your best work?

"Are 'Friends' Electric?" and "Down in the Park" from *Replicas.*

Do you mention "Are 'Friends' Electric?" because it was your first hit?

I just think it's simplicity taken to an art form. That sounds a bit big-headed. I don't quite mean it that way. It's so simple, yet it works so well. I think that's nice. I like the way the lyrics fit into the riff. Actually, the lyrics go against the riff yet still fit exactly into it. It has four themes in it, including the chorus. I don't know why I like my own stuff, I just like it [*laughs*]. I don't like all of it. I think "Engineers" [*Pleasure Principle*] sucks. It's a horrible song; don't like it at all. I don't like "You're in My Vision" on *Replicas* one bit.

Why not? Is it too simple or does it no longer express what you feel?

I like the lyrics on "You're in My Vision" and "Engineers"; I like what it's about, what it's trying to say. I just think the song itself, the line with the Polymoog on it, is boring. I

A SELECTED GARY NUMAN DISCOGRAPHY

Replicas Redux
Jagged
Hybrid
Exile
Live Dark Light
Strange Charm
Telekon
The Pleasure Principle

WITH TUBEWAY ARMY
Tubeway Army
Replicas

FOR MORE INFORMATION ON GARY NUMAN, VISIT www.numan.co.uk.

do it too often. It doesn't bear enough. I should have put a lot more in it. It's almost like a song I wrote quick to stick on the end of an album. "You're in My Vision" is just so straight rock; it's boring for that reason.

Do you plan to add more keyboards to your setup?

Definitely a Prophet. Everyone's talking about the Prophet.

What would set the Prophet apart from your other synthesizers?

For a start, the amount of sound you can get out of it, the memory on it, is very handy. I also like the actual quality of the sounds it does. A Minimoog is nice. You see, you can't fault a Minimoog until you put a Prophet beside it and compare. Like a white noise sweep on a Minimoog. Then do it on a Prophet and hear the difference in the quality of it.

What will your next album be like?

The next album will be called *Telekon*. All the songs are written for it. There are 12 at the moment. It isn't as futurist as the last ones have been. *Replicas* was really my futurist album. *Pleasure Principle* had two or three songs on it that were futurist, but really I was just getting rid of them. Basically, the next one concerns me and what's happened to me because of this success, what I'm going through, and what people think I'm going through. All of a sudden, friends won't ring me up anymore because they think I've changed, and here I am wondering why everyone's stopped ringing me up. It's about the little queer things that happen like that. I've actually done a romantic futurist song. All the other songs I've written about the future I've considered all to be possible, ideas that could happen.

They're rather bleak, wouldn't you say?

Oh yeah, but I'm a pessimist anyway. I think we're all doomed, one way or another [*laughs*]. But I've got a romantic song about the last electrician in the world. There wouldn't be any more electricians because everything would be nuclear. Everybody would have their own little nuclear plant in their backyard.

Dispensing the Cure, mid-'90s: Roger O'Donnell goes emo with a Kurzweil PC88 and a thinly disguised Roland XP-50.
(Jeffrey Langlois/Getty Images)

10 ROGER O'DONNELL

TRUTH IN SYNTHESIS

by Tom Brislin

Portions of this chapter originally appeared in the September 2006 issue of Keyboard *magazine.*

Following his recent departure from the groundbreaking band the Cure, Roger O'Donnell went searching. Armed with one Moog Voyager synth, he created *The Truth in Me*, an album spawned from an integration of spontaneous monophonic musical moments and developed into a cohesive musical expression. With his new label, 99 Times Out of 10, he has gone searching for new and emerging talent that is bursting onto the indie scene.

On the inspiration for the album, Roger muses, "When I first started talking to Moog about having a relationship with them, they told me about a documentary that was being made about Bob (*Moog*, by Ryan Page and Hans Fjellestad), and they said they'd love to have a song in there by the Cure. And I was like, 'I'll ask Robert', but we were right in the middle of making an album. But it's a lot of pressure on him, it's his band, and he carries the writing process. So he said he'd love to, but he'd have to pass.

"So I thought I would write a song for the soundtrack. And I thought back to my early days of writing music and very limited instrumentation—I had a Fender Rhodes, a Micromoog, and a Prophet 600. I would write a song just using the Voyager; it would be a really nice thing, a great tribute to Bob, and I thought I could make it work. I know the Voyager is incredibly versatile; I just have to make it musical and emotional. So I wrote the song, and it worked."

That's a characteristic O'Donnell understatement. To say that producer Ryan Page really liked the song hardly begins to describe what happened next. "We were having dinner and Ryan said, 'That song, I think it's really important to electronic music right now. I think it's saying something that nobody else is saying in electronica.' And I said, 'Really?' Because I never take anything I do too seriously.

"I think it was an interesting process, and also it's hugely restricting to use just one instrument, especially one that plays one note at a time. At the time I was working on a solo album because I really wanted to do something outside of the Cure. I thought, 'I'm in a band, and I work with a drummer and a bass player every day. Why don't I try something that really is just me? Why not I do it on an instrument I really feel I can express myself on?'

"So I sat down and started to write songs. And I thought, 'I'm just going to write totally outside of myself. Not holding back. Not trying to craft them as songs, I'm just going to let it happen.' And that's what I did. It just came really quickly. And I felt really comfortable with it."

To serve the individuality, and the spontaneous moment, Roger refrained from using any preset sounds on the album. "I'm not a big fan of presets. In the '80s, when I was using a lot of Sequential Circuits gear, I remember using presets, because whenever we would play San Francisco, we would always invite all the guys from the factory. I'd stand there playing presets, and then you could look out and see them smiling because they recognized their sounds.

"A lot of the sounds on my record are really subtle. The difference between one sound and another is so slight. In going back and try to recreate the sounds to play them live, I've realized that each song is kind of like a growth from the original sound that triggered the song. Because when I would write a song, it would come as much from the sound itself, which would trigger a melody or a bass line, or some kind of musical motif. And then I would progress from that base, so whatever wave shape that sound was, the rest of the song would kind of progress from there. Sound would suggest melody. Melody would suggest structure and progression. So most of the songs don't have very big chord changes in them. They're kind of like a movement from one place to another. So it's about what you can do around that base; that's how they work.

"I'd play a line, and I would think, 'Okay, that needs another line on top of it, and the sound needs to change just a little this and that.' And I would have to play that line or I would have lost it, 'cause it's only in your head for that fleeting moment. I didn't save anything."

The one guiding rule throughout the whole process for Roger was that the moment itself was the most important thing. "I don't think I had any choice. It's just about capturing—it's such a fleeting, inspirational moment. I'd go into the studio, switch the Moog on, and immediately start playing. I wouldn't wait for it to stabilize the tuning. So each song is in tune with itself, but not in tune with the next song on the record. It was such an instantaneous, inspirational thing. And you can't mess around with that, or you just lose it. Everything was improvised.

"I would play a phrase, four bars, eight bars, I think there's one that's 40 bars long. And I would just loop it, and I'd build up the foundation of the track. Then I'd play over that. And I would play the lead line, though I wouldn't learn it, I'd just go and play it again. And so the subtle differences give it that intricacy. Because some of the loops would be so long, I would forget what would be at the beginning. So it would come around and I'd go, 'Oh cool,' and I'd be playing the same thing. And that's how it kind of all built up.

"So I would get the foundation of the track going, like the rhythm track. Then I'd play a theme, and sometimes try to recreate that theme without learning it, so it would be slightly different every time. And then there would be other sections, like what you might call choruses but they weren't really, and then I would play a free line over the top of it, just entirely inspired by what was there."

"Sound would suggest melody. Melody would suggest structure and progression."

The recording process was an individual affair, with Roger recording all of the tracks in his own studio. "I recorded it using [MOTU] Digital Performer, which I've been using since 1987. I never was a staunch [Apple] Logic user. I went to Cupertino and August '04, told them that I used DP, and nearly got shown out of the building. Phil Jackson, who is one of the main Logic guys, took me through three locked doors, made me sign my life away, and gave me a three-hour demo of Logic. I was blown away. I thought 'I want to start using it tomorrow.'

"Everything went through my mixer, and so I've always got delay and reverb, like two effects, outboard. I put time delay on, but that was just to monitor in the recording process. I recorded everything dry. I used a wah-wah pedal on one track, and I used Moogerfooger on another ("This Grey Morning"), and that was it."

When bringing the tracks to mix engineer Mario Thaler, they discovered that some of Roger's spontaneity during the tracking process meant not always recording at optimal levels. "We actually mixed it twice. The first time we ran it out to a vintage Neve, put it through effects in the studio, re-miked stuff, re-amped stuff, and all we managed to do was add three levels of hiss. Because I engineered it myself, and I was working in this kind of stream of consciousness way where everything just had to get played. So if I came up with a sound, and it needed to be quieter than before, I just turned it down; I didn't record it at the same level. So Mario said he would bring up the tracks, and he'd zoom in with Logic, and it would still just be a thick line, because there was no level on the tape. So we ended up with a bunch of hiss, and we tried a de-hisser, and it just ate through the frequencies. I mastered it, got it home to my studio, and I was just like, 'Oh, my god.' I wanted this to sound pure, and analog, and it ended up with all these digitalized artifacts on it from this de-hissing process. So we went back and remixed it again entirely in Logic."

With the whole musical statement complete, Roger felt it would be important to reach out to other artists and remixers to hear what they would do with the tracks. There are now remixes from Console, Acid Pauli, Fourtet, Vincenzo, and Dntel (Jimmy Tamborello of the Postal Service). "I think we owe a big debt to Jimmy and Postal Service for making keyboard-based music mainstream again. He's such a nice guy, as well. I call him an 'e-quaintance' because I've never actually met him. When I finished the record, I thought, 'Okay, let's get some remixes done.' Because my record is very basic, there are no drums on it, and no other instrumentation. It's perfect for people to remix. The first person I actually thought of was Jimmy. I sent him a CD with the files on it in January, and then one Saturday morning, I logged in to get my email and there was the remix. It's just really nice to work with people you respect, and it's just about the music."

In addition to the remixes, Roger enjoys discovering new music on the web and in the independent music scene, which led to the formation of 99 Times Out of 10. Now handling a dozen artists, the label recently released the compilation CD *Nothing Concrete*. "My plan was to release a sampler featuring unsigned talent," says Roger, "and the bands we found are incredible. Each is very unique in sound, yet when we put their songs together on this album, they work perfectly together. The label is really an extension of my wanting to help bring interesting and new music to people, and to help bands be heard that never otherwise would be."

Whether with his own music or through his discoveries, Roger's desire to explore speaks to the artists who first inspired him to take up music. "Luckily, for the diversity of my style, my first major influence was Frank Zappa," he says. "And because he had such complex musical tastes and such a large number of influences in his music, it just opened my ears to a whole new world. I was like, 'Whoa, this is pretty cool, this is kind of like blues, but it's got this kind of different edge to it.' So I kind of followed that, and that's when I discovered Herbie Hancock. And Herbie Hancock is like my mentor. He's just been there all the way through my career. It probably sounds funny to people who know my playing from the Cure, because obviously his influence doesn't figure very largely in

A SELECTED ROGER O'DONNELL DISCOGRAPHY

SOLO

Songs from the Silver Box

The Truth in Me

WITH THE CURE

The Cure

Wild Mood Swings

Disintegration

FOR MORE INFORMATION ON ROGER O'DONNELL, VISIT www.rogerodonnell.com.

my Cure work. But he was always there as I am influenced by his sensibility and orchestrations. I remember reading an early *Keyboard* interview with him about the way he used instrumentation, and I still think about that today. Little tricks.

"I saw him play early last year, which was just before I left the Cure. And he's onstage, exploring entirely new areas of music, working with musicians who are young enough to be his children. And I thought, this guy's still exploring new areas and he's relentless in his musical explorations. And here I'm in this group—and I don't intend to put down the Cure because I'm very proud of it—we're playing the same music, and we're not really going anywhere. We're not challenging ourselves, or our music. And I thought, 'This guy is a good hero to have.'"

The man who never cracked a synth manual: Prince onstage during the *Purple Rain* years. (Waring Abbot/Getty Images)

11 PRINCE

SYNTHS GET SEXY

by Ernie Rideout and Ken Hughes

Portions of this chapter originally appeared in the January 2000 and August 2004 issues of Keyboard *magazine.*

The vibrant summer foliage of the Minnesota countryside lines the gently winding road, empty but for a distinctive purple roadster. Outside the air is still, benign cumulus dotting the sky, but inside the car it's a world within a world. The massive sound of *Rave Un2 the Joy Fantastic*, the first album by the Artist in three years to be distributed by a major label, fills the cockpit. "This is my favorite way to listen to new music," says the Artist as he shifts into high gear. The title cut, an airtight classic Prince jam from 1988, gives the car's suspension a workout. Public Enemy's Chuck D raps over "Undisputed," a characteristically dense mix, alive with sonic one-liners and interwoven tonal messages.

"My mixes have always been terrible," he says with a slow, deep laugh and a humorous gleam in his eye. "All of them. Listen to anything—'1999,' 'Darling Nikki,' 'Purple Rain.' They're all that way." Twenty years of bad mixes? Most of us were probably too busy dancing to notice.

We pull into a cul-de-sac with a handful of modest homes on it, and angle into a driveway. A wrought-iron gate bears a heart and a peace symbol, and beyond it is a large but not ostentatious purple house. "That's where I used to live, in much less clear days," he says. "That's where I recorded '1999,' 'Purple Rain,' all that stuff with Apollonia. My dad lives there now."

Less clear days? Whatever was going on behind those gates notwithstanding, there's nothing unclear about the albums he came out with during that time. Sure, the stylistic contrast between 1999 (1982), *Around the World in a Day* (1985), *Sign o' the Times* (1987), and *Lovesexy* (1988) caused a great deal of confusion. But the result is a remarkable body of booty-shaking work documenting the growth of one of the greatest musical forces of these times—a major instrumental and vocal talent who believes in the power of that venerable institution, the live band.

He turns onto another rural road, "Greatest Romance" rocking the car. A layered synth horn line snakes by, an unusual sonic pairing that rapidly mutates into frenzied reverse-loop mayhem. He does this brilliant stuff all the time. The questions can't wait any longer. What synths, what production secrets lie in store for us?

"Look at that sky," he says, gesturing at the clouds and sunlight through the windshield. Purple rosary beads and a pair of purple panties hang from the rearview mirror. "How could anyone look at that and not think that a higher intelligence created it?" A pause. He smiles. "I'll show you the synths when we get back to Paisley."

Longtime readers will have noticed that this is the first time the Artist has ever agreed to be interviewed by *Keyboard*. From the'80s Revolution through the New Power Generation of the '90s, we've had great luck talking to several of his keyboard-playing associates, but the Man himself was never accessible. Our January 1991 cover proclaimed, "Not an Interview with Prince." Frankly, it drove us nuts; such incredible keyboard work and production, such massive grooves, yet so little opportunity to get behind the music.

But here we are, hanging on to the end of 1999. Whether you believe in the party or the apocalypse as portrayed in "1999," can it be a coincidence that the Artist chose to open up to us now, nearly 20 years since our first inquiries? As always, the answer is in the music.

"This is the deepest record I've ever made," he says once we're seated in the control room of Studio A. Quite a claim coming from the creator of such dancefloor bombshells as "Sexy M.F.," "Let's Go Crazy," and "Days of Wild." But a lot went into the making of *Rave Un2 the Joy Fantastic*, and at the heart of the entire disc are two secret weapons.

The first is a pristine Linn LM-1, pulled from the mothball fleet deep in the vault at Paisley Park, the very LM-1 that featured prominently in many of Prince's earlier recordings. Now it occupies an altar-like position in the control room of Studio A, surrounded by a fiber-optic sculpture and a framed drawing by Ani DiFranco. "Nothing has the timing of that thing," says the Artist. "It locks up differently than any other drum machine. And believe me, I've had every drum machine ever made. When I put my own internal rhythm on top of it, there's nothing like it. Kirk Johnson [drummer for the New Power Generation] did some of the programming for the album, too."

The second surprise lies in the production credits. Advance publicity for the album indicated that the Artist wanted to work with a producer with whom he was familiar. "That's why I asked Prince to produce the album," says the man who changed his name in the early '90s legally from Prince to the Artist to distance himself from contractual hassles, imitators, and his own past. We could debate the meaning of this relationship for pages, but suffice it to say that when you listen to the album, it'll come to you. "I can sound like Prince should sound in 1999, now that everyone's gone the other way," he explains, not without humor. "I always wondered what he'd sound like now."

The album features collaborations with several artists who are in fact not the same person. This is by no means in itself an unusual move for the Artist, and the results are remarkable. On the ballad, "I Love U but I Can't Trust U Anymore," the Artist played a lush, sustained part on his 7' Steinway, singing the lead vocal simultaneously in a single take. He brought Ani DiFranco in to overdub acoustic guitar, and the part she laid down was characteristically idiosyncratic, resulting in some intriguing and unusual accents. The Artist overdubbed synth parts matching the guitar's rhythm, and the result is an orchestrated track that seems organic yet completely composed. He also teamed up with Chuck D for the rap on "Undisputed," with Sheryl Crow on "Baby Knows," with James Brown's sax mainstay Maceo Parker on "Pretty Man," with Gwen Stefani of No Doubt on "So Far So Pleased," and with Eve, his current favorite vocalist, on the deeply grinding "Hot With U." "Eve is incredible," he says. "If you don't say anything else, at least tell everybody that."

Another common element between *Rave Un2* and the Artist's previous work is the presence of a couple of lush orchestral arrangements by Clare Fischer, the Los Angeles-based jazz piano virtuoso and arranging phenomenon. Though they've collaborated since the early '80s, they've never met. "At this point," muses the Artist, "I wouldn't want to jinx it by meeting him. His arrangements are incredible. I just send him a tape, we talk on the phone, and he sends me the finished orchestra tracks. Hear that?" He points at the monitors as the arrangement emphasizes a chord substitution in the Artist's original track, thick with jazz extensions. "I'm gonna get that chord on the radio, baby!"

The Artist is infamous for his incredibly thick bass lines, and they abound on the new album. The secret is in how he layers the bass sounds, often three deep. Occasionally an electronic kick drum becomes a bass sound, too, adding two-fisted punch to already bowel-shaking analog synth lines. One line in particular seems like it could be felt back in Minneapolis, but when queried, he smiles, "Sorry, that one's a secret." Damn. Now how we gonna make that booty boom?

Whether you agree with the Artist's earlier assessment of his mixes or not, they are often packed with guitar lines doubled with keyboards, whimsical synth licks that appear and morph into sampled snippets, countermelodies layered in dissonant intervals, and many other techniques that keep pulling you into the tunes. *Rave Un2* is filled with prime examples. Does he make these up as he overdubs, or does he have them in his head from the beginning? "I see everything in my mind," he reveals, "but as I overdub synth parts, I flip through the presets I like until I find the sound I want for the next phrase. I listen to what tone goes with what color. I usually don't change the sounds themselves."

One ear-catching sound design technique pops up in the hi-hat part on "Rave Un2 the Joy Fantastic." The tone of the hi-hat seems quite unusual, but really effective in the song. A synth hook at the end of the phrase belies the fact that it and the hi-hat are coming from the same synth patch. "It's a gate effect," says the Artist, "triggered by the hi-hat. When the hi-hat hits, the gate opens, and all you hear is the synth patch while the gate is open, but it sounds like a hi-hat."

> "Most keyboard players don't have good rhythm. You have to have an intimate relationship with the beat. And you either have it or you don't. You can't learn it."

The Artist's instrumental virtuosity is legendary, and his playing seems free of technical limitations or concerns. His albums have consistently been keyboard and synth showcases, and in his view, synthesizers have always represented freedom itself. Keyboardists who have worked for him report tales of running up against their own technical limitations when trying to execute a keyboard part, only to have the Artist demonstrate to them how it can be done.

One of the most amazing live displays of his prowess occurs from time to time during live shows as he takes a guitar solo, then after a few phrases, fingers the guitar with his left hand while doubling the improvised line with his right on a synth. After 20 years of recording your own keyboard and guitar lines, you might expect that this would follow. But then he'll harmonize his improvised line with one instrument or the other. And then he'll improvise two independent, contrapuntal lines. And they'll both burn. He may latch onto an ostinato pattern on keyboard, then he'll drag someone up from the audience to play that part while he invents additional lines on top of that. Whether it's 3 a.m. at Paisley or 10 p.m. onstage, the guy just doesn't stop.

Interestingly, he has no keyboard heroes in particular, whereas he's obviously a Hendrix and Santana fan on the guitar side. "I think the keyboard player I'm most influenced by is Sly Stone," he says. "But I never have studied anyone's style or licks."

For the Artist, the most important element of good keyboard playing is rhythm. "Most keyboard players don't have good rhythm. You have to have an intimate relationship with the beat. And you either have it or you don't. You can't learn it."

The Artist is hands-down one of the most prolific recording artists in pop history. A glance at his discography is like looking at the tip of an iceberg, though; there's no telling how many partially finished or completely mixed recordings he's got sitting in the vaults of Paisley Park, ready to be brought to the light of day. *Crystal Ball,* his five-disc independent release of last year, is a compilation of just such buried treasures. (It has reportedly sold upwards of 250,000 units from www.newfunk.com, his website.) The title cut of *Rave Un2* is a late bloomer itself, having been laid down in 1988; the rest of the tracks have only recently been completed.

How does he do it? Well, it's certainly helpful that he regained full ownership of Paisley Park studios a couple of years ago after having operated it as a public facility for years. (REM recorded there, and *Grumpy Old Men* was filmed on the main soundstage.) That means he has 24/7 access to three interconnected state-of-the-art studios and one of the best, most devoted engineers in the business, Hans Buff.

But for the Artist, 24/7 means just that: He works around the clock without sleep for days at a time, sometimes working from initial drum tracks straight through to mixdown, at other times flitting from one song to another. "My job is mainly to make sure to document the sounds he's making," says the soft-spoken Hans. "He works the board himself [a fully automated digital SSL occupies the control room of Studio A], and when he's tracking his vocals, he doesn't even let me in the room."

So what's it like to work on a tune with the whole thing visualized in your head, from start to finish? "The question is always, 'What needs to be here right now?'" explains the Artist. We sit at the massive console, him reaching over from time to time to pull a fader up or down as we listen to the new tracks. "It's not about what's hittin'. What sound needs to be here at this moment? It's all about trust, and keeping the channel clear. 'The Greatest Romance Ever Sold' [one of the new tracks on *Rave Un2*] already existed. I just yanked it out of the sky."

How does he get these airborne sonic visions to stick to tape? Does he just yank gear familiarity from the sky, too? "I don't ever read manuals," he says. "I don't want to have a preconception about what a piece of gear should or shouldn't do. I just start using it, I start pushing buttons, and I discover the sounds that I can make with it. Sometimes a particular sound will give me a whole song, like the harpsichord sound on 'Manic Monday.' [He plays air harpsichord and sings the intro, made famous on a recording by the Bangles.] That sound just dictated that part."

Okay, seems pretty easy. When you work a hundred times harder than your muse, you're bound to have a pretty well-oiled creative process—especially after more than two decades of phenomenal concentration and self-discipline. But what comes up next is surprising. "I'm new at this freedom thing, though," he says. Now, freedom is a loaded term where the Artist is concerned, what with his highly publicized contract battles with Warner Bros. in the mid-'90s and the recent redefinition of his relationship with his partner, Mayte. But the freedom in question is of the creative spirit. How could anyone be artistically freer than the Artist is already?

"When Ani DiFranco first came in here," he explains, "she curled up underneath that chair over there, and we started talking. She didn't sit in it, she curled up underneath it, like a child. Ani has known freedom from the first record she ever made, when she was still a kid. So it's natural. I never was able to be like that, until now. Freedom is something I'm still getting used to."

Fast forward to 2004. The Artist regained the use of his name shortly after (or perhaps during!) the interview you just read. He also retains the ownership of his master recordings as well as the right to distribute and sell them, and he hits the road in support of a new recording, *Musicology*. In fact, *Musicology* is made up of songs that were nearly complete in 1998, and with its release, the press has been all atwitter with talk of Prince's "comeback." But where, exactly, is he supposed to have gone, and when? From the last media blitz, surrounding 1996's *Emancipation*, to now, Prince has released ten collections through both online and traditional channels. *Musicology* is just the first since Emancipation to receive major media attention. So maybe it's his comeback to media-darling status. One thing's for sure: He's as musically powerful as ever. *Musicology* is packed with deadly James Brown-esque "park it on the one" grooves (as in the title track), echoes of 1999 and *Purple Rain*'s rock ("Cinnamon Girl," "If Eye Was the Man in Ur Life"), the psychedelia-laced feel of *Parade* ("What Do U Want Me 2 Do," "Reflection"), and the gospelly R&B/jazz vibe of *Rainbow Children* ("Dear Mr. Man"). Remarkably, though, *Musicology* somehow escapes coming off as just a retrospective pastiche of Prince's many musical phases.

The live show provides all the retrospection a longtime fan could want, even as Prince and the band drastically re-imagine many of the songs. His uncanny knack for assembling ultra-heavy musicians is undiminished, too: The current unit incorporates longtime associates Mike Scott on guitar and Candy Dulfer on sax and vocals, Rhonda Smith on bass, Renato Neto and Chance Howard on keys, drummer John Blackwell, the great Maceo Parker and Mike Phillips on sax, and Greg Boyer on 'bone.

It's a powder keg of scandalous talent and showmanship, and the fuse is found in the diminutive figure standing at center stage wielding his trademark Hohner Tele copy from behind a gold microphone and matching stand.

Minutes before the match was struck, Prince sat down with us to discuss the music, the record, the business, and his two keyboard men, Renato Neto and Chance Howard.

While "crusade" is probably too strong a word, you seem to be on a mission to see live music honored the way it used to be. The lyrics of "Musicology" talk about it, and your all-live show seems to drive the message home.

One of the things that's happened as a result of all the manufactured groups is that young people now have another prototype to aspire to—it used to be if you wanted to be successful in music you had to be a musician. Now that's not necessarily true. Some of these people are truly talented, but we also now have a whole lot of groups that can't play, can't write songs, people that sing with no control or taste. There's an alternative.

But your bands have always been so impossibly tight, are you ever concerned that folks think they are listening to something pre-recorded?

People are smarter than they're given credit for. I think, as tight as the band is, that the audience understands we're giving them 100 percent live music. And for those that don't, we tell 'em.

See, when I started, the thing to do to be different was use all the electronic stuff. We went out with electronic drums and such, and that got people's attention because it was new and different. Now it's the opposite. The new and different thing is to go out without any pre-recorded elements at all, and people seem to like it. They know it's live, and that's exciting. You'll see it; take a look around at the audience during the show.

There's some cool stuff being done with software and computers, but you can't just hook up a little keyboard to your computer, trigger some pre-made loops, and call yourself a keyboard player.

Speaking of keyboard players, what does Renato bring to the table?

Renato brings a very accomplished technique with him, and a sense of harmony that's informed by where he grew up and what he was exposed to musically. It's a cool flavor to add to my music. If there's anywhere where he and I have anything close to difficulties, it's in the area of staying out of the way of the vocal. One really cool thing about Renato: Unlike other keyboard players, I've never heard him work in licks he's learned from somewhere else, and I listen for that. Every night it's something new.

And Chance?

I first became aware of him as a bass player and singer. He plays mostly synth bass but he plays some funky keyboard parts too, and because he's a singer he naturally knows, from accompanying himself, how to stay out of the way of the vocal. Ray Charles had that skill, as did Aretha Franklin, who is totally underrated as a keyboard player. Chance came to jam one day and as time went on he started doing more and more, and he just kinda edged his way onto the tour. [*Laughs.*]

You've always been a very strong keyboardist yourself. Why give it over completely to someone else?

I'm more of a colorist on the keyboards, but I can usually get my ideas out. Renato has a whole other level of harmonic understanding.

You've gone almost totally independent and D.I.Y., business-wise. How's that working out?

So far, on this tour, there's been one million tickets sold. Since the CD is included in the price of admission, and since SoundScan now has to count everything, we've gone platinum at this point. We're planning a platinum party and Sony is upset about it, because they haven't sold a million copies. [*Laughs.*] We could theoretically go on forever; that's one reason we called it the "2004ever Tour." I'm having a ball on the road, and I'm not feeling ready to stop yet.

If we were still doing things the old way, I'd be number one right now. But you've seen the benefits to the way we roll now. Without all the corporate nonsense, it's peaceful back here. You've seen it; ain't nobody rushing around all uptight, several of the guys have their wives with them, nobody's trippin'. [*Indeed, the tension index was several dozen orders of magnitude higher when we visited the same venue just days later for a Madonna tour report.*] Nobody's worried about getting paid.

Shortly thereafter, we sat down with Renato Neto himself. What's this Brazilian jazz cat doing in Prince's band? Adding an entirely new dimension to tunes conceived during the tenures of previous Prince keyboardists Matt Fink, Lisa Coleman, Tommy Barbarella, Rosie Gaines, and Morris Hayes, that's what. At each show, Renato Neto's staggering range of abilities is on full display—he opens the show with an atmospheric sound sculpture using his Korg Triton, Yamaha Motif, and Clavia Nord Lead synths, faithfully covers certain "sacred" keyboard parts like the blistering baroque lead on "When Doves Cry," subtly tweaks convention on classics like "Take Me With U" and completely re-invents the harmonic structure of other songs, injecting blissfully sweet, highly sophisticated jazz substitutions under Prince's indelible melodies. Then he closes the show by deftly blending the explosive ending of "Purple Rain" into a playback of the ethereal string epilogue from the album cut. Impressive he certainly is, but where did Neto come from and what was he doing before rock royalty summoned him to Minneapolis? Neto graciously sat down with us between sound-check sessions to tell his story.

What kinds of things have you learned from Prince?

I had played some funk before, I grew up listening to Earth, Wind, and Fire too, you know, and George Clinton, Herbie Hancock, all that stuff. But mainly it was Brazilian music. It's a little different, when you talk about groove. Now I know really deep what's up with the funk.

Prince told me the mixing between my Brazilian style and the jazz I've been playing for years is a really good combination. It's my own sound. That, I think, is the most important thing for a musician; you have to have your own way to express yourself. Try to be as unique as possible.

And you get a lot of freedom to do that in this gig, don't you?

Yes! Especially on the *One Nite Alone* tour. That was in smaller venues, and was more jazzy. Prince was promoting *Rainbow Children*, with all those interesting great songs. The lyrics, melodies, everything was pretty deep, with a lot of influence of jazz. He loves all that. He loves Miles [Davis]. It's a great culture.

It was a small band, just a four-piece plus sax and trombone. He played the guitars all the time, so there was a lot of space to be very creative. This show is the greatest hits. I have a space to be myself, of course, but it's more about the pop songs.

How much re-interpretation of the songs has there been?

That's another thing that's interesting about Prince; what's on the album is one thing, but he wants to do something different live. It keeps it fresh, and I think the audience likes that, to hear something a little different from the album. It's a good idea, and I think a lot of artists are afraid to do that. They want to do it exactly as recorded, but the people can listen to that at home. Live, it should be something new—a surprise in some way.

Since you've been in the band, you've been the sole keyboard player and you've shared duties with another keyboard player, and sometimes that was Prince. How do you guys divide up who's going to play what?

It's more up to Prince, but sometimes I can give advice because I've been here longer than Chance. Mostly the piano and string stuff Prince likes to keep in my hands. Chance plays synth bass, helps with hits and stabs, and he can sing too. He's a great singer. It's pretty new for him, but he's doing a great job.

Prince gives most of the guidance; "You do this, he'll do that," and so on. He's kind of the MD guy. He gives me a little bit of the arrangements to do, sometimes he wants ideas for taking things in a more jazzy direction, but most of the time it comes from his head. He leaves me alone with harmonic ideas sometimes, because it's very natural for me to do that stuff. So I think he likes the freshness or the surprise of it. But he definitely knows what he wants. [*Laughs.*] He really knows.

Prince was once notorious for booking studio time in the middle of a tour, bringing the band in to work on some new material, and a few months down the line there'd be a new single or B-side. Does that still go on?

Oh, yeah. The *N.E.W.S.* CD that is sold through the website was a project like that. One night at around 11:30, he called us: "Come down to the studio, I need to record something." It was me, Rhonda, [saxophonist] Eric Leeds, and [drummer] John Blackwell. We'd been working all day, and got started on this at around midnight.

And you'd never heard the material before.

No! [*Laughs.*] But this is the great thing; I'm serious, it makes all the difference. I wish all pop music was done like that. You can be creative. You must be creative in that situation. So he says, "OK, we're gonna do four songs, 15 minutes each. They're called 'North,' 'South,' 'East,' and 'West.'" And that was it. Somebody said, "What key?" "C minor." I think it was C minor [*Laughs.*] We started playing, and when we got close to 15 minutes, we stopped. Two hours later, we left the studio. Prince stayed a little longer and did some overdubs. One day, months later, we got into a limo to go to a lunch, and he played it in the car. I couldn't remember the stuff I played: "That was me?" [*Laughs.*]

A SELECTED PRINCE DISCOGRAPHY

20Ten

LotusFlow3r

3121

Musicology

N.E.W.S.

The Rainbow Children

Rave Un2 the Joy Fantastic

Emancipation

The Love Symbol Album

Graffiti Bridge

Lovesexy

Sign o' the Times

Parade

Purple Rain

1999

Dirty Mind

For more information . . . you're on your own. After the release of *20Ten* as an on-cover giveaway with the British tabloid, *Daily Mirror*, in 2010, Prince shut down his website, declaring the Internet to be dead.

Renato Neto may be the resident muse, but we'd call Chance Howard Prince's secret weapon. From behind a keyboard rig that includes Prince's wild Plexiglas Rhodes and a vintage Roland Juno-2, this top utility man plays synth bass and fills in anything and everything Renato Neto can't physically get to at any given moment; funky wah-wah Clav, lush Rhodes, strings, horn section sweetening. And he sings beautifully. We caught up with Chance at the Dallas tour stop.

What have you learned from Prince?

Wow. Where would I start? [*Laughs.*] I would say discipline. Prince is a real stickler for discipline. I'd been playing keyboard bass up until then, and he kinda threw me into becoming a regular keyboard player. So I really had to put the time in, and prove to him that I wanted the gig bad enough to take my skills to the next level. So he really helped me raise my game. I thought I was just gonna come in and do my thing, and he had this whole keyboard rig set up for me. I said, "What am I gonna do with all those?" [*Laughs.*]

There's a dead-simple but crucial synth bass part on "Controversy." What's the key to making something like that live and breathe?

You have to be willing to just play it straight, without embellishment. That groove in particular has a lot of things going on that make it tricky. A lot of times in Prince's funk tunes there's a real straight rock beat up under it. The bass plays around it, and the guitar plays around that. In order for that groove to work, all the parts have to interlock. A lot of keyboard players think the more they play the funkier it is. Most of the time the opposite is true, especially if there are other instruments playing. The idea is not to clutter it up and let each part do its job.

What does the Roland Juno-2 give you that no other synth does?

Aw, now don't make me give up my secrets! It's just really simple to program, and it has that great sound. Most people think of a Minimoog when they think of synth bass, but the Juno-2 just does it for me. I used it all over a Nikka Costa record. Her producers loved it, and Prince didn't want me leaving home without it, either. It's definitely a well-kept secret. Until now anyway! [*Laughs.*]

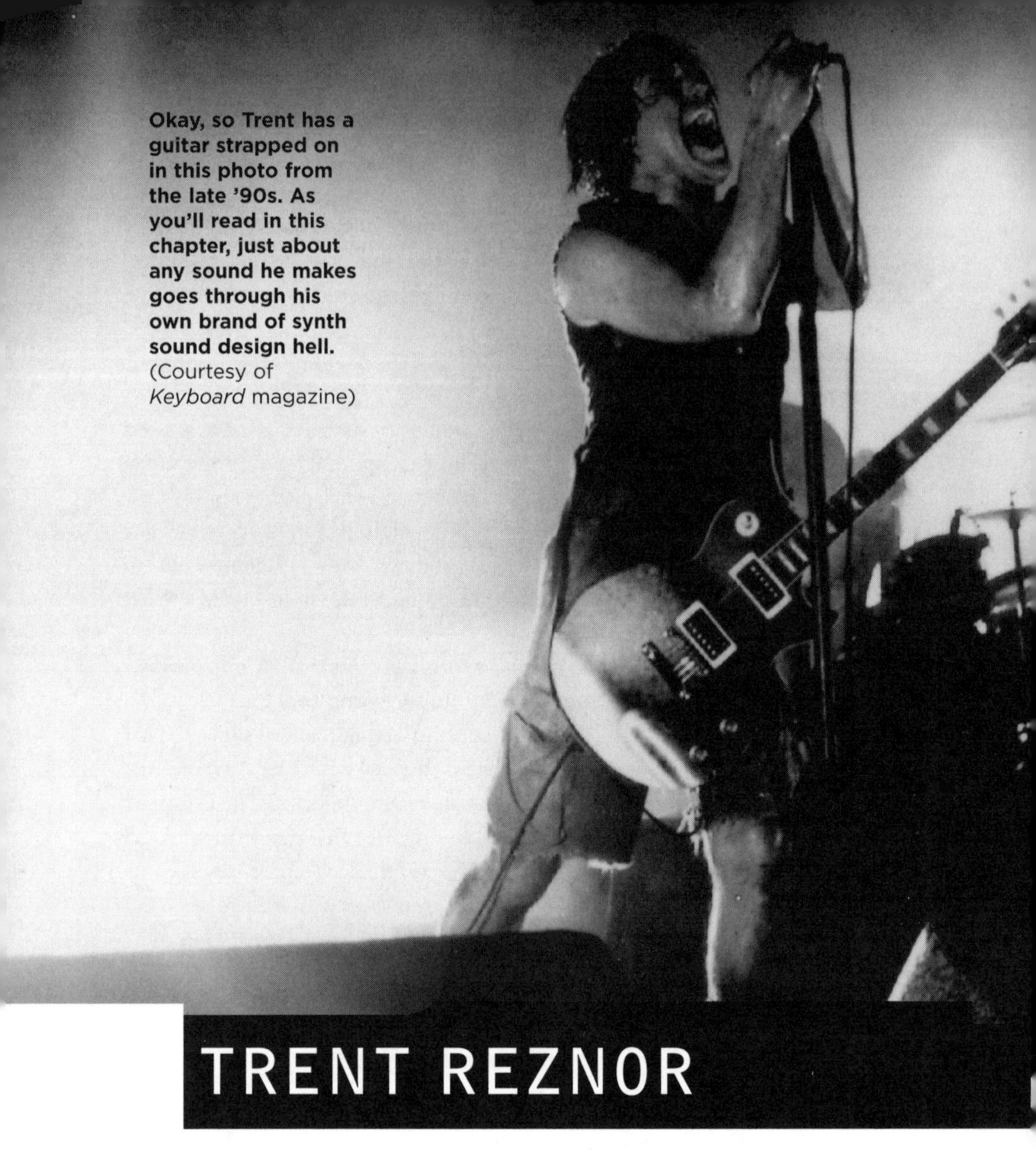

Okay, so Trent has a guitar strapped on in this photo from the late '90s. As you'll read in this chapter, just about any sound he makes goes through his own brand of synth sound design hell. (Courtesy of *Keyboard* magazine)

TRENT REZNOR

12 ANALOG ECSTASY MEETS DIGITAL DESTRUCTION

by Greg Rule

Portions of this chapter originally appeared in the February 2000 issue of Keyboard *magazine.*

One sentence. One simple sentence that hit like a hammer. "Most of the album is actually guitar," declared Trent Reznor in a press release about *The Fragile*. Just as it felt when the great Michael Jordan announced he was leaving basketball for a career in baseball, Trent Reznor dealt the synth world a low blow by admitting

that he'd made a "guitar album."

Or had he?

"There's a general theme of systems failing and things sort of falling apart," says Trent of the record. "In keeping with the idea of making everything sound a little broken, I chose stringed instruments because they're imperfect by nature." But a closer examination of the two-disc opus reveals that Trent hasn't abandoned his black and whites. Far from it. The synths are there, and are employed more creatively than ever. You just have to dig a bit deeper at times, listen a bit closer. And even when the guitars come crashing through the mix like bulldozers, such as on "The Day the World Went Away," it doesn't take long for the mood to shift. In that case, the grinding riffs give way to a whisper-soft piano interlude ("The Frail").

When the sonic landscape is non-keyboard, Trent and company cut, paste, twist, and mutate the audio in brilliant NIN fashion. "When it came to instruments that I didn't really know how to play, like the ukulele or the slide guitar," he says, "we were able to get some interesting sounds by making the studio the main instrument."

What studio techniques is he talking about? What happened between the end of *The Downward Spiral* and the launch of this tour? What programming tips and tricks did the Reznor collective employ on this record and for the subsequent tour? You're about to learn the answers and more as *Keyboard* goes behind the curtain with two of Trent's techno wizards, Charlie Clouser and Keith Hillebrandt, plus a special road report from keyboard tour tech Bruce Hendrix.

THE FRAGILE

Not only did the personnel change for the making of *The Fragile* (longtime drummer/programmer Chris Vrenna departed the Nine Inch Nails camp, to name one), so too did the process of writing and recording. Trent had started to pen new material during a sabbatical in Big Sur, California, but it wasn't until he returned to New Orleans that the tree started to bear fruit. "Trent had these basic categories of songs that he wanted to fill," explains Charlie. "There was a blackboard on the wall, and it said things like: old style NIN jams, rap-influenced drum beats, Atari Teenage Riot level of chaos, and so on."

While there was no one way of developing a song, Charlie says that ideas often started with a foundation groove. "Trent would be working on bass and drum tracks; he'd start with a rhythm of some sort, a drum part or a synthesizer part, and build it from the bottom up. The lyrics and vocals usually came at the very end, after the song was well developed. For a good year there, we were all listening to instrumental tracks with no vocals on them. One collaborative song, 'Starfuckers,' for example, grew out of a Quasimidi Rave-O-Lution [309] through a fuzz pedal jam that I had done upstairs in my studio. That had fallen into the 'Atari Teenage Riot' category of song ideas. It was just something I'd spent about a day and a half fiddling with. I'd gotten some crazy sounds, and I created a basic bass and drum track that I dropped onto the server, and Trent pulled it downstairs. Then, in his weekly or monthly review of song ideas, he picked that one out and said, 'I want to add some things to this.' So he added some bass, some guitars, and eventually wrote the big, heavy riff that comes in the chorus. The final resulting song bears little resemblance to the original track idea that I had laid down, but the original data that I had put in there—the Quasimidi through the fuzz pedal—is the drum track in the verses. So working in the computer let us keep every scrap from our demo ideas, 'cause it was all recorded correctly from the beginning."

The process also worked in reverse. "Trent would sometimes have a very sketchy idea that might not have many instruments on it," Charlie explains. "It might be just drums and bass and a couple of keyboard sounds and a guitar loop or something, and then Danny and I would pile on so much stuff up in our studios that Trent was able to pick through all of our overdubs and find bits and pieces that accentuated the mood that he was trying to get to. So on some of the songs, we were all generating track ideas and swapping them off."

Sound design ace Keith Hillebrandt was brought into the fold early on to create a gigabyte of fresh samples for the album (more on this later), but his role expanded. "We were working on 'The Perfect Drug' remix at the time I arrived in New Orleans," says Keith. "I was under the impression that I was pretty much going to be running the sequencer for Trent and coming up with sounds, but when I actually got here, I realized that my contribution would be greater than I initially anticipated. It was everything from running the sequencer, recording Trent, and editing the sequences to coming up with sounds, manipulating them, and arranging a lot of the demos that Trent was coming up with. He gave me a lot of free rein to pick out the parts that got used. He played a lot of guitar on this album. In some cases there were up to two hours of guitar tracks for a single song, and I would basically sift through all of that and find the parts that I liked." One of Keith's proudest moments on the album was the middle break and the guitar solo of "The Fragile." "We looped the middle section of the song and Trent just kind of banged away on a guitar, and worked out all these dissonant things. Once we had recorded it all in, I cut it up and turned it into this strange dissonant build that leads into the guitar solo. The solo was something that, again, was the result of looping the section. Trent played a series of four-bar phrases, and at the end of playing, he left the room and let Alan and I sift through all the different bits, which eventually turned into the guitar solo you hear on the record. It turned out to be one of the highlights of the album—the way the guitar solo builds up into the end of the song."

> "In keeping with the idea of making everything sound a little broken, I chose stringed instruments because they're imperfect by nature."

If you haven't guessed already, *The Fragile* was recorded digitally. "Everything was going to hard disk," says Keith. "We only started going to tape when we were running out of hard disk channels, which, when we had 72 tracks of hard disk channels . . . we knew we were pushing the limits. There were things like 'We're in This Together,' which turned out to be a massive undertaking. We had so many guitar tracks on that, it only made sense to start dumping them off to tape because even until the last week or so of working on that track—I think that track took nine weeks to complete—we were still not sure exactly what kind of guitar balance we wanted. I think at some point we had maybe 40 or 44 different guitars playing in the chorus. Alan was experimenting with different combinations of guitars and things like that for the chorus, so I think at that point we started dumping tracks off to tape because it was getting a bit chaotic. There was everything from Trent's very low, muddy 'swollen pickle' guitar sound to some fuzzier Tone Machine type sounds."

SYNTHS AND STUDIO GEAR

A mountain of gear was used in the making of the record, but a few key items made repeat appearances. "The main tool in my studio was a Macintosh computer with [Digidesign] SampleCell and lots of TDM plug-ins," says Charlie. "Instrument-wise, the [Clavia] Nord Lead had just come out as we were beginning this record. Trent has always relied heavily on some of the old favorites like the [Sequential] Prophet-VS and the Oberheim Xpander—two unique-sounding synths. But when the Nord Lead first came out, it kind of cracked open the door for a lot of new synth technology."

Trent used "a Nord Lead on almost every song," says Keith. And not just for leads or synth bass. "It was pretty much all over the map. There wasn't any real definitive synth bass. I mean, we used the Minimoog, we used the Nord, we used the [Novation] Bass Station on 'The Wretched.' There wasn't anything that we always went back to for a specific sound, but if he had a melody in his head, the Nord was always the first synth he'd walk over to. He'd basically flip through sounds until he found something in the ballpark, then we'd record in the synth line, and then tweak the sounds as the sequence looped around."

The Access Virus and Waldorf MicroWave also played prominent roles on the record. "In my studio," says Charlie, "I basically rely on three synths—the Nord, the Virus, and the MicroWave—as well as the Nord Modular, which is also a big part of this record. A lot of the processing and drum sounds were actually done on the Nord Modular, which Trent is really good at programming. He's always been really good at using white noise, sweepy drum sounds—not so much synth drum sounds, but synth sounds used in a drum context. And a lot of those kinds of things were done with Nord Lead and Nord Modular.

"I'm also a big fan of the Prophet-VS and the Xpander," he continues. "I found an Xpander that has external audio inputs to the filters, which have a unique musical character and quality, and a bunch of interesting filter types. The Waldorf family of synths are featured very heavily on this record. Their Pulse analog synth was used on quite a few songs, and the family of MicroWaves has been a huge success in our building. Trent owned an original MicroWave module. When the MicroWave II came out, we all got those. Then, of course, the day after we all bought IIs, they came out with the MicroWave XT, which has knobs all over the front."

The main samplers used on *The Fragile* were E-mu E4s. "At the start of the album we got E4s," Charlie says, "which at first were slow. The screen redraws and stuff on the things used to be painfully slow, but we just got the new E4XT Ultra, and sonically it sounds better than my SampleCell card. Even though my SampleCell is TDM and it's coming out the [Digidesign] 888/24, and it should be the cleanest possible signal, there's some subjective quality about the E4 that makes the same sample sound bigger, somehow. I don't know how. I don't know if it's doing something bad to my sample to make it sound better. But we did make very heavy use of the E4s on the record because of the sound and because they have lots of interesting filter types and that sort of thing."

As the album progressed, Charlie also started getting into boxes "like the Quasimidi Rave-O-Lution, the Jomox XBase 09 drum machine, and the FutureRetro 777 303-clone, which are all strange and wonderful devices. Many happy accidents occur when I use those types of devices as opposed to something like a [Korg] Trinity. We don't really have many sample-based workstation-type keyboards in the studio, except for the Kurzweil K2500."

The NIN team started out using Opcode Studio Vision, but switched to Emagic Logic halfway into the sessions. "Initially we were working in Studio Vision," Keith confirms, "but that was before we threw our hands in the air and switched over to Logic. It got to the point where Studio Vision just wasn't reliable enough for us to work with consistently." How seamless was the transition? "I had been a Studio Vision user for six years," says Keith, "so it took a little bit of time to learn Logic, and to learn to use it in a professional manner according to what Trent and Alan were used to. There was a point where we had a guy from L.A. come out, Paul DeCarli, who's a brilliant programmer. He took the reins for a bit and in the meantime was really helpful in getting me out of the way of thinking of Studio Vision and into the way of thinking of Logic—seeing it as more of a transparent interface than what I was used to in Studio Vision."

Switching platforms is easier said than done, and for many reasons. Trying to convert the band's elaborate demos, for example, was anything but a picnic. When they switched, "Everything was in a demo form, which was over 40 tracks that we had to convert," says Keith. "It took a while, and there were some bugs in trying to get it to sound the same way the demos sounded. For instance, if an audio track didn't have the same plug-in on it, or if the correct sys-ex for a synth didn't get sent along with the sequence. Trent's process for synth sounds is basically to dump a single track into the sequence he's using, not to do big dumps. I mean, there are so many synths in the studio, it kind of makes sense. So for every song we had a single sys-ex dump of each Nord Lead, the Virus, the MicroWave, depending on which synths were used on that song. But things like that did make the transition a bit sketchy, and it also made it a little bit tough to bring up the recalls when Trent wanted to further develop a song."

The magic combination for Keith and company turned out to be Logic with Digidesign hardware. Pro Tools software came into play later in the process. "We weren't using the Pro Tools app that much, until we got to the compilation stage—compiling the sequence of the album. But using Logic as a front end for the Digi hardware, it was pretty much flawless. Logic is a very impressive sequencer. It's a lot different than what Trent and I were used to, since we were both Studio Vision users. Charlie made the transition pretty seamlessly."

SOUND DESIGN

Keith Hillebrandt first came to the attention of Trent Reznor for his sound design magic on the *Diffusion of Useful Noise* sample CD. When he got the call to join Nine Inch Nails in New Orleans, his first order of business was to create a 1GB sample library exclusively for Trent. "A lot of stuff was similar to what I'd done on *Diffusion*," says Keith, "a lot of strange, evolving drones and a lot of envelope-triggered loops, which were basically noises that I ran through my [ARP] 2600 and then had the envelopes triggered by drum loops. That would create strange peaks and valleys, kind of giving you the feel of drum loops, but it didn't sound anything like your standard off-the-shelf CD-ROM drum loops. There were a lot of effects-type sounds, things I processed through [Digidesign] Turbosynth and [Prosoniq] SonicWorx. I created a lot of the stuff that way. I'd get off on a little tangent in SonicWorx, and before I'd know it I'd have 20 sounds that came from those processes."

How much creative latitude did Keith have in designing the sounds? "Charlie gave me some ideas for rhythmic loops. As far as the more tonal things, like drones and samples that you could transpose and actually play melodically, Trent kind of gave me an idea of things he was interested in hearing. Things that would complement the ideas he was coming up with. He was really interested in sounds that evolved, that sounded more alive. Not just simple two-second loops. Things that were ten to 20 seconds long that had a development stage. He was looking for things that had a kind of organic nature in and of themselves, so he could drop them into tracks or use them as segues between pieces. He wanted things that would create an evolving feel, as opposed to an obvious three-second loop. He really gave me a lot of free rein. Continually over the two years of recording the album, we were always able to go back to it and find things that we hadn't listened to before or hadn't yet exploited."

You can hear Keith's handiwork throughout *The Fragile*. For example, "there's a shriek-

A SELECTED TRENT REZNOR DISCOGRAPHY

The Slip
Ghosts I-IV
Year Zero
With Teeth
And All That Could Have Been
The Fragile
The Downward Spiral
Pretty Hate Machine

FOR MORE INFORMATION ON TRENT REZNOR, VISIT www.nin.com.

ing type of sound in the verse of 'The Wretched' that kind of peels off into this odd stereo space. There's an evolving drone in 'I'm Looking Forward to Joining You' that moves around in the background behind his vocal."

How did he create these signature sounds? "I would get my source material from all over the place, from pulling it off AM radios or the television to sticking a microphone outside my car window as I was driving home. But I know that the sound in 'The Wretched,' that very sharp stereo peeling out sound, was created in Turbosynth using the Diffuser module, which actually turned out to be quite a great device for creating unique stereo effects. It wasn't something that sounded like it was run through, say, a spatializer kind of plug-in. It wouldn't create that kind of effect. It would create something that always seemed to move a little bit further out beyond the speakers."

Charlie Clouser contributed his fair share of strange noises and loops to the record as well. "We did rely heavily on processing on this record," he reveals, "because there were so many new tools around. A few years ago our choices were limited to basically running stuff through the filter input of the Minimoog or putting it into the Eventide H3000. Those were the two main choices in those days. Now there are piles of plug-ins and crazy processing tools. We used the TC Electronic Fireworx effects unit a lot, which has some interesting filters and such. We also did a lot of passing audio through the filter inputs on the Access Virus module and the Roland JP-8080."

Case in point: "The pulsing synth-type line that runs throughout 'Into the Void' is Trent playing guitar through the MicroWave XT's filter inputs, and the big, heavy sub-bass sounds that come in on the song 'The Great Below' are, I think, Quasimidi Rave-O-Lution through the filter bank on the JP-8080," says Charlie. "There are also a lot of ambient drones on the 'The Great Below' and 'The Way Out Is Through' which are, I believe, a [Steinberg] ReBirth bass sequence running on a Macintosh passing through the filter inputs on the JP-8080. So there was a lot of starting with one thing and ending up with a completely unrecognizable result by basically removing 99 percent of audio from a sound, and just winding up with a delicate little squeaky noise when the original was a screeching, squalling sequence."

Trent's studio complex has no shortage of Macintosh computers, but PCs were integrated into the studio setups along the way. "About halfway through the album, a couple of us bit the bullet and got Windows machines," Charlie says, "because there is a lot of shareware-level audio software for PCs that we wanted to try. Programs like AudioMulch and, on the professional side, [Native Instruments] Reaktor, Generator, and Transformator, which are modular synthesizer-type situations in software that offer a different set of module choices than what you get in a Nord Modular. We also got the Pulsar audio card from Creamware, and I believe on one song we actually used the simulated Minimoog that comes with the Pulsar. We mostly used the PCs for audio processing and drone creation. Basically it was a whole new world. I mean, we didn't learn most of these programs from top to bottom; it was more like, plug it in, bring it up on the console, and see if anything interesting comes out. You know, you're putting in a vocal, and what's coming out is a small crackling sound. The PC, with all these strange shareware programs, provided just another color to the spectrum. But we still did all our sequencing and audio recording on the Macs. The Logic Audio/Pro Tools combo is a lot more evolved on the Mac, and many more plug-ins exist. Plus, we kept breaking our PCs' operating systems by installing audio drivers and shareware stuff, so we couldn't rely on them too much."

If you happened upon the Nine Inch Nails website during this time, you might have noticed the virtual tour of the Nothing studios. In one room, there was an array of stompboxes that had to be seen to be believed. "Keyboards were run through [the pedals] occasionally," says Keith, "but for the most part they were used on guitar. Before Trent would record a guitar track, he would describe to Alan the kind of guitar sound he wanted and Alan would get about five pedals, plug them all in, and start dialing in sounds according to what Trent was looking for. But on occasion we did do things like putting drums through the stompboxes and things like that. A lot of the sounds that I developed for the album were run through Electro-Harmonix pedals like the Screaming Bird, which basically only lets everything above 8kHz through, and that created some nice upper frequency ambiences. But, yeah, I did use quite a few pedals in the sound-design stage of the album."

Dave Smith answered the phone himself in 1976, and he still does so today. This pre-Prophet photo shows Dave Stempson in the back, checking over circuit boards for the model 700 Synth Programmer. (Courtesy of Dave Smith)

13 DAVE SMITH

THE PROPHET RETURNS

by Richard Leiter

Portions of this chapter originally appeared in the September 2007 issue of Keyboard *magazine.*

And lo, it came to pass on the cusp of the second millennium, the voice of the Prophet was heard in the land. And it was big, and it was fat, and it was on a gazillion records. And it wouldn't have happened without Dave Smith. In fact, here's a partial list of other things that wouldn't have evolved the way they did without Dave

Smith: MIDI (he thought it up), the Korg Wavestation, Sequential Circuits, and the very first soft synth that ever ran on a personal computer. You'd think that a guy with this kind of impact on an industry and a world of artists would be sitting on a mountaintop somewhere playing guru to generations of soundmakers. Well, he is off in a glorious part of the world (Napa Valley), and he is a guru. But he's sure not sitting still.

Dave realized when he was still in school that he wasn't going to set the world on fire playing guitar in his band, so he gave up and got an engineering and computer science degree from U.C. Berkeley. This was in the late '60s when engineers weren't the techno gods they are now. He got a low-paying job doing what calls "real stupid work" for Lockheed in what we now call Silicon Valley. One day in 1971 a friend phoned him and told him about this new invention called a Minimoog that he'd seen in an unlikely little shop in Santa Clara. "It was just a tiny store and I have no idea why they had the synth there because they shouldn't have," recalls Dave. "But they did and I bought it. It was a perfect combination of my musical background and my technical background. It was like, whoa!" Bored by his day gig, Dave started to build stuff that made the Minimoog cooler. "I decided to build my own sequencer based on looking at pictures of the big Moog sequencers," he says. "I wasn't even sure how they worked. It was one of the classic three-row, 16-knob analog step sequencers. I played around with it and then I realized other people might want them, so I decided to sell them. I ended up selling four. That's when Sequential Circuits started, in 1974." Ah, so. Sequencers. Circuits.

This is where things get really interesting. In the day of the Minimoog just about all synths were monophonic. Which means if you wanted to play a four-note chord you needed four synthesizers (and four hands), or a four-track tape recorder and lots of time. You can imagine what the thrill was like when, in early 1978, Dave introduced the Prophet-5, the first completely programmable polyphonic synth. Even though the Prophet-5 cost $4,595—and people paid full retail then—everyone bought it just to get five marvelous voices under their grateful fingers. In fact, it's shorter to list the artists who didn't use it than those who did. It wasn't long before other companies like Oberheim and Moog came out with their own versions of the polyphonic synth, but by that time the Prophet-5 occupied an iconic niche in the pantheon of modern music. In the ensuing decade, Dave introduced a slew of variations on a theme: The Prophet-10 contained two Prophet-5s and a 10,000-note sequencer in one big box—it even had two keyboards. Then came the Pro-One, which regressed to one voice but sported a sequencer and arpeggiator for a ridiculously low $645. It was no wonder the One outsold the Ten 10-to-1. Then in 1983, Dave introduced two synths that changed everything again: the Prophet 600, which was a six-voice synth with all the bells and whistles and that new-fangled MIDI thing for under two grand, and the T8, which had a real wood piano keyboard with flying hammers and polyphonic aftertouch. And the inventions kept coming: a MIDI-capable drum machine, a sampling drum machine, and an instrument that used vector synthesis, which pros still use today. In fact, Dave borrowed the vector synthesis technology when the Korg R&D division (which he created and helmed in 1989) developed the Korg Wavestation—the first affordable synth that offered sound production so complex and interesting that it was truly one-finger-soundtrack time.

Even though it was evident that Mr. Smith was the master of all the technologies he surveyed—digital and analog—it was in the world of analog that he reigned supreme. He'd never really gotten over the wonder of producing the special atavistic sounds that only analog can provide. "What analog is really good at is being imperfect," he says. "It's funny, as an analog designer, you spend most of your time trying to get rid of the bad parts of analog. You're trying to keep it in line, close enough to stay in tune, and not too sloppy and not too noisy. Then you have to worry about crosstalk between circuits. So you spend all this time trying to clean

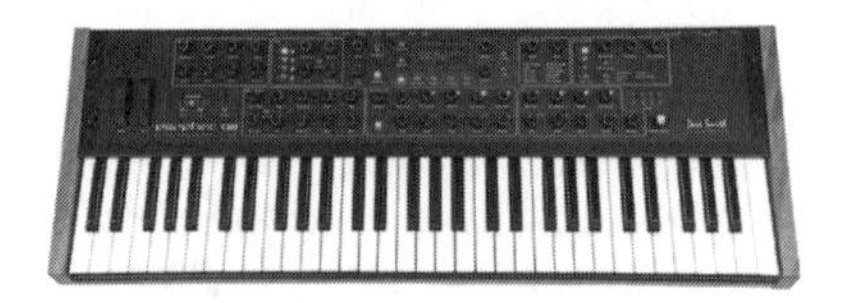

The Prophet of old (top) and the Prophet '08 (bottom).

it up. But when you're designing a digital synthesizer, you spend all your time trying to muddy it up and dirty it up and make it more like analog, because analog has this natural slop to it. With analog, every time you hit a note, it's going to be a little bit different. And the next note will be a tiny bit different from that. Not audibly, but when you play them all together, it really adds up to something that's just more lifelike. It's not a digital recreation. It's the real thing. There are plenty of good-sounding digital synths and they have their own edge and their own special sound, but analog is just . . . different."

"The idea was not to just do an old-style analog synth, but to take it further with a lot of highly integrated digital circuitry. And so it has the best of both worlds."

Most of the electronic instruments we play today use some form of digital manipulation of recorded waveforms. So even though they're technically synthesizing sound, they start with a recording and use a processor to change that recording. Analog synths started with the simple building blocks of Electrical Engineering 101. In the beginning there were oscillators that generated waves: sine waves, square waves, sawtooth waves. They are sounds that don't exist in nature, but are pretty elemental. Now, when we start to run these sounds through filters, things get listenable, and designers like Dave Smith wax rhapsodic. "It really gets down to the analog filters," he says. "They're really the key. Oscillators, yeah, they contribute a lot to the sound, but the filters are probably the most important part. A filter is no different from the tone controls on your stereo. Think of it as a treble control; if you turn it up, you get more brightness. If you turn it down, you get less. That's basically what a lowpass filter does. When you turn it down, you get fewer high frequencies; when you turn it up, you get more. That's all it is." Ah, but the devil is in the details; and there are loads of details. Early analog synths gave you fingers-on control of the envelopes that encased the sounds: the attack, decay, sustain, and release. You could dial in white noise and pink noise and bend your pitch with a voltage control attached to a lever or a wheel—which put the fear of God into a generation of lead guitar players and their precious whammy bars.

Naturally, analog designers complexified their inventions to create more and more fascinating sounds and wonderful ways of controlling the parameters. But for Dave Smith the analog instrument was more than a matter of circuitry. It had its own unique personality. "It's like a guitar," he says. "You buy it one day and ten years later it has the same six strings and the same three knobs, and it works exactly the same way. You know all the intricacies. You know what sounds good, what doesn't sound good. You know how to use it—it's your axe. It's a real instrument. I think sometimes synthesizer players have kind of gotten away from the instrument side—the musicality of having a real instrument in front of you."

But don't soft synths do the very same thing, just on a computer? "To me, a musical instrument should be something that you can hold," says Dave. "You can play it, you can turn knobs. It's a constrained design. It doesn't get updated forever. You come back ten years from now and you turn this knob, it will do the same exact thing it did when you bought it, as opposed to a soft synth that you have to update every couple years, not only to add ten more layers of menus and features, but also because operating systems and computers change." In 1994, Dave, heading the team at Seer Systems, invented Reality, the world's first professional soft synth. It was clearly a little too far ahead of its time, and in some ways, way behind it. "Our Reality system won't run today because the operating systems have all changed," he says. "So as a designer, you end up spending half your time porting the same design year after year to different plug-ins. What is it today, VST? AU? What? You've got to work with all this stuff and Mac and PC and this version and that version. It just gets silly. With soft synths you can keep going forever—let's do this, let's do that! There's no argument that soft synths sound good. But I don't think they sound quite as good—or play as well—as a real analog synth does.

"We see this at trade shows year after year. Someone who's never played one of our synths comes up to us and says, 'I've always heard about this but I haven't had the chance to play it.' And they play on it for about ten seconds and then look up and smile and say, 'Oh, now I get it.' It all becomes very clear what all the talk is about—what analog really means. What having an instrument with real knobs really means. It's something special."

To understand what happened next, it's important to understand that in Dave's mind there's no holy war between analog and digital synthesis. It's like chocolate and vanilla—they're both wonderful. Which explains why, in 2002, Dave drove his analog bus into the wonderful world of digital processing and came up with the next step in electronic music: the Evolver.

"The idea was not to just do an old-style analog synth," explains Dave, "but to take it further with a lot of highly integrated digital circuitry. And so it has the best of both worlds. I found that a lot of things you couldn't do (or shouldn't do, digitally because they hurt your ears and were just big mistakes) did work when you ran them through analog filters because the filters tamed the

FOR MORE INFORMATION ON DAVE SMITH AND HIS AMAZING INSTRUMENTS, VISIT www.davesmithinstruments.com.

sound. I do a lot of feedback stuff in the Evolvers—that's one of the main features. And feedback is a whole lot of fun to play with." Keep in mind that this is not your grandfather's shrieking feedback loop. One of the Evolver patches is just a tiny pinch of white noise in the loop that goes through a tuned digital delay and back into the analog filter and round and round. What might be termed a plucked string sound evolves into a huge, compelling creature of acoustic dimension that lurks in a stereo jungle. And the stereo spread is created not by a single digital black box, but by separate analog filters and delays and an independent feedback loop on each channel. There's a built-in imperfection in the sound that Dave calls "slop" but you or I might call "organic" or even "awesome." Dave seems to be drawn to the unpredictability of sounds that will occasionally blow up, things that can hurt your ears in the digital domain. But pulling them back into the analog circuitry tames those beasts and makes them into wild but useable sounds. And what's more, the sounds are never static—they shift and change and alter themselves—just like an instrument would in the real world.

Not too long ago, Dave realized that he was coming up on the 30-year anniversary of the very first Prophet-5. The Evolver had matured so elegantly—and generated such an active global community of users—that he felt he'd like to spend a little time back with his analog roots. So many fans had come knocking, over the years, asking for an updated version of the original Prophet-5 that he decided it was time to go back to the drawing board. First step: He got on his bike and began to imagine a 21st-century (but still all analog) version of the groundbreaking original. As he cycled through the vineyards of California's wine country, he visualized the basic circuitry of his new re-invention. Each time he returned from a ride, he'd sit down at his computer and lay out schematics on a sophisticated virtual circuit board. In what amounts to a Rubik's Cube of voltage, Dave could tease out all the vexing intricacies of crosstalk, glitchy proximity, and the dreaded FCC emission challenges. This is how one invents a synthesizer in the new world. When he knew in his heart that he'd taken his schematics as far as computerly possible, he started on the layout design for the circuit boards that would be in the instrument. Once the layouts were done, he emailed them to a circuit board maker, and in four days, Dave received the soul of his new machine: four little green boards with lots of silvery lines and little square doohickeys. To create a user interface, he popped the top off one of his Evolvers and plugged in a generic keyboard and presto! The Prophet '08 was born. This might be a slight oversimplification, but in Dave's words, "To locate a part for the design, you hop on the Internet and type in a few search parameters. You go to a site and find a part you think might work. You download the data sheets on it and then you know exactly how it works. Then you go to another site to see how much it costs and you do all of that. And you know immediately whether it's the part you want or not. So the resources are just incredibly fast now, compared to 1978."

If you liked the Prophet-5—or even the idea of the Prophet-5—you're going to die for this instrument. "I thought it would be fun to go back, even though I said I'd never do something like this, and do a pure analog instrument where the audio chain is completely analog," says the proud designer. "It still does quite a few different things that the original Prophets didn't. Also, this one is going to be under $2,000, it's got eight voices, and it's quite a bit bigger sounding, but with the same basic filters and the same basic structure as the original."

The Prophet '08 is a passport into another time and musical place. Like all the other Dave Smith instruments, it's an instrument end-capped with real wood. And when you call up Dave Smith Instruments, you get . . . Dave! And if a circuit board goes down, you won't spend two frustrating weeks emailing back and forth with tech support overseas. Dave will just mail you what needs to be fixed. Of course, if he sells a million '08s this will all change and you'll wind up dealing with phone menus and overworked nerds. But in the meantime, Dave is committed to doing it his way—the expeditious way. "What's amazing is how efficient you can be when you do everything yourself," he says. "I don't have a marketing department, so I don't have to listen to what's supposed to be. If you think about how a normal company works, they have sales guys and marketing guys that say, 'We need a product that does this!' And then they have to go to engineers, and engineers don't really know what they're doing, except to say, 'Okay, we need this many filters!' And then they go out and try to do it and somebody says, 'Well, it costs too much!' Meetings, meetings, meetings, and time, time, time—it just takes forever to get something done that way. "For me, I just sit down and make all these decisions on the fly. I can decide that for only $2 more, I can add this great new feature by adding this one little piece of hardware. Or I can save $10 if I take this part out and do that other part in software. It's just me talking to myself, basically, and I don't have to answer to anybody else. So it just makes it incredibly fast to do." And yes, it will have full MIDI implementation. And yes, it will look handsomely retro like its forbearers. And yes, it will never go out of tune in the middle of a song—unless you want it to. But that's beside the point. Dave Smith's vision of musical pleasure is once again with us. And he'll be proud that no matter how many instruments he sells, he'll always be making an excellent Prophet.

Edgar Froese activates an audience from within one of the three synth-packed stations that were a part of every Tangerine Dream performance in the early '80s. That's a VCS3 in the foreground. (Courtesy of *Keyboard* magazine)

14 TANGERINE DREAM

SYNTHESIZER CONSCIOUSNESS

by Dominic Milano

Portions of this chapter originally appeared in the April 1981 issue of Keyboard *magazine.*

Tangerine Dream makes music for your eyes as well as your ears. It evokes images and takes you places you may never have been before. The layers of synthesizer sound are an audio version of a surrealist painting. And more than one reviewer has remarked on this German trio's huge influence on other practitioners of electronic music.

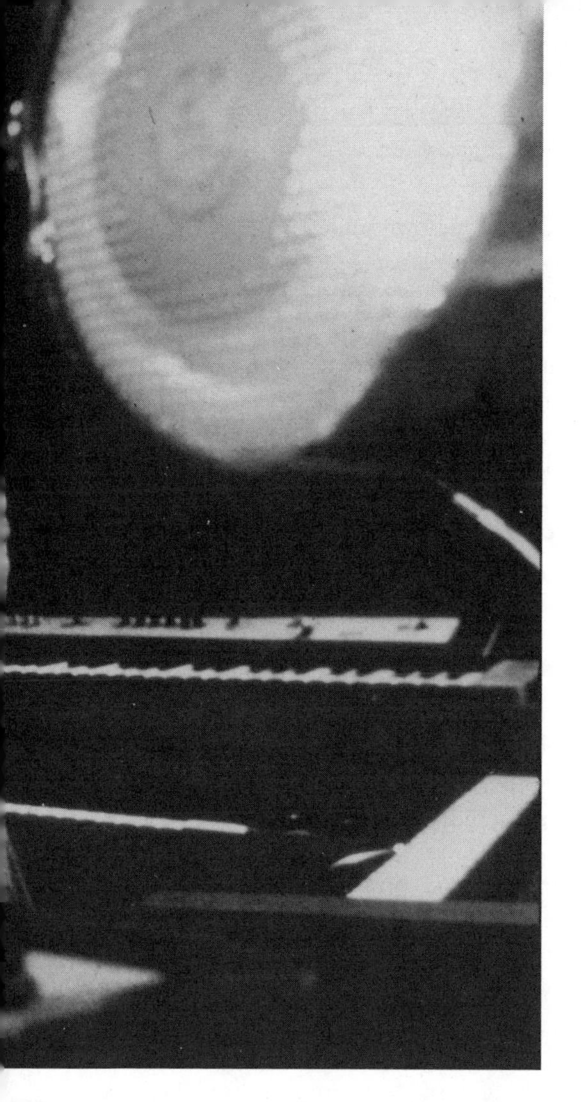

Tangerine Dream was formed in the late '60s by Edgar Froese, then a guitarist. Originally, their music was traditional psychedelic rock with traditional instrumentation and traditional volume levels (it was loud). Working within this format, it was hard for the band to establish any kind of original sound, and as Froese puts it, "Playing that type of pop music became unsatisfying. We weren't saying anything new to our audiences or to ourselves."

So in 1969, the band began exploring the synthesizer, much to the initial dismay of its growing European audience. At the time of this interview in 1981, Tangerine Dream had become, arguably, the most influential electronic band in the world. Their mixture of hypnotic improvisation and driving sequencers laid the foundation for much of the electronic and dance revolution that characterized the '80s.

Also by this time, the band had been through several changes in lineup and instrumentation, with Edgar Froese anchoring the sound and keeping the band's vision intact. In 1980, the band released *Tangram*, which showcases Tangerine Dream at what may be the most interesting moment in the latest phase of their development. Edgar still plays synthesizers and a bit of guitar, and Chris Franke is still playing synthesizer and taking responsibility for the sequencer rhythms within the trio. They've been joined by keyboardist Johannes Schmoelling, and you can perceive some subtle alterations in the classic Tangerine Dream sound: There are more dynamics in the music, and coupled with their machine-like rhythms is a hint of emotion and some feeling that goes beyond New Agey mellowness.

Schmoelling joined the band after a chance meeting with Froese in a Berlin studio, where Schmoelling was completing some work with another band. His background, he explained to us, is in classical music and more traditional jazz and rock keyboard playing. He worked as an engineer in various recording studios and studied electronics as well. He saw joining Tangerine Dream as a chance to make use of his skills in both playing and electronics. Onstage, his instrumental duties involve playing some of the more traditional keyboard parts on such instruments as an Oberheim OB-X, a Prophet-5, a Yamaha electric grand, and a Minimoog.

Speaking of which, Tangerine Dream is infamous for the vast amounts of synthesizer gear with which they cover the stage. Froese and Franke each have huge customized modular synthesizers that dominate the stage setup, dwarfing the many other keyboard instruments used by the band. Many of these instruments aren't as stock as they seem, and the number of technological advances that this band has made is enough to make any equipment fanatic drool.

We caught Tangerine Dream in Los Angeles just after they had finished up their latest American tour. We spoke first with Chris Franke, and about halfway through the interview we were joined by Edgar Froese. We spoke to Johannes Schmoelling over the phone from Berlin later. The entire band was eager to talk about their unique collection of instruments, their perceptions of the music industry, and future directions that they're going to explore.

How much modular equipment is the band making use of currently, and has it been modified to make live performance a little easier to cope with?

Franke: We have three modular systems, which have been modified rather heavily through the years to make live performance easier. I think we have 200 modules or so. Our service engineer in Berlin became more and more involved with our problems, and he started to design his own modules, which are not for sale anywhere else. They are designed just for us. His company is called Projekt Electronic. This company is very useful to us in the analog field. Digital, or course, is a different story altogether. Our modular systems are about 50 percent Moog and 50 percent Projekt Electronic.

What kind of problems have you had to overcome on the modular systems?

Franke: That's very easy to explain. The natural problem with modular systems is that they don't have any programmable computer interface facilities. You have no preset programs. You have so little time between songs and within songs to change patches and to set up new registers. That is why we have our systems modified. We have added a lot of CV [control voltage] busses for the oscillators, a lot of signal busses, a lot of busses for controls like keyboards and sequencers. All of these things can now be routed very easily. We even have sequencers set up to control these routings.

How do you decide which sequencer is going to control which voltage?

Franke: The sequencer, which we use a lot, is an important controller for us. There are a couple of different sequencers programmed onstage, but we use another to control routing. This routing sequencer is in control of routing the other sequencers to the oscillators and saying how often sequence A is played and how often sequence B is played. This way you get some kind of structure already programmed. Another modification we've had to make is to have completely different power supplies. We have had to stabilize all the oscillators, and all the mechanics we've had to change drastically. Those were the main problems in preparing our system for use onstage. We have just played 30 countries, and our systems are still holding up. Five or eight years ago, there were tremendous problems. Now we're prepared for them.

> "But we still think that ideally, music should awaken people. It should make them think, not make them passive."

How did you deal with the problems back then?

Franke: We went to Australia and the modular gear was completely smashed. We played the tour with a couple of Minimoogs. That was a particularly hard time. I still wonder how we were able to use the standard Moog sequencers, since the steps are not quantized and the temperature changes affected them all the time. Now I have a very special quantizing arrangement. I can define the intervals of the quantizing. My oscillators also never run out of tune. I can't believe that I used to go through all the trouble that I used to go through. I guess the motivation for going through that much was supplied by the interest in doing something new. Every night we were afraid of having things not work, so we spent most of our income on improving the live situation. We always wanted instruments that were programmable and had polyphonic facilities. We even built our own programmer before there was any other programmer out. Then we started using the Sequential Circuits programmer on our modular units when it came out, and we started using synthesizers like the Prophet-5 and the OB-X when they came out. We also used the Oberheim Four-Voice because this was the first polyphonic synthesizer we knew of and Oberheim instruments have always been avant-garde in technology.

What other types of keyboards does the band make use of?

Franke: We use ordinary keyboards like a Yamaha CP-70 electric grand, a Hohner Clavinet/Pianet Duo, a Wurlitzer electric piano, and string machines like the Solina, Elka, Crumar, and Korg units. Every instrument has a special position in our music. You have to clarify where to use each instrument through your own experience, because they all sound a little different. Sometimes an instrument only sounds its best in one octave, so we make use of combinations of all of them. We are also getting into purely digital machines.

What other experiences have you had with digital instruments that are on the market now?

Franke: We own two instruments, the Crumar GDS and the PPG Waveframe Computer, which comes from Germany and isn't available in the States. We feel that the Crumar GDS is by far the most advanced and developed digital instrument in terms of software. It also has some of the best hardware in it. Some people feel that it's not good to use such dedicated hardware because you have no idea where digital sound synthesis will go in the future. Will it be additive? Will it be FM? Will it be something else entirely? Nobody knows for sure. And every system is still limited in certain ways. The Fairlight people say that a system that is totally software-oriented is the way to go, because it's easier to develop and change. I don't think that idea will go too far. Microcomputers and microprocessors are just far too limited in sampling speed.

Tell us something about the PPG system.

Franke: Edgar is using this system. There are small versions of the system available that cost about $5,000. These have 100 presets, 40 of which you can define yourself. Then there is the big machine, which lets you define all your own waveforms. There are eight voices, which can be used as notes, sequences, or independent tone colors. In each voice set there are 64 waveforms, each of which can be defined by splitting it up at 256 break points. You define waveforms by defining the break points, and then you use the envelopes in the machine to sweep through all these different waveforms. That is what makes it sound natural. That is the key to making a synthesizer sound good. The manufacturer has to decide what circuitry to use to make sound change. Using a filter is nice, but it cuts off frequencies.

That is why I like to use digital machines. They make the sound appear so clean and crystalline. Electronic music has always sounded too soft and not as brilliant as it should be. You must imagine what this Waveform Computer sounds like with these rich harmonics sweeping about. It gives you the effect of having a filter, but without all the dullness that a filter imposes on a sound. Then you can also arrange the harmonics in strange orders to get a previously unheard effect.

Getting back to other types of equipment that the band uses, what about effects and signal processors?

Franke: We use Moog parametric equalizers, and we use delay lines, of course. I have a very nice delay line made by KlarkTechnik called the DN-36 that I use for chorus and flanging effects in stereo. Then we have the 360 Systems programmable parametric, and some graphic equalizers too. Almost everything has at least three effects on it. We use flanging and chorusing effects quite a lot, because they make your brain think that the sounds are moving around more. In the future, it would be nice to see someone come out with flanging, chorusing, and echoes which are programmable and can be tied in with synthesizer voices directly. On side two of *Tangram* I put my OB-1 synthesizer through a very old fuzzbox. That made it sound like a saxophone in the lower registers and a guitar in the upper registers. Many people mistake that sound for Edgar's guitar.

What type of fuzzbox did you use?

Franke: It is only the Electro-Harmonix Big Muff fuzz which is usable for this effect. I even play my Prophet through five Big Muffs.

Five!

Franke: Five of them, one for each voice. This is because if you play a chord on the Prophet and run it through a fuzzbox, you get white noise. So I run each voice out to its own fuzzbox. This gives me an almost digital sound quality. Sometimes we use Hot Tubes, which gives you a little more sharpness and a little dirt. Electronic instruments sound better sometimes if they're run through an old Marshall amp or through a Leslie. I like to try unconventional setups to see how the instruments will be affected.

What about the vocoder effects on *Tangram*?

Franke: For those, I'm using a Moog vocoder in conjunction with a Gentle Electric pitch-to-voltage unit. I haven't used it onstage yet. I haven't found the right singer for it yet. Also on *Tangram* we used the vocoder with a rhythm machine. We have had our own studio for a year and a half now, and we have all the usual stuff in it, which was used for *Tangram*. We have tape recorders that are used for delays and an EMT plate reverb. It is a breakthrough for us to have our own studio, because we can go ahead and breathe now. We can get used to having things in the same place and having the room always sound the same. You need to feel comfortable in an environment when you're doing improvised music, and you need to feel no pressures from time, which we always had when we were renting studios. It's also very important to us to have rehearsal space where you can record as well, and the studio could easily fit 250 people in it. Unfortunately, electronic music is expensive to make. It's something like making an animated film. You work with a whole lot of tracks in electronic music, and in that respect it resembles animated film. Maybe we're doing animation music.

How much of a part do visual images play in your music?

Franke: There have always been visuals in our music. In the beginning, things were pretty surreal. They were landscape kinds of things. A lot of our music removed you from time and gave you the feeling of flying in a dream. We always tried to express our visuals through our music. We experimented with using slides and video projections in our live shows, and we did a tour with laserium. We will definitely do a video disc sometime in the future, but for now, people need to learn to accept lots of new information. Some people close their eyes when they're presented with too much visual experience accompanied by music which they don't know too well yet. I wonder if there will ever be a film that we write music to that no one would ever see. They would just hear the music that we've composed for it. The film would structure the music, but no one would ever see what we used to create the structure. Since we don't use vocals to determine timings, we've had to find other things that will define those parameters for us. We still feel that we don't want to do vocal music, and we want to find new sound colors that will create a new fantasy for the audience.

How do you actually go about organizing a piece? Does it generate itself in the studio?

Franke: There are a lot of different ways. Sometimes we're just fooling around improvising and we come up with a theme. Sometimes you're setting up a special color that is so extraordinary that you can only play certain tunes on it. Sometimes sound colors dictate the tune you play, and sometimes it's a certain structure in your mind. At the moment, our recorded and live approaches are mixtures of all those things. We always work around the structured parts and the improvised parts. The structured parts last from five to ten minutes and then you have the improvised parts, which are centered around certain rhythms or keys and that's about all. There are always places left for solos, and there are places where we do abstract kinds of sounds and abstract transitions from totally composed pieces to free-form ones. One nice feature about my editing system is that it can read out what has been played on a keyboard. That is nice, because we will be able to have a printout of what was played during an improvisation. It's very difficult to try to remember what you played, and it's nearly impossible to transcribe what three guys improvised when you're dealing with echoes and three different synthesizer players. This editing system gives you the opportunity to go back and look at what was played and to edit it together.

You could also go back and alter tone colors.

Franke: Of course, this can always be done. So we are not afraid of doing spontaneous music even in a live performance context, even if there is the danger of having something not work and not sound quite right. Our following knows that we are improvising, and that makes it more exciting for them because they know that they will always hear something different.

One of the most characteristic sounds of Tangerine Dream is the ever-present use of sequencers.

Franke: It's one rhythmic structure which, when we use it, you can always hear it. The sequencer is a great instrument. The type of repetition it creates is used a lot in African music and minimal music. Bach also has some great sequences. The sequencer makes it great to go into modal music. It makes it much easier to get away from certain types of harmonies, and that's important to us in making music work for the mind. I was a drummer and always was wondering how I could make these bloody drums be in tune. It was just impossible. I wanted percussive sounds that were in tune and that bore some tonal relationship to what the rest of the band was playing. I used to use tape loops, and for years people thought that that's how we did it. They didn't know that we had switched over to sequencers.

What about digital sequencers?

Franke: I don't like that type of sequencer. I like sequencers that you can use like an instrument, where you have access to certain parameters and you can cause it to change over time, so you have an ongoing structure happening. If you are good and you have the right instrument, you can have astonishing patterns happening. We have a new sequencer which looks analog from the outside, but is really digital, but not the kind of digital that people sell on the market. You don't control pitch with them, you use them as a clock, because we had trouble creating polyrhythmic things. We had to find a way to sync two different sequencers running two different rhythms. Our engineer came up with a wonderful phase-lock-loop system that synchronizes them. We can sync up to five or six sequencers at once.

How do you control the pitches?

Franke: I have switches for quantizing the pitches to whatever I would like. I only have two stepless pots, to control the outputs to the VCAs and the filters. I use these for accents. But I can adjust any semitone that the switches on my sequencers put out, so I'm not locked into playing within a tempered scale. On my new Prophet I can also play in these tunings and I can do the same on a Korg polyphonic synthesizer, which lets you tune each oscillator individually.

What do you do when you change key?

Franke: On those two instruments, you can set up a new scale, but it's limited to one key, unless on the Prophet you use a different program position with the same sound but a different scale tuned to the new key. I use a bass pedal to tell the computer when to change keys. I press a note and the computer knows what to detune and what to readjust to make the scale work in the new key.

You're not worried about being accused of using robots to play your music?

Franke: No. There is a person in Berlin who has built a robot that plays the flute. There is a little motor that blows wind into the flute and relays that play the keys, so it is a perfect flute sound, but every time a flute player listens to it he will get a little sick, because he doesn't hear the sound of the flutist breathing in [*laughs*]. I don't mind having robots around in the studio which can play, but actually more important to me are devices like Master's Touch, the EVI, Lyricons, Humanizers, and so on, because they start making electronic music sound more alive. It's so dead when you hear a static tone from a synthesizer. You need something to make the sounds move more. You need to make them sound alive. Pitch-to-voltage converters are going to be better and better for guitars, vocals, and wind instruments. This is always very important. You can't be an artist by just playing notes. You have to be versed in all the different left-hand controllers. Jan Hammer was just the start of pitch-bending on synthesizers. Now with the touch-sensitive keyboards that companies like Yamaha are designing, people will have even more to think about. The keyboard alone is really boring.

In much of the band's newer material, you can hear more dynamics than used to be the case. Is that a conscious thing?

Schmoelling: Yes, it is a goal that we all have as a band. It is something that we are striving for.

Franke: The only guy who has done it well in electronic music so far is Tomita. Sometimes he is so very strange, though. His tone colors are so very Japanese. Still, one has to give him credit for his dynamics. It is one parameter that gets overlooked too often. Dynamics are very hard to control. One can always use a computer mixing console to adjust them, but you have to keep in mind that they are a big thing. The electronic keyboard instruments haven't had that much control over dynamics, at least not when compared to the piano, but they're coming along now. It's the new age of electronics. You have more control, so the expression will be much greater in the future.

Does your music serve any purpose for you other than exploring tone colors?

Froese: Many different hardwares can be addressed by software, and both together

A SELECTED TANGERINE DREAM DISCOGRAPHY

The Bootmoon Series: Aachen

Inferno (Live)

The Seven Letters from Tibet

Mars Polaris

Tyranny of Beauty

220 Volt Live

Melrose

Canyon Dreams

Firestarter

Tangram

Force Majeure

Stratosfear

Phaedra

FOR MORE INFORMATION ON TANGERINE DREAM, VISIT www.tangerinedream.org.

can be used to change consciousness, and that's what we want to go for. By using new sounds and new technology, we are changing a program that exists outside of our human process. Hopefully, that will lead to a change, in a positive sense, of our internal programming, the subconscious matrix. That's a very high aim, and I don't know how far we can progress in trying to reach it, but this is what we would like our music to do. We don't want to try to occupy everyone's life or try to tell them what to do. We just want to help people start thinking for themselves again. We want to make them more independent in deciding what they're going to do next. It should make people ready for some new way of thinking.

Franke: A lot of music is used as therapy for people when they are frustrated and troubled. They go home and switch it on and then they feel good. It is therapy. It's something that helps them to forget. But we still think that ideally, music should awaken people. It should make them think, not make them passive.

Froese: Activating people is what is important. We don't want to put them to sleep.

Isao Tomita with his object of desire: The Moog Modular he painstakingly built and learned how to program that was the basis of his huge hits in the mid-'70s. (Michael Ochs Archives/ Getty Images)

15 ISAO TOMITA

FROM CIRCUITS TO COLORS

by Mickey Yoshino translated by Steve Fox

Portions of this chapter originally appeared in the August 1977 issue of Keyboard *magazine.*

From the vantage point of 1977, scarcely more than a decade into the era of the synthesizer, the magnitude of its impact on the world of music remains to be determined. Like any other device, it can have only as much effect as the people who use it have talent. The face of rock and jazz is being transformed by dozens

of prominent synthesists whose understanding and application of electronics becomes daily more sophisticated. In contemporary classical music, there is likewise an army of dedicated artists making use of the instrument, though of course their work is heard by fewer people.

The bastions of 19th-century symphonic music have, however, proven more formidable. Although the synthesizer would seem to offer comparatively effortless access to the range of sounds that composers have traditionally required a hundred or more musicians to produce, the synthesists who have so far attempted large-scale electronic realizations of symphonic works can be numbered on the fingers of one hand. Of these few, the one whose work has recently generated the greatest critical acclaim and popular interest, thereby showing how bright the future of electronic orchestration may be, is Isao Tomita.

Born in Tokyo in 1932, Tomita had already firmly established himself on Japan's music scene through his work on film scores and TV commercial soundtracks, as well as through having received several important commissions from the Japanese government, when his first album of synthesized symphonic music, a Debussy collection called *Snowflakes Are Dancing*, was released in 1974. After *Snowflakes* followed his versions of Mussorgsky's *Pictures at an Exhibition* and Stravinsky's *Firebird Suite* (the album *Firebird* also contains Debussy's *Prelude to the Afternoon of a Fawn* and Mussorgsky's *A Night on Bare Mountain*. With the release this spring of *The Tomita Planets* based on Holst's *The Planets*, Tomita's career has reached an all-time high: The album rocketed to number 67 on Billboard's pop chart and to the number one slot on the classical chart, assuring him of the continuing attention of an international audience.

When did you start studying music?

I began seriously concentrating on music study after I entered senior high school. I went to a class in the arts section at the YMCA and learned music theory and composition. Today, there are many classes like this available, but this was not so much the case in those days.

Did you start with the piano?

Yes, the piano was almost the only musical instrument available. I took lessons from an instructor of classical music and progressed to where I was playing some of the simpler sonatas. I began with Beyer and went through Czerny and various other methods. But I started only after my father bought me a piano when I was a sophomore in high school, so I'm not that good at it.

Weren't you also interested in electronics?

Yes, I was. At the same time I was taking a class at Keio University in aesthetics and the history of art, I was enjoying tinkering with electronics. I often went to the shops in Tokyo's Akihabara district that dealt with electrical equipment. You could buy a sack full of parts of demolished airplanes for 20 or 30 yen [about 10¢], and often the sacks contained tubes, relays, and many other precious parts that couldn't be bought anywhere else at such prices. Using these parts, I once made a device that would ring a bell when somebody passed through a doorway—a sort of a burglar alarm. At first, my interests in music and electronics were quite separate. It was the marketing of synthesizers that unexpectedly merged my two hobbies.

What motivated you to go into music more seriously?

The Asahi newspaper was sponsoring an all-Japan chorus festival. When I was a sophomore in college, I sent in one of my compositions to them and won a prize. This was my first motivation for entering the world of music. At about the same time, I got involved with taking care of radio programs and arranging music for schoolchildren. So by the time I graduated from college, I didn't have any trouble getting work in the field.

How did you come into contact with the synthesizer?

It started when I listened to Walter Carlos' *Switched-On Bach* for the first time. I had known that NHK [the Japan Broadcasting Corporation] was spending hundreds of millions of yen setting up an electronic music studio, but I wasn't really interested in working in them, because they had a large staff of composers, engineers, and sound-effects people. In the case of normal music, melodies, chords, and rhythms are expressed with notes, and consequently there is a solid object, the score, which can be discussed in the same way that one would discuss a blueprint of a building. But the concept of a sound that hasn't yet been electronically created exists in the mind of one person, and can't be discussed in the same way.

For instance, suppose that there was no such thing as a violin in the world, and that the sound of the violin existed in the mind of one person. The person couldn't convey the sound until it was actually produced by a violin. Because of this limitation, the development of electronic music has tended to be rather haphazard. But the synthesizer can be operated by one person alone. This means that a music producer can directly create the sounds he or she wants by connecting circuits. It was this possibility that made me think electronic music was worth producing. I was impressed by *Switched-On Bach*, and subsequently I bought a relatively expensive synthesizer.

> "The musician, unlike the painter or the sculptor, has never been able to search for colors other than those that were given. But with the synthesizer, we have a palette comparable to that of the painter."

How did you acquire it?

Nobody in Japan knew about the synthesizer at that time. I even made an inquiry to Hong Kong in vain. However, I discovered that the Aichi Prefectural University of the Arts in Nagoya had just acquired such a device, and I went to the University and asked them to introduce me to the dealer. I finally acquired an instrument around the end of 1971.

What equipment did you buy at that time?

I bought a Moog III and a sequencer. The operation of this equipment is pretty complicated, but of course it's easier to handle than the electronic music devices of decades ago, and much less bulky than if vacuum tubes were still being used instead of transistors. And once you understand how it works, the equipment of today lets you handle sounds to perfection.

Did you encounter any difficulties when you first set the device up?

Yes, I did. I had the importer install the equipment in my home, but I didn't know how to operate it. I felt as if I had bought a load of scrap iron. However, a fifteen-page operations manual came with the instrument, and a Mr. Shiotani, who had worked in the NHK electronic music studio and who I believe is now an assistant professor at a university in Osaka, was kind enough to come to my home on two occasions to explain the machine. Because of my electronics background, I could understand to some extent the various functions of the modules. But I imagine that the techniques I acquired for using the equipment are sort of unique, because I developed my understanding of the various functions almost without being instructed by an expert. I didn't exactly intend to go about learning in this way, but that's how it worked out.

How did you pay for such an expensive instrument?

It was a headache. I had to pay back about ten million yen. But it was a relief to know that there were almost no other synthesizers in Japan except for a small number of Minimoogs. So I teamed up with a group of sound-effects producers, and we received a substantial number of orders for TV commercial soundtracks. In a normal case, the cost of producing music for one TV spot is about 500,000 yen [about $1,800], which is allocated to the composer, the studio rental, and payments to the musicians and conductor. We offered better music for the same cost. And if we made three commercials a month, we had an income of 1,500,000 yen. This enabled me to pay back my loan little by little. But I wasn't satisfied just to be doing that kind of work. I knew that the synthesizer was capable of more, so I started working on Debussy's "Claire de lune" [released in the U.S. on *Snowflakes Are Dancing*] on my own. Walter Carlos had already put Bach's music into electronic form, but I wanted to try doing the same thing to pieces by the Impressionist composers. As I experimented, the number of finished tunes I had grew until I had five for each side of an album. So I went to a record company with the material.

What was their reaction?

Japanese record companies refused to put out records of such music, because they said it wouldn't sell. They felt that my music was merely experimental. One of the biggest problems was that they didn't know how to classify electronic music within the conventional categories of classical, popular, and jazz. As a result, they didn't know where they would put the records of electronic music in a record store. I checked to see where *Switched-On Bach* was being put in the stores and found one shop selling it as a sound-effects record. The Japanese record companies said that records with no appropriate place in the racks in the stores don't sell well. They also said that the considerable success attained by *Switched-On Bach* lay in the fact that it was done by an American. They implied that no such record made by a Japanese would be as successful.

What was the next step?

I gave up trying to sell the tapes to Japanese record companies and took them to Mr. Yamamoto at RCA, who told me about a certain Mr. Peter Munves at RCA in New York. Munves had handled *Switched-On Bach* when he was at Columbia. He listened to my tapes and immediately agreed to put my music on records. Another American who helped me is Thomas Shepherd, who is presently a vice president at RCA. He also worked formerly for Columbia, where he produced a record entitled *Switched-On Bolero*. He has had the experience of actually operating a synthesizer.

How long did it take you to complete the first album?

Working more than six hours a day, it took me about 14 months. Two or three hours each day were required just for setting up the equipment and stabilizing the sounds.

Did you encounter any difficulties in overdubbing?

Of course, the amount of noise increased, but also the quality of the sounds sometimes changed in unexpected ways because of repeated overdubbings.

How many tracks did you have to lay down?

It varied according to how complex the passage of music was. In some passages I dubbed the sounds more than a hundred times. All this had to be done on a four-track machine. Sometimes, it seems to me that the actual work involved in creating electronic music is more like making a documentary film on how to make Persian carpets than it is like playing music. I've heard that on Mike Oldfield's *Tubular Bells* there are literally thousands of overdubs.

Did you intend "Claire de lune" more as a demonstration of a synthesizer sound collage, or as pure music?

It is intended to offer one particular sort of pure music. To most people, it doesn't matter how many people have worked to create the sound, or that the synthesizer was used to create it. New things tend to encounter many barriers before being accepted. My music meets with a lot of curiosity, but merely being a curiosity doesn't guarantee success.

Which is your favorite among your first three albums?

The Firebird. The tunes on the back side of that album are somewhat inferior in quality, because I did them even before I did *Pictures at an Exhibition.* But *Firebird* is one of my biggest technical successes. Ideally, it should be listened to through a four-channel system. You see, my music is four-channel music from the beginning. I try to create a certain acoustic space. There is, however, no fixed direction that the four channels ought to have. The listener can sit anywhere among the four speakers; it isn't even necessary to sit in the exact center. If you're close to a speaker, you might experience the sound traveling away from you, while a listener in the center would feel the sound shift from the right to the left.

You did a live tour of Europe, didn't you?

I toured Europe from February to April of 1976. I borrowed Pink Floyd's audio equipment and toured West Germany, the Netherlands, and Britain. I had always wanted to reproduce my music in a vast sound space that could accommodate as many as two thousand listeners. I thought it would be a dream come true if my music could be played in such halls with good audio equipment. You know, most music critics use a two-channel system to listen to my music, but when the front and rear channels are combined, the music sounds too flat. This results in unjustified reviews. It seems to me that this is like scratching an itch through an overcoat. It's a hopeless case. But really, a live performance of this genre of music is absolutely impossible. So I was playing simple sounds on the synthesizer on the spot, while the rest of the music was coming through a four-channel tape system. The promoter of the tour, however, didn't understand things like this. Many people appeared to have the notion that all the sounds could be produced at once. I was quite perplexed with the whole situation. In addition, although the posters said that Pink Floyd's equipment would be used, in London the posters showed Hammersmith Odeon. This naturally led people to think that the concert would feature live performances. It embarrassed me a lot.

So you were the only performer?

I did concerts of part of *Pictures at an Exhibition* with a pianist. The sound of the synthesizer came from the tape, and I operated the mixing console, and the pianist performed while listening to the tape. On *Firebird*, I had the pianist play the orchestral piano part that Stravinsky had written. The rock group Renaissance also performed on these concerts. We performed in this manner in nine places, I believe. Another problem was that European fire laws prohibited the placement of speakers in the balconies of the larger halls, and as a result, the two rear channels of the four-channel sound were in front of the balcony seats. This was almost always the case in Germany and the Netherlands, though the situation was a little better in London. And of course, the critics always sat in the balcony.

Aren't many of the sounds created by the synthesizer just imitations of the sounds of conventional instruments?

Some people think that the fixed mission of the synthesizer is the quest for sounds that could be produced using conventional instruments. But I feel that the emergence of the synthesizer makes it possible for players and composers to do better than past achievements, because the limitation of having to deal with given sounds is no longer there. The musician, unlike the painter or the sculptor, has never been able to search for colors other than those that were given. But with the synthesizer, we have a palette comparable to that of the painter. There is no rule that dictates how this palette ought to be used; it can produce both imitative and non-imitative sounds. Also, you could reproduce your image of a soprano so high that the human voice couldn't produce it. You see, if you want the sound of a violin, you can always use an actual violin. But if your sound images are somewhat different from the sounds of any actual musical instrument, the synthesizer will allow you to create sounds similar to your image. If a listener relates to the synthesized sounds as imitations, it doesn't matter to me, because in any case the origin of the sound is in our minds. It will take many years of use, though, before the best method of using the synthesizer is determined. Good methods will remain, while others will vanish. It seems to me that history will have to evaluate the various possible uses of the synthesizer. Right now, we're all seeking to find good methods, so each user should find his or her own way. In the past, we could already imagine beforehand, just by knowing the style of the composer and the instruments that were available during that period, the kind of sound that he or she would produce. The sounds of the synthesizer, however, cannot be imagined in advance. But there are a lot of possibilities. Who knows? Imitative synthesis might someday take the place of conventional instruments. I imagine, though, that in synthesizer orchestration, imitative and non-imitative sounds will continue to exist side by side. Take the paintings of Salvador Dali, for instance. In certain paintings, you will have an image as realistic as a photograph placed next to another that isn't so together. The same thing can also be said with music. It's the personal feelings of the musician that will determine the quality of the music.

In what direction do you see the synthesizer moving in the future?

The synthesizer has just made its debut. When automobiles first appeared, they had to be started with a hand-crank, and they needed fresh water every kilometer or so. Like the automobile, the synthesizer will be quite different within a few years from the way it is now, and these early models will be recalled with nostalgia. What I expect from the synthesizer is a better capability of producing the kind of sounds that users want. Now, it sometimes takes an hour or more to get the sound I want out of the machine. According to the people who make the hardware, the type of hardware created depends on what kind of software is wanted. And the software demand then changes in response to the new hardware. This reciprocal progress is sure to be seen in the case of the synthesizer. For instance, look at my 16-channel board. When 16-channel devices first became available, they had so many amplifiers and volume knobs built in that they looked like a chest of drawers. The hardware almost overwhelmed the user. But now I have one with no volume controls. It reproduces the signal at the same volume at which it was fed into the board. If the signal is too loud, it comes out distorted, but the carefully fed-in sound comes out in good condition. Thus there is no need for volume controls. All the machine needs are selectors for record and playback. And although it's considerably simplified, the device offers no inconvenience compared with older models that had lots of switches. So in my opinion, the synthesizer can be gradually simplified while retaining the capability of meeting musicians' needs. The image of a sound can disappear from the mind if the synthesizer can't produce it quickly enough; for example, when it takes more than two hours. Eventually, you start wondering what it was you were trying to do in the first place. It's the same with live performance: The quest for a certain feeling becomes futile when the musician keeps doing the same thing for too long. So eventually the synthesizer should be able to produce immediately whatever sound is wanted.

Then it could be used effectively onstage. Right now I'm not able to get the maximum from my synthesizer. I still have to search for possibilities for software. I'm satisfied with the present functions of the instrument, but the access to them should be made more convenient.

What plans do you have for future albums?

I have lots of plans. I particularly want to take up the mentality of the Japanese people and put it to music. Up to now I've just been rearranging Western classical music. I want to use music to convey such typical Japanese stories as *Yukionna* (Snow Fairy) and *Miminashi Hoichi*. In the latter, a blind hero (Hoichi) plays a biwa, a Japanese lute, before the ghosts of the Heike warriors. Without knowing it, Hoichi shuttles between reality and the land of the dead. I want to describe such a story with four-channel music somehow. Rock artists like Rick Wakeman are using their own folk tales as a basis for music, and I want to do the same thing with tales that are full of Japanese atmosphere. Right now I'm in the process of solidifying in my mind the methods that I'll use.

Are you planning anything that would incorporate more conventional piano playing?

I'm not that good at normal keyboard technique. My music works best when I overdub sounds to create a certain color. I put a lot of emphasis on tone color. I do plan to do an album in which only the color of the sounds varies. I want a sound without rhythmic pulses to shift its colors like the changing colors of a light show.

What advice would you give to someone who wanted to own a system like yours?

The first thing is to obtain the main body made up of oscillators, filters, a simple mixer, an envelope generator, and a VCA. The Roland company, for instance, is making a System 700 and a System 100 similar to the setup that I have. Then you can add other modules later in accordance with your financial ability and your needs. For people who are mainly interested in imitative synthesis, simple preset devices, or a Minimoog, should be enough. But even if you want to use the instrument to reproduce sound images from

A SELECTED ISAO TOMITA DISCOGRAPHY

Grand Canyon
Space Walk
Back to Earth
Daphnis et Chloe
Kosmos
The Tomita Planets
Firebird Suite
Pictures at an Exhibition
Snowflakes Are Dancing: Electronic Performances of Debussy's Tone Paintings

FOR MORE INFORMATION ON ISAO TOMITA, VISIT www.isaotomita.com

your mind, you don't need to buy a huge system right at the beginning, because parts of it may prove useless to you. What you need to convey your images is something that matches the level of your personal development. So first you should buy the core of the machine. My Moog III is a combination of various modules, and it's possible to buy only the casing of it first and then insert the necessary modules one by one. This prevents unnecessary buying and enables you to get a better understanding of the instrument by learning about one module at a time. One more thing: If you're planning to use the synthesizer in concert performances, you should acquire a live preset panel, which will give you easy access to the sounds you've created. In order to do this effectively, of course, you need to have a good enough instrument that you don't run into any unexpected mechanical trouble onstage.

What composers have most deeply influenced you?

Since my student days, I've been seriously influenced by Rimsky-Korsakov, and also by those who followed him, such as Ravel, Debussy, and Stravinsky. Bach's music to me sounds like drawings with lines, but no color. The notes can be played equally well by an organ or by strings, or can be sung by a choir. But Rimsky-Korsakov started using different instruments like the different colors in a painting. In *Scheherazade* he used not only melody, harmony, and rhythm, but included the important factor of color as well. And Stravinsky and Ravel both learned this from Rimsky-Korsakov. It appears to me that they composed symphonic works by mixing together the colors of the various instruments. Painters and sculptors can use their favorite colors, while musicians can't work with such visible qualities. Nor can musicians create new instruments to produce the sounds they want. But Stravinsky and the others did create wonderful colorful music within such a limitation. If they had had a palette like the synthesizer to work with, I feel that they would have produced a completely different kind of music.

16 VANGELIS

SYNTHESIZERS OF FIRE

by Robert L. Doerschuk

Portions of this chapter appeared in the August 1982 issue of Keyboard *magazine.*

This year's academy award for Best Soundtrack marks a milestone in the career of Evangelos Papathanassiou, known for years to his fans and now to the world by the name Vangelis (pronounced, incidentally, with a hard g, as in agree). But more than that, it has a special meaning for the music world in general. Not only does it take the synthesizer one step further as a principal compositional and orchestral tool in

The man behind the synth scores of *Chariots of Fire* and *Blade Runner* plays in a decidedly non-electric and analog moment. (Courtesy of *Keyboard* magazine)

movie scoring; the Oscar also signifies its undisputed arrival in the community of instruments.

The ascendancy of Vangelis, a self-taught artist whose melodic and colorative gifts soar unencumbered by his inability to read music, demonstrates that synthesizers, like pianos, violins, and every other accepted Western instrument, can cater to any and all compositional schools. Wendy Carlos takes center stage in adapting them to the precise demands of Baroque performance, and Kraftwerk pioneers their application to a blend of neo-Futurism and rock, but Vangelis is the great romantic, the inheritor of mid-19th century approaches to lush mixtures of sound and the sweeping thematic line. He is, compositionally, the electronic Tchaikovsky.

It is another reflection of the times that Vangelis has done what he has done without the benefit of a formal musical education. The great composers of the past generally could not have written full scores without having had some basic grounding in the complexities of transferring their inner music onto paper effectively enough to bring the sounds out into the open. But in his London studio, surrounded by banks of keyboards, percussion instruments, and recording apparatus, Vangelis is able to let his imagination run directly onto tape, improvising the basic melodic track first, then augmenting, altering, and enhancing as his mood dictates.

Some traditionalists in the musical world complain that the impact of technology has been to drain music of its life force; they fear that the process of filtering their expression through electronics will somehow move it further from the fingertip immediacy to which acoustic musicians are accustomed. This may be true in the work of certain artists, but to the general public Vangelis is surely the first clear and undeniable exception to this idea: This burly bearded Greek expatriate is no white-smocked technician; he is as emotional in his conversation as in his art, at times verging on the mystical in his expostulations on the relationship between his music and his equipment. He, perhaps more than any other synthesist, has demonstrated that technology can be brought to the service of romantic expression.

Though he seldom performs live these days, preferring to spin complex synthesized webs in the shelter of his studio, Vangelis has been through the pop star experience. At one point, he was even invited to replace Rick Wakeman in Yes, a post many multi-keyboardists would have killed for. Yet Vangelis turned it down, since the pressures of fame, and the compromises it would have demanded on his work, were unacceptable to him.

For similar reasons he is somewhat uncomfortable with his Academy Award. Proud as he is of *Chariots of Fire*, Vangelis does not see it as his high-water mark. Music to him is not a flood, a contest to pile one wave higher than the next against some measure of public acceptance. In Vangelis' eyes, it is more of a river, a steady stream of inspiration, twisting here, falling there—perhaps to accommodate dramatic action in a film, for example—but always flowing outward, from the heart. If the Oscar seems to represent a standard for him to beat in his future work, Vangelis may well at times wonder whether he would have been better off without it.

Now nearly 40 years old, Vangelis was born in Volos, Greece, and raised in Athens, 200 miles to the south. He began experimenting with music at the age of four, composing his first piece (for piano) and exploring other, more unusual sound sources by playing with radio interference and stuffing the family piano with nails and kitchen pans. Attempts to subject him to piano lessons proved fruitless; an indifferent student, Vangelis preferred developing his own ideas to playing those dreamed up by someone else in some distant time and place.

Rock attracted him at an early age. At 18 he acquired his first Hammond organ, and soon formed a group with some student friends. Called Formynx, it quickly became one of the top bands of the early '60s in Greece. However, partly because of limited opportunities for musical progress in his homeland, and partly because of the ominous political atmosphere stirred up by the 1968 Greek military coup, Vangelis packed up and moved to Paris at the age of 25.

By the time of his move to London in the mid-'70s, Vangelis was already well on his way toward his goal of building a self-contained music studio, or "laboratory," as he calls it. Today it sits in London, tucked away near Marble Arch behind an unobtrusive side-street door. Inside, up some stairs, it unfolds in two enormous rooms. The ceilings tower overhead, dark and indistinct, but a wonderland of keyboards and equipment spread out brightly below. A simple walk-around tour offers a taste of the Vangelis arsenal: a Minimoog, Yamaha CS-4OM synthesizer, Roland CSQ-100 digital sequencer, Yamaha CP-80 electric grand, Roland

Compuphonic synthesizer, modified vintage Fender Rhodes electric piano, CSQ-GOO digital sequencer, Roland VP-330 electric piano, Roland CR-SOOO Compurhythm, Yamaha CS-80 synthesizer, E-mu Emulator, Sequential Circuits Prophet-5 and Prophet-10, Simmons SDSV drum machine, Linn LM-1 drum computer, Roland JP-4, nine-foot Steinway grand piano, Yamaha GS-2, 24-track Quad-8 Pacifica mixing console, and an RSF one-octave Blackbox synthesizer. And, on an elevated platform overlooking the whole array, three timpani, a trap drum set, and rows of gongs, chimes, and exotic bells.

Of course, the laboratory is never quite finished. New additions come along, old instruments are stored. But despite the changes, Vangelis is comfortable here. He visits with friends amidst this maze of hardware, playfully punctuates his conversation with rim shots on a nearby snare drum, and ambles from one keyboard to the next, trying out new sounds, musing over new ideas, and storing them on tape. This is a home of sorts for Vangelis. It was here that he put together his popular solo albums, like *Heaven and Hell*, *Albedo 0.39*, *Spiral*, *China*, and *See You Later*; as well as his duo albums with singer Jon Anderson of Yes (*Short Stories* in 1979 and *The Friends of Mr. Cairo* in 1981); his 1978 project with Greek actress Irene Papas, who sang traditional Greek tunes to his less traditional accompaniment in *Odes*; and his other film or television assignments, like the ethereal theme to the Carl Sagan PBS series *Cosmos*, the Costa-Gavras movie Missing, and his most recent effort, the Ridley Scott adventure film *Blade Runner*.

And it was here that *Keyboard* met Vangelis. The bustle of the city seemed far away as we settled down in the stillness to discuss music and the machines that make it.

Recently, a magazine article in America claimed that you had studied piano for a while, contrary to reports you were self-taught. Which is true?

The second one, actually. I started very early, around three years old. My parents tried to push me to go to the music school, but they failed. It was just an attempt.

Why did you object to the idea of attending music school?

Because I always believed that there are things you never can learn, and I never liked the idea of becoming a computer or a performer performing someone else's compositions. To me, music was more fundamental and more important than the thought of becoming a musician. I never felt like a musician. I don't feel like one now. Music to me is nature. It is not a music school, it is not a kind of job; that to me seems completely schizophrenic. You can learn some technical things in school, but the best thing is to build your own technique. You want to do your own thing, which is the way that you feel.

Can you remember your first musical thoughts as a child?

I remember, but it's very difficult to put into words, because whatever we say through this whole interview will be about two kinds of music. One is natural music, and the other is what I call social music. This means you have to split the human being in two. There is his natural existence, with his natural behavior to everything, not just to music. Then you have the social existence, where people learn how to behave. As you learn how to behave in society, you learn at the same time a music which derives from that by going to music schools and becoming a violin player, a keyboard player, or whatever, in order to play what is there already, to perform. You build a machine, and then you put in memories of how to play Mozart. Now, natural music is a different thing altogether.

"To me, success is a vehicle for me to keep this place, my laboratory, alive, and to buy more synthesizers."

So if someone is trained as a pianist, for example, you see that as a barrier that person must get past.

Not necessarily. Now, even if I am a fully qualified piano player from a school, I don't think that means I can do anything in front of a synthesizer, because that's a new instrument which requires a new technique, a new dialog altogether. If a pianist does play the synthesizer, it isn't because he is a pianist; it's because he was meant to do it. The synthesizer is like a mirror over the world, which is the same as nature.

Does it get harder for you to create as you become more famous?

Oh, it's a tremendous problem. Sometimes I'm completely panicked, like now, for example. I'm living in constant fear that I have too many social values, which creation doesn't have. Creative values are completely different from social values. Creation comes first, then analysis and evaluation come later. By putting the evaluation before, you kill the creation. Creation is completely unpredictable and free.

What do you do to keep your own music free?

This comes only from consciousness and awareness. That's all. But sometimes I fail at this because I'm a human being and I live in society. I go through all the usual everyday problems that everybody else has, so my problem is to keep the balance between this side, which is success and fame and all that, and the creative side, which is pure and has nothing to do with fame. To me, success is a vehicle for me to keep this place, my laboratory, alive, and to buy more synthesizers. Nobody is going to just give me money for that. You have to make it yourself.

At least you must feel good about that aspect of financial success.

It is a fantastic situation, like going to some fantastic place. If you go to India or China or someplace else that not too many people experience, then you will call me, because you are a friend of mine, and say, "Come with me next time." You want to share that. What I am saying is that I try to share with other people. With two or three million people buying my albums, I share not my ego with them, but what I experience through this. This is the main reason why I am working before the public. Maybe in a few years, if I don't feel the need to do it, I won't do it anymore.

Do you feel a limitation in how much you can share, though, by going through as impersonal a medium as recordings, rather than by playing directly to live audiences?

Oh, those are two different things. You see, what I'm doing on records is completely spontaneous. It's like playing in front of you now. When you have a picture, whether it's of a battle or a bird, you have what it was at that moment forever. This is the recording. You can repeat it, and every time you repeat it you can feel it and see it in a different way. This is the power and the beauty of music. Now, if I play without recording myself, the music is lost forever. This is also fantastic, in a different way, but we humans have a tendency to preserve things. Maybe in a different theological society this would be wrong, but we do.

On those rare occasions when you do give a live performance, do you try to enhance your communication with the audience through multimedia techniques?

No, no. I hate visual effects. I've never believed that music is an entertainment anyway. It's not my job, and the concert is not for me an opportunity for success. It's an opportunity of sharing and questioning.

As a creator or composer, do you ever regret not being able to read music?

No, not at all. I don't need to. My score is my tape. I score on the tape, not on paper.

So you don't even have your own system of notation.

No. My orchestration occurs during my playing because I developed the technique of playing different synthesizers at the same time.

Do you feel, though, that it's important for synthesists to eventually develop a standard notation that would allow them to communicate their work to one another on paper?

Yes, I think that's very important. I believe that in the future there will be orchestras and ensembles with synthesizer players, when the synthesizer will be as established as the piano. If you want people to play live and repeat what you've done, there must be a way. It's very difficult, because you always have the personal way in which you play. The way that Mozart or Handel or Bach played their music is not the way that we play it now. They had different instruments and different techniques. Still, I believe that this standard notation is going to happen.

Has your way of composing changed dramatically since you began writing at the age of four?

No, because when you are four years old that is a different age from when you are 20, but the fundamental thing never changes. I have the same essential need now that I had when I was four years old. Sometimes I go through tapes I used to make on my little domestic recorder and listen to them, and although it's not exactly the same thing, it's the same root. Sometimes I can't believe that I've created that music with almost nothing.

When you begin composing, do you hear the music as an abstract theme, or as a specific sound?

As a sound. I might call it a violin, but I don't know what that is. Then it's a strange feeling. You feel that you have to start creating. It's like you feel when you have to go to the toilet. Then I just push the tape, and it happens when it happens. I don't know how it happens. I don't want to know. I don't try to know. It's like riding a bicycle. If you think, "How am I going to do it?", you fall down. If you think about how to breathe, you choke. But when you do things dramatically, they happen like that.

Do you usually begin on any particular instrument?

It just depends. Every day is different.

Do you play often without turning the tape on?

Many times. Sometimes when I play, I don't mind if I don't keep it. Sometimes I do things then that may be better than the things you hear. But even though they are lost, so what? Actually, they are not lost. We think they are lost because we can't hear them again, but they are actually there all the time.

What was your first synthesizer?

It was a very cheap, small Korg. Quite nice, quite humble, a primitive, simple instrument. I've done a lot of things with it. But the first time I heard synthesizers, I was very disappointed. I never liked this *oueee-ooo* sound. It's a very cheap, small, uninteresting sound. So when I saw pictures of this great big Moog or whatever it was, I said, "My God, this is what all that's about?" The reason it sounded so bad, actually, was because of the way that people played it.

I see that there are no modular synthesizers anywhere in your studio.

I never liked the fact that you had these big instruments and you had to plug in all those things. It was a waste of time to have to program like that. A little later, in the early '70s, we started having instruments that we could play immediately—poor synthesizers in some ways, but quite nice.

Did you sense from the beginning what freedoms synthesizers would allow you as a composer?

It was a different freedom. I never condemned the conventional instruments. They are beautiful. They will always be there, and they are what they are. But synthesizers are what they are as well. I can't imagine myself using only one thing. It's impossible.

How do you feel about the way the synthesizer is being used in the music world today?

[*Sighs.*] You see, I am not here to discuss or criticize other people. The only question I can ask is, why do people do it? Why do people play synthesizers? They do it for fame, as I said, and for fashion. That doesn't get you very far. But if you do it because you can't do without it, then it makes sense.

What about audience reactions to synthesizer music? *Chariots of Fire* was enjoyed by many people who probably would never have thought they would enjoy listening to electronic music of any kind.

Well, many times I've heard people who were looking at a painting of something like a flower say, "Oh, it's so beautiful. It's almost like real!" And when they see the flower itself, they say, "It's so beautiful that it's almost not real anymore." Both things are absurd. In both cases it's a very intellectual way of accepting something. In music, it's not because it's a synthesizer or not a synthesizer. I like it or I don't like it, that's all.

That's true, but still there are many people who shut the door on synthesizer music only because it is played on synthesizers.

It's unfortunate for them, but that's not my problem. There's nothing I can do. It's a psychological problem for people who need to accept other things in society too. It has nothing to do with me anymore.

But as an artist, don't you feel a responsibility to try to communicate with these people?

No. The only responsibility I feel is to myself because of my popularity. I must ask myself, why is my music so popular now? Have I done anything wrong? I feel that it is possible for people with a lot of popularity to give something to listeners that could be very damaging.

Why do you think the theme to *Chariots of Fire* has been so successful? Does it sound different to you from the other music you've been doing over the years?

No, not at all. It's exactly the same, no difference. I never did it for success. It's only another piece of music.

Did you study footage of the film as you wrote the soundtrack?

Yeah. But I didn't do music for 30-second bits. I did it for the total. I tried to put myself in the movie. I tried to become a contemporary of the people in the film, with a kind of memory of that period. [*Chariots of Fire* is set in England and France during the early 1920s.] I didn't want it to become period music, but I didn't want it to become contemporary music either. That was the difficulty of this film.

That, at least, must have made this project different from your other recordings.

Yeah, mainly because I had to work with something specific, a film. Now, in many ways *Blade Runner* is a completely opposite kind of film. It requires a lot more music, suited to many different situations. You don't have the unity you had in the music to *Chariots*.

But the compositional process is the same?

Yes. I still watch the film. But normally, when I'm not working on soundtracks, I am very spontaneous. I don't work with any specific thing—only the moment and nature. That's all.

Still, your albums do often have thematic unity. How, for example, did you come up with the idea for *Albedo 0.39*? That title, of course, indicates the light-reflective capability of the Earth.

As I've said, nature and space are always very important to me, although I try to avoid words like "space" because they are now very common and fashionable. Fashion is something from the social world. It comes and goes, but space and all those truths are always there. Even if you take the albedo out and put in another name, it doesn't change anything. At that moment I was very into that kind of thing. I am now as well, but on the day I began creating that music I was in, let's call it, an inspired kind of situation. But, you see, I never record to make an album. I record because I record, and from what I have I decide to release an album. It's not like, "Now I'm going to do an album, and when I finish it I will continue with the next album." Even if I stop releasing albums I'm going to continue to compose.

On your album *China*, it sounds as if you studied Chinese instruments as models for your programming.

I never did, actually. Many people have told me this, but I've never been to China

A SELECTED VANGELIS DISCOGRAPHY

Blade Runner

1492: Conquest of Paradise

The City

Invisible Connections

Chariots of Fire

Opera Sauvage

China

Albedo 0.39

Heaven and Hell

For more information on Vangelis—at least for official information directly from him—you may have to wait. As of this writing, www.vangelisworld.com is still under construction. Wikipedia, anyone?

and I don't have one Chinese album at home. I can learn more simply by looking into a Chinese face. I never pretend to play like a Chinese musician.

The solo line in "The Long March" from that album creates the impression of a string instrument very strongly.

I think I did that with the CS-80. I used that a lot on that album.

What about the violin lead line in "Lotus Blossom"?

That really was a violin, played by a friend of mine.

You play what sounds like a pipe organ in the introduction to "Nucleogenesis," from *Albedo 0.39*.

Oh, yeah. That was actually a very small synthesizer. I can't even remember the make, and I think I don't have it anymore. It was like a children's toy. Again, it's the way you play things, when and how you use them, that's important in creating a certain effect. Sometimes with very cheap instruments you can produce incredible things.

But you won't go into detail about what instrument you use and how you use it to get certain specific sounds?

The problem is, I don't know what happens! You see, there are people who know exactly what they are doing; they program this, think about that, and so on. With me, it just happens.

As you accumulate new instruments, do you ever get rid of older ones?

Oh, no. I always keep my keyboards because of the good memories. They can always be useful. Each instrument keeps its own character. Nothing changes.

Are there still sounds in your mind that the instruments of today cannot release?

Yeah. I have in mind a different way for using synthesizers, but I'm first going to have to get together with the people who make them.

What changes would you like to see them make?

It's difficult to explain sounds by words. And, again, all those things are personal to me in connection with my technique, so whatever I might have built for me would be completely irrelevant for other people. That's why you don't see these machines, because of marketing. The question shouldn't be one of economics; the question is to make a better instrument for the sake of making it. For years and years, every time I ask them to do something new in a synthesizer, they say, "Oh, come on, you ask the impossible," but then four years later they do it. Now I know they are going to do it, so why not do it now?

And if I were one of those synthesizer designers, what would you ask me to do?

I'd ask the impossible.

RICK WAKEMAN

17

YESSYNTHS

by Dominic Milano

Portions of this chapter originally appeared in the March/April 1976 and February 1979 issues of Keyboard *magazine.*

Whether Rick Wakeman needed Yes to receive recognition for his keyboard playing or whether Yes needed Wakeman to become known as a band is a question some might wonder about. There are those who think that *Fragile* was the first Yes album, when it was really their fourth. But it was the first Yes album that multi-

Rick Wakeman onstage with cape and with his beloved Minimoog, circa 1979. (Evening Standard/Huton Archive/Getty Images)

keyboardist Rick Wakeman played on, and it was also the first Yes album to give birth to a hit single in the United States, the well-known "Roundabout." Without question, the union of vocalist Jon Anderson, bassist Chris Squire, guitarist Steve Howe, and percussionist Bill Bruford with Rick Wakeman was beneficial to all concerned. The keyboards Wakeman brought into the band provided a firm foundation for them to build their orchestral sound upon.

Prior to joining forces with Yes, Wakeman had been a very successful session player, recording with David Bowie, Cat Stevens, and many others. He had studied at London's Royal Academy of Music with the ambition of being a concert pianist prior to playing sessions, which he turned to as a way to support himself. While playing in a pub, Rick met guitarist Dave Cousins of the Strawbs. Rick was asked to join, and played with the Strawbs for 15 months and appeared on two of their albums, *A Collection of Antiques and Curios* and *From the Witchwood.* Rick left the Strawbs and joined Yes in 1971, shortly before *Fragile* was released.

Less than a year after that, *Close to the Edge* came out. Some hardcore Yes fans would argue that this is unquestionably the best album the band has put out to date. It featured only three cuts, all of them very progressive for their time. The Yes sound developed on *Fragile* and *Close to the Edge* was imitated by many a band.

In 1973, Wakeman's first solo recording came out. It was a keyboard treatment of his impressions of the characters of *The Six Wives of Henry VIII.* The album was placed on *Time* Magazine's 1973 list of best recordings of the year. It was also at about this time that Wakeman started edging out Keith Emerson in polls such as the *Playboy* pop music poll.

Rick's second solo album, a musical production incorporating a live orchestra to retell Jules Verne's *Journey to the Centre of the Earth*, was recorded in 1974. It was the beginning of the Wakeman tradition of mingling rock bands with full orchestras, choirs, and assorted spectacle-creating units such as troupes of ice skaters. But even as *Journey* was being recorded, trouble was brewing between Wakeman and Yes. *Yessongs*, the three-record set of the 1973 Yes tour recorded live, had already been released, and Yes had completed recording the controversial *Tales From Topographic Oceans*. Drummer Bill Bruford had left the band and had been replaced by Alan White. Wakeman told us in 1976 that he didn't enjoy the direction of the music on the double-record-long concept album, and he left Yes after completing the European tour in 1974.

The albums produced during his two years spent away from Yes include *The Myths and Legends of King Arthur and the Knights of the Round Table*, *No Earthly Connection*, the soundtrack to the Ken Russell film *Lisztomania*, and the soundtrack to the 1976 Winter Olympics film *White Rock*. Wakeman's *Criminal Record* won top honors in *Keyboard's* 1978 Readers' Poll as best new keyboard album.

In 1976, Wakeman found himself in a Swiss studio helping out on the recording of a new Yes album after Patrick Moraz had left to pursue his own solo career. What was supposed to have been just a session turned into a permanent thing after Rick heard the new direction Yes was heading in. In his words, "We had taken different paths to get to the same end." Two Yes albums have been released since that rejoining: *Going for the One* and *Tormato*. Both albums show a slight shift in the Yes sound, a loosening in the feel of the music. The rock and roll influences in the band have been let out of the bag, and the orchestral feeling has changed somewhat. For better or worse, it may be due in part to the way the keyboards are being treated now. They seem to be mixed farther in the background with less timbral variation than before. Wakeman has also been limiting himself to using fewer keyboards, with the main focus being on pipe organ, Polymoog, and Birotron.

In the early days of your career, how extensive was your studio experience?

I used to do about 15 a week for around two and a half years. I should think I worked for just about everybody at some time or another. In fact there were times when I didn't know who I was working for.

Was it through session work that you met Strawbs guitarist Dave Cousins?

Yeah. The first session I did for Dave happened when I was working at the Top Rank Bowl in Reading, and Tony Visconti phoned me up and asked me to come down to do what was called a BBC session at the Paris Studio. It was to play piano for a folk group called Strawbs. I did it and became quite good friends with Dave. I ended up doing all their stuff for them. Things just seemed to culminate and I fancied to join them. I had become disillusioned with session work. I was getting good bread, but I wasn't getting a chance to be part of the music: You're in there for three hours and then you're out again. So that was it. I joined Strawbs and stayed there for 15 months.

What made you leave?

I got more and more on the outside of things, with Dave himself doing all the work. In the end, with the musicians that were in Strawbs at the time, things had gone as far as they could. There would have to be a complete change-around or it would have rotted away. Yes was having a change also, and asked me if I wanted to join. I said no, but went to one of their rehearsals anyway. I was only going to stay ten minutes, but I ended up staying about three years.

What gear did you use on the *Tormato* tour?

This time around, the object was to cut down a bit. We've been noticing that for the last two or three years every band around has been taking more and more junk with them. It's getting to the point where there will be so much equipment onstage that you won't be able to see the band. So now we've gone full circle. Instead of seeing how much we can put onstage, we're seeing how little we can put onstage. That meant finding instruments that could do two jobs instead of one. So first of all, I hid all of my amplification under the stage. I used Moog Synamps. Then I only took the Hammond C-3, the Polymoog, the Sequential Circuits Prophet, two Birotrons, two Minimoogs, a Yamaha CP-30 electronic piano, an RMI Keyboard Computer, and a grand piano. That was it, besides the obvious little gadgets, like some Sequential Circuits sequencers and things. The object was to cut down and make the show a little more visible to the audience. If they can't see anything because of three tons of junk onstage, they can't enjoy it. The Keyboard Computer took away the need to carry the Mander Pipe Organ this time. The new Keyboard Computer is really very clever. It's far more advanced than the first one. The Prophet has taken away the need to have a lot of stuff onstage too. I can't begin to tell you how many instruments that replaces. The Yamaha CP-30 lets you do without a Rhodes, a Wurlitzer, the RMI Rocksichord, the Hohner Clavinet, and the Hohner Pianet. The only problem

> "I still love the old Minimoogs. They're magic. I've got a strange affinity for them."

comes up when you want to do something like play Clavinet and Rhodes at the same time, but then you just turn to the Prophet. Between the Prophet and the Yamaha you can almost do a whole show—almost. I need what I've got out there.

What kinds of things are you using the Polymoog for?

It's an interesting instrument. On the last tour and on the *Going for the One* album I used it mainly as a filler, a brightener. I used it as a coloring instrument, but for the *Tormato* album and also for my own album, *Criminal Record*, I used it more for soloing and filling. I think the first thing you tend to do when you buy the Polymoog is to look at it as a polyphonic instrument, and go flat out and play as many notes at once as you can on it. That's a mistake.

The updated Polymoogs have slight differences in them, like the strings have a faster attack. Do you like those differences?

Yeah, the strings do have a considerably faster attack. What I preferred most on the newer ones was the keyboard balancing between the presets. Every instrument has small niggly things that annoy you a bit, and they seem to have worked those out. It pleased me no end, because the Polymoog is the instrument I use the most.

What about the Prophet?

I think the Prophet is the best thing to come out in the last . . . I was going to say the last ten years, but most of the stuff has only just come out in that time. But it's definitely a revolution. The Prophet is a gold mine. I think it's a superb instrument. For the amateur or pro who wants a machine that's not super expensive but doesn't want to buy a piece of junk, and who wants something that he or she can be proud of, then the Prophet's the machine. It's just absolutely superb, and I'm not saying that as an advertisement for Sequential Circuits, because I don't endorse them. I wouldn't mind it though; they're that good at what they do.

What kinds of things have you done with the Prophet?

The first thing I did was to go through all their presets and decide which ones I liked. Then I took one of my Prophets—I have two of them—and wiped off all the presets. Then, without looking at the sound charts that Sequential Circuits gives you, I tried to duplicate their presets on the blank machine. That way I got to know the instrument. It's the quickest way to learn an instrument. Then I reset the presets however I wanted them. I only kept about five of the original ones.

Do you miss having a touch-sensitive keyboard on it?

No, because I don't really like touch-sensitive electric keyboards. It's always seemed phony to me. That's because of the fact that I'm a piano player. With the piano, the touch sensitivity is a little more obvious. With electronic instruments you can alter the note after you've played it. I find it very confusing to do that with my fingers. I don't like it, I feel like it's cheating. But here's the strange thing: I'll do it with my feet. I feel like I've got more control if I do the effects with my feet.

How do you approach playing all these different instruments?

First you've got to know that no two keyboards are the same to play. The touch is dissimilar on all of them, and every instrument has its little idiosyncrasies. That's the thing you have to get used to. When you get your instrument, don't just take it on the road straightaway. Take it home and practice on the thing until you know it inside out; until you know if it's going to do something silly and why it's doing it. One of the hardest instruments to adapt to is the straight harpsichord, because the keys are smaller. You really have to be on your toes, or else you will end up with 30,000 split notes.

Do you do any warm-up exercises before you go onstage?

Yeah. About 36 cans of beer, and only about two bottles of wine. [*Chuckles.*] Really, I practice a lot. I try to put in three hours a day, otherwise my fingers stiffen up. And that practice can be anything. Sometimes I might have a day when I like to get out the old Bach 48 [*The Well-Tempered Clavier*] and bore myself to death. On another day I might leap through scales and arpeggios. It just depends, you know. It's important to keep your technique up because you write according to it. That's the one fault with anybody who writes for themselves. They write what they know they can play. So if you keep working on your technique, constantly improving it, then that must help your writing, as it gives you a wider variety of things you can play. I think there's a lot of self-written crap going around because people are writing according to their technical ability. That's why we end up with these three-chord rondos.

Do you have any other effects machines running in the setup?

We have about four Roland Space Echoes going. We also have two Sequential Circuits Model 800 sequencers and a Moog sample-and-hold that I use with the Minimoogs. I still love the old Minimoogs. They're magic. I've got a strange affinity for them. I don't think I've ever gone on the stage without at least a pair of them. It would be like having something missing from my life. Getting back to the effects, most of the phasing and flanging units are built into the instruments. Rather than having tons of boxes and pedals and switches laying around we put everything inside the instruments. Other than cutting down on leads, it lets you know just where a problem is. It makes things easier for the road crew. Everything went very well on this tour, though. San Francisco is the only place we had bad troubles. Right at the beginning of the set everything was fine, but then everything went haywire after about five minutes. I had to do the whole set on the top manual of the Hammond. I didn't know what was going on. There was this nice burning smell and everything. It was a nightmare. What had happened was one of the AC junction boxes went haywire and sent all of my equipment surges of 220 volts for about ten minutes. That, of course, burnt everything out instantly and utterly. We were up all night getting everything fixed for the show the next day. The damage was very sad. But the amazing thing was that most of the damage was done to the effects. For example, the Polymoog withstood those surges. Once it cooled down it was fine. The same for the Prophet. The piano mixer blew up, but the two I would have thought would have been hurt the most, the Polymoog and the Prophet, were fine. That says something for the way they make keyboards today. At least you know they make them to a good standard. They're not making them to be chucked away.

The old Polymoogs were susceptible to static electricity problems.

That's right. And radio interference as well. I've run into a lot of instruments that love to pick up radio. It can be very funny at times, but it's annoying. It's funny when you're picking up a radio station very clearly. You can just sit back at the end of a sound check and press the volume pedal down and listen to the radio. But if you get a bad station, it can be miserable. The only time it annoys me is when it gets into the oscillators and starts playing games. Then you've got no such thing as tuning anymore. I used to really worry about all these things onstage. If one little thing went wrong I used to get very upset. Now, I don't care anymore. If one little thing goes wrong, I've still got tons of other stuff that I can make do with. It might make life a little more difficult, but you might end up doing something better. So I don't worry anymore. The only time I get ruffled is when everything goes, like it did in San Francisco. But when something goes so wrong that you can't play anything, I just sit on the stage and play cards with the roadies [*laughs*].

A lot of people would probably like to know about your Birotrons.

It's my fault that the Birotron didn't come out, because it was finished about a year and a half ago. What happened was that when the instruments were done, we had a studio test, which I was pleased with, and we made a few alterations. Then we went out on the road for the *Going for the One* tour. We found a few little things wrong. They did very well overall, but they didn't have enough output, they were a bit too dirty-sounding, and we found a few mechanical and electrical things that only show up when you're on the road. Nothing serious, though. So then we had them fixed and refined. But when we started the European tour, we found that all the refinements didn't fit the good old European market. I don't mean the market for selling, I mean the electrical needs. The power requirements were too precise. Don't ask me the full details, because you'd be asking a dumbo, you know? But that was the basic problem. We had the choice of either making models for England that ran on 240 volts, ones for Switzerland that ran on 220, ones for Brazil that ran on 120, and ones for America that ran on 110, or we were going to have to make one that would have transformers in it for all those places.

The last thing I wanted was an instrument that was rushed out. I don't mind having the teething problems to deal with myself, but I don't think it's fair to have other musicians paying for instruments and then having to deal with teething problems. We also want to keep the price down so there are still some decisions to be made. There are about 30 to 35 working models in existence now, but none of them are really finished models. I'm not going to let anything out that I'm not totally happy with. We had four different machines on the road with us this time out. Not one of them had everything we wanted on it. There were little bits and pieces of each one that we want on the final machine. We've now finished the final one. We got the major problems solved. The one major problem was getting all the tape heads aligned right. Then we did some tests that hopefully no normal band will ever have to deal with. We did things like drop them out of airplanes at 20 feet to see if the casing stood up and if the engineering stood up. With luck, touch wood, we should be shipping in reasonable quantities by the end of 1978. Another thing we wanted to make sure we had was an after-sales force. The people who could deal with problems and service after the machine has been sold. We're going to do all this and still keep the instrument under $2,000. Well under. It will be more like $1,500. It depends on the quantity we can turn out. We're operating on a really low profit margin. I would have liked to have seen the machine out a long time ago, but it wasn't just right before.

What kind of tape sounds were you using on this tour?

We've had very few sounds with us this time around. There were about 20 different sounds altogether. I had male choir, female choir, single violin, string quartet, mixed violins, single 'cello, mixed 'cellos, flutes, jazz flute that has the breathing included. One thing that's always missing from electronic imitations of flutes is the breathing. And things like that. We've almost solved the problem of getting plucked sounds from strings, which would be really nice to offer people. I may wind up with a full orchestra tape. That doesn't mean everybody playing every note, but having the instruments playing in the registers that they're designed for. We haven't made the decision as to what to put in the basic tape rack when you buy the instrument. It will have three to four sounds at least, but we can make anything anybody wants, and I imagine that the cost would be about $100 for a rack. I think the basic rack will have flutes, violins, a mixture of strings, trombones, and trumpets, which sounds really weird but is a nice full sound, and then a mixed choir.

How big is the keyboard on the Birotron?

Three octaves.

It uses electronic keying and eight-track tapes that run in loops, doesn't it?

Yeah. The tapes run continuously, so you get instantaneous touch control. You can have as much attack and decay as you want. It also has a tuning switch. You can go up or down an octave, which I wouldn't advise really because you lose stability when you run it to its outer range. But going up or down a fifth is great. You can play as fast as you like and get clarity, which is a tremendous advantage. That lets you do choral runs that are impossible to get with the real human voice. The notes last as long as you hold them down. The machines will come with two identical sets of tapes so when one set wears out, which will happen in about 100 hours of use, you send that worn-out set back and use the second set. Then we replace the other set for the cost of the tape, which is very minimal. So there's never any need to have people without tapes. We've tried to make sure that people don't run into the same problems that I've run into with other manufacturers. Things that have annoyed me like no after-sales service, no spare parts, and so on. We've even gone a bit too far on that, but I think it'll be worth it in the long run. I doubt if we'll ever make our money back, but that's not the object of the exercise. We just wanted to do an instrument that no one else was doing right. There's no way we can ever compete with the synthesizer manufacturers. I don't even know how they compete with themselves.

You've used a lot of different electric pianos in the past. Can you relate your feelings about them?

The Rhodes is a nice machine. It has a nice sound, but I have to say I've always found it cumbersome. I still use them, but

A SELECTED RICK WAKEMAN DISCOGRAPHY

SOLO

Out There

Almost Classical

Preludes to a Century

Cirque Surreal

Heritage Suite

Black Knights at the Court of Ferdinand IV

White Rock

Criminal Record

Myths and Legends of King Arthur and the Knights of the Round Table

Lisztomania

Journey to the Centre of the Earth

The Six Wives of Henry VIII

WITH YES

Keys to Ascension

Union

Yesshows

Tormato

Going for the One

Tales from Topographic Oceans

Fragile

Close to the Edge

FOR MORE INFORMATION ON RICK WAKEMAN, VISIT www.rwcc.com.

they're not my favorite electric piano. It's hard to keep the keyboard even. Wurlitzers are nice because you can take them up to your hotel room and play them, because of their little built-in speakers. I'm not knocked out by their sound. The same with the RMI Rocksichord. I don't like the sound that much. It's a bit whiny for my liking, although I love the KC-II. The little Yamaha CP-30 is the electric piano I love most. Not the little electric grand, the electronic piano. I think it's the best one I've come across. I love it. Good touch, good sound, well built. The Clavinet's the great old die-hard, but I think it's going to have problems now that the Yamaha CP-30 and the Prophet can do what it can plus a lot more. And also the Polymoog can do it. My vote definitely goes to Yamaha for the electric piano. But it doesn't go there for synthesizers. I've had bad luck with the Yamaha synths.

Have you ever modified your Minimoogs?

Yeah. I've had lots done to them. I've had all new cards put in for the oscillators, and all the patching on the back is different so I can use the Sequential Circuits things. I've got read-out lights that tell me if there's a fault and where the fault is. I'm also having another set of oscillators added, which is something Moog just started doing. I really love the Minimoogs. They're like my children.

Edgar Winter in a non-Frankenstein setting, with an ARP/Solina String Ensemble atop his Fender Rhodes 73, and a Hohner Clavinet D6 in the background. (© Len DeLessio)

18 EDGAR WINTER

FRANKENSYNTH

by Joe Bivona with Dominic Milano

Portions of this chapter originally appeared in the December 1976 issue of Keyboard *magazine.*

Edgar Winter, the white-haired, thunder-throated leader of such bands as White Trash and the Edgar Winter Group, was once described as a traditional Texas gentleman. Nowadays, that description might be a little hard to swallow given that in concert this "gentleman" can be seen bouncing across the stage with a synthesizer keyboard slung around his neck while pulling notes from everywhere in his four-octave vocal range—creating the kind of hard-hitting musical performance that turns good rock songs into full-blown, high-powered extravaganzas.

A native of Beaumont, Texas, Edgar grew up in a musical family. His first instruments were the ukulele and banjo. At the age of eight, Edgar, along with his older brother Johnny (who also played ukulele and banjo) appeared in talent shows and even on television. As Edgar recalls, "We used to do Everly Brothers things like 'Wake Up Little Susie,' but we weren't really serious about it." Winter's mother played classical piano, and Edgar used to listen to her for hours on end. He credits her as a big influence on his early playing.

By the time Edgar was 11, he was playing drums and piano in a rock band with his brother, who had by then graduated from ukulele to guitar. "Then I decided I wanted to play saxophone," Edgar recalls. "But Johnny said, 'I don't want no saxophone in my band.' So I started my own." The brothers were to be reunited in a band called Black Plague a few years later. They played in go-go clubs throughout the South, doing music by Wilson Pickett, Ray Charles, and Otis Redding—mostly rhythm and blues things, in which Winter found himself playing lots of saxophone and organ. Black Plague disbanded when, as Edgar puts it, "The car fell apart, and nobody wanted to buy a new one."

Winter then received his high school diploma through a correspondence course, and almost enrolled in a music college. But, on advice from friends attending the college, he joined a band instead. He explains, "The guys told me I could learn just as much playing in a band, and that suited me fine. I had always hated school because my poor eyesight made it hard to do the stuff you have to do."

Meanwhile, Edgar's brother had been signed to the Columbia label. And it wasn't long before Edgar was called in to play sax on Johnny's first album, *Johnny Winter And.* Steve Paul, who had signed Johnny to Columbia, began talking to Edgar about making an album of his own. After much deliberation and five weeks in the studio, Edgar's *Entrance* was released.

The album did little toward establishing Winter as a figure of note, so he set about forming a commercially oriented band. Pulling together some friends and local musicians, Winter launched an eight-piece group, White Trash. It received wide acceptance, and their first record, *White Trash*, far outsold *Entrance*. In 1972, a double-album set entitled *Roadwork* was released, a short time after the band had actually broken up. It provided Edgar with a firm foothold in the pop music world.

The next stage of Winter's development was the Edgar Winter Group, which at various times featured guitarists Ronnie Montrose and Rick Derringer, bassists Dan Hartman and Randy Hobbs, and drummer Chuck Ruff. Their first album, *They Only Come Out At Night*, included a tune called "Frankenstein," which was just tacked on to the end of the recording. Edgar didn't think it was commercial enough, yet shortly after the album was released, "Frankenstein" became a million-selling, number one hit. It showcased some of Edgar's first synthesizer work. The Edgar Winter Group released two more albums before biting the dust, *Shock Treatment* and *The Edgar Winter Group With Rick Derringer*.

Winter also has another solo album to his credit, *Jasmine Nightdreams*, and his next project, scheduled to begin shortly, is an album with the legendary disco team of Gamble and Huff.

What effect did the synthesizer have on your music?

I got my first synthesizer when White Trash broke up. I realized that it would never fit into a group like White Trash: We had been playing R&B, and I found that we were doing mostly unoriginal material. I didn't think that that was a very creative contribution to the world. I wanted to expand the music I was doing. The synthesizer helped shape the direction that I went in.

How did you get your first synthesizer?

I just went into Manny's Music Store in New York and said, "Hey, you got any synthesizers?" And the guy said, "Oh, sure." I bought an ARP 2600. I had heard synthesizers on records and thought that they sounded great. I wanted one. I had no idea what it was supposed to do, but I knew that I didn't want to start out on a small one and have to graduate to a larger one.

Did you take any lessons on the 2600?

I'm very impatient, so I took lessons from the guy that does work with Stevie Wonder. He gave me three lessons. He'd drill me and I felt like I was back in school. I was very technically minded in school, but in this instance I just wanted to learn as much as I could in a short period of time. I didn't want to hear about waveforms and such. I learned enough from that to take it on my own. I could understand what was going on pretty much, because I used to mess around with electronics when I was younger. I'd try to build radios, but I'd always burn my face or singe my hair or something. I wasn't totally in the dark about synthesizers; it wasn't so much like groping. I think that somebody who doesn't have preconceived ideas about something attacks it more objectively. They can come up with something more original. They don't have that much knowledge of convention. Somebody who has learned by a method can be limited. It's hard to break away from conventional things. I've always wanted to be the adventurer and figure things out for myself.

> "I've always wanted to be the adventurer and figure things out for myself."

Is that the way you approach learning the piano also?

It's always been the way I approach things. I had piano lessons for about three years. And I just played from memory because I couldn't see well enough to sight-read. I listened to my piano teacher and then played the passage that she played by ear. I've always had the ability to listen to somebody play a line and then sit down and play the same line. My piano teacher liked that. It made her job easy.

Did your piano training help you with the synthesizer?

Yeah. Knowledge of piano to me is basic to understanding music. It's the easiest thing to learn theory on. You can see the keyboard and visualize the concepts. It's not the same as if you had a guitar and someone pointed at the frets and said, "this makes a fourth." You can hear that, but you can't visualize it. I learned the most about music from playing in my brother's band, though.

Do you still utilize theory, consciously thinking, "I'm playing a sixth here, a fourth there"?

All the time. I set up control oscillators to raise the pitch a fourth, or lower it a fifth. All those kinds of things use theory. It's indirect, but it enters into things.

What about your actual approach to the synthesizer?

I think it is less technical than most people's because I like the flexibility of bending notes. In most cases I try to play it as expressively as possible, utilizing the mechanical functions that you have at your disposal. I intend to get more into new sounds—things that I haven't heard before. I haven't heard anything that's totally unfamiliar to my ear.

Then you're not into mimicking the sound of other instruments with the synthesizer?

I don't think that's what I want to do. But I love Tomita. I love listening to his strings. They don't sound exactly like strings—in fact, they sound a little better than life. Too real. Too perfect. There's no way you can use an electronic instrument to mimic acoustic instruments perfectly because it leaves out the human element of imperfection. With an electronic instrument you will always get the same overtone pattern. It's programmed. A human playing a violin still has that random element in it. I have written some studies for the piano that might lend themselves to an electronic orchestration. I'd like to try to out-do Tomita with them.

Have you ever attempted anything like that before?

The closest I've come to anything like that is dubbing five string parts on top of each other in "Miracle of Love" on the *Shock Treatment* album. After that I bought one of those Solina string units. I get tired of hearing it, though. They don't sound like strings. They just create the same impression—the atmosphere. I stopped dubbing string parts with the 2600 after I got the Solina, but the sound I've gotten from it has never been realistic enough for my purposes. When I do those etudes, I'll probably end up using real strings. What I really want to get into, however, is spacey, weird sounds.

You've stuck with the ARP 2600 synthesizer from the start?

Yes. I have eight of them that I carry around on the road with me. You can never tell. They're pretty stable, but we have to have a voltage regulator to make sure they stay in tune. I'm an intonation freak. If something is out of tune it really bothers me. That's the reason I have so many 2600s. They do strange things when they get moved around. I have to make sure that the units are turned on two hours before I get to the hall. We have someone watching the stage voltage at all times, because that can have an effect on the tuning too. There are better synthesizers than the 2600, but I haven't played any of them. I got used to the 2600 to the point of not having to look at the panel to know where everything is on it. I've wanted to get an ARP 2500 for a long time, but I've never had the time to spend learning a new piece of gear. It's been hit the road, get back, organize the material for the next record, hit the road again, and so on.

Do you use patch cords?

I use them in recording, but when I play live, it's just too difficult to switch them around. Since I wear my synthesizer keyboard around my neck, all the changes that I make have to be quick. What I usually do is have little strips of masking tape that I preset in the dressing room so that I can just push the sliders and they're where I want them. For recording, I experiment with the patches until I come up with something I like. I don't write them down, because it seems I can never get exactly the same sound twice. I like to treat each time I'm at the synthesizer as if it were the first.

Are your ARPs modified?

No. They're stock 2600s. The only real thing of technical interest that I'm involved with is a unit called the Cromulizer, which will convert the alto sax into a synthesizer triggering device. It has pads under the keys that read which ones are pressed and convert that knowledge into the proper control voltage. Then that feeds into the 2600. I think that synthesizers are still in their infant stages, but they're going to come into prominence pretty soon. Many of the components that are in synthesizers have been around ever since science fiction movies have been. They had oscillators and filters—all that stuff. It's just that someone came along, threw them all into one package, and called it a synthesizer. What I'm waiting for is for someone to come up with a pitch-to-voltage converter, so you can plug a guitar into a synthesizer. I don't think that the Walter Sear unit [the Synthesar] is very good. It doesn't work that well, and costs something like $15,000.

Do you still use a Univox electric piano?

I haven't used that for two years now. The main advantage of it was mobility. But one of the first shows I played with it slung around my neck was with Billy Preston. Right after that I saw him doing it. I was sort of taken aback by that. I don't suppose I could have patented the idea or anything, and I'm sort of flattered now. But I got tired of playing electronic-type keyboards. There's really very little expression to them. You just touch a key and there's a note. You can beat it as hard as you like and the same note will come out at the same volume. The Univox had a trashy sound too. We had to use a lot of equalization on it to get it to sound even fairly decent. The amps we used, Ampeg SVTs, didn't help much either. I'd much prefer feeding everything direct into the PA. It's much cleaner that way. The only thing I'll put around my neck anymore is the synthesizer keyboard. But I just started playing acoustic piano again. On the last tour I did with the Edgar Winter Group I was using a Steinway grand with a Helpinstill pickup. And on a later tour I did with my brother Johnny, I didn't have room onstage for a grand piano so I used a Rhodes. I've always liked them. They don't sound quite like a piano, but the sound they do have is nice. I only used the synthesizer on about three tunes with the Edgar Winter Group, when we played live. In the studio I'd use it for bass lines and things, but onstage "Frankenstein" was the main number I used it on.

What other kind of equipment did you use with the Edgar Winter Group?

I had two 2600s onstage. One was mobile, the other was on a stand. And

I had the Univox. As I said, the amps I used were Ampeg SVTs. Monster, 300-watt amps. I tried to keep the situation onstage as simple as possible. The drawback I have is that my vision restricts me. I can't possibly have a whole bank of equipment like Keith Emerson. Having to look at all that stuff would be too much of a problem. The lighting onstage is always changing, and that makes it kind of spacey as it is.

You mentioned that you had a Solina string synthesizer. Have you ever used a Mellotron or Chamberlin?

I have a Chamberlin. I used it on our very last album, *The Edgar Winter Group With Rick Derringer*. I used some flutes, 'cellos, vibes, and violins. That's a very sensitive unit, too. I was afraid to take it on the road, because I knew what would happen to it. But it's good. The tapes that go along with them are a problem. How can you possibly get good tapes? You tell some string player that he's going to record some notes for an instrument that's going to put him out of work, and he's not going to be very inclined to do that.

Has your saxophone playing influenced the way you play the synthesizer?

The saxophone is my favorite instrument, and it has definitely influenced my synthesizer style. I think that the more instruments you play, the better your overall concept of music will be. Since the instruments are technically different, I play things on sax that wouldn't lend themselves easily to keyboard and visa versa. I do transpose lines that I've figured out on one instrument to the other, though. When I first started playing synthesizer, I did things that you might normally hear played on other instruments. The difference would be that they had the synthesizer sound rather than their normal one. I think that's a more realistic approach for a beginning synthesist to take. I didn't want things to be overpowered by synthesizer. There are already people doing that—Keith Emerson being the most obvious example. I wanted to take a different approach. I didn't want to compete with those other people. I just wanted the synthesizer to be another voice in the group's texture.

A SELECTED EDGAR WINTER DISCOGRAPHY

Jazzin' the Blues
Winter Blues
The Real Deal
Not a Kid Anymore
Mission Earth
Standing on a Rock
The Edgar Winter Album
Jasmine Nightdreams
Shock Treatment
They Only Come Out at Night
Road Work
White Trash
Entrance

FOR MORE INFORMATION ON EDGAR WINTER, VISIT www.edgarwinter.com.

Do you change your keyboard style at all when you play with Rick Derringer as opposed to your brother or Ronnie Montrose?

No, what I play on keyboards is never affected by what the guitarists play. There are other things that I alter, like scat singing with Ronnie Montrose. That was more like a duel than a duet.

What are your impressions of what synthesists are doing today?

You hear synthesizer players all the time now, but you don't hear too many new sounds. On most things you could figure out what they're doing with little or no trouble. With an instrument that's about as unlimited as any instrument can be, I think there's more that can be done on the creative level. That's what I'm aiming for.

19 BERNIE WORRELL

BURNING DOWN THE HOUSE

by Robert L. Doerschuk

Portions of this chapter appeared in the September 1978 issue of Keyboard *magazine.*

According to the Gospel of P-funk, many of us are trapped in the zone of zero funkativity, never having enjoyed the blessings of supergroovalisticprosifunkstacation as dished out by the chocolate-coated freak in habit form and his cohorts. It is entirely possible that we might not even know what in the world this sad diagnosis means in plain, stale English. But there is nothing mysterious about this not-so-

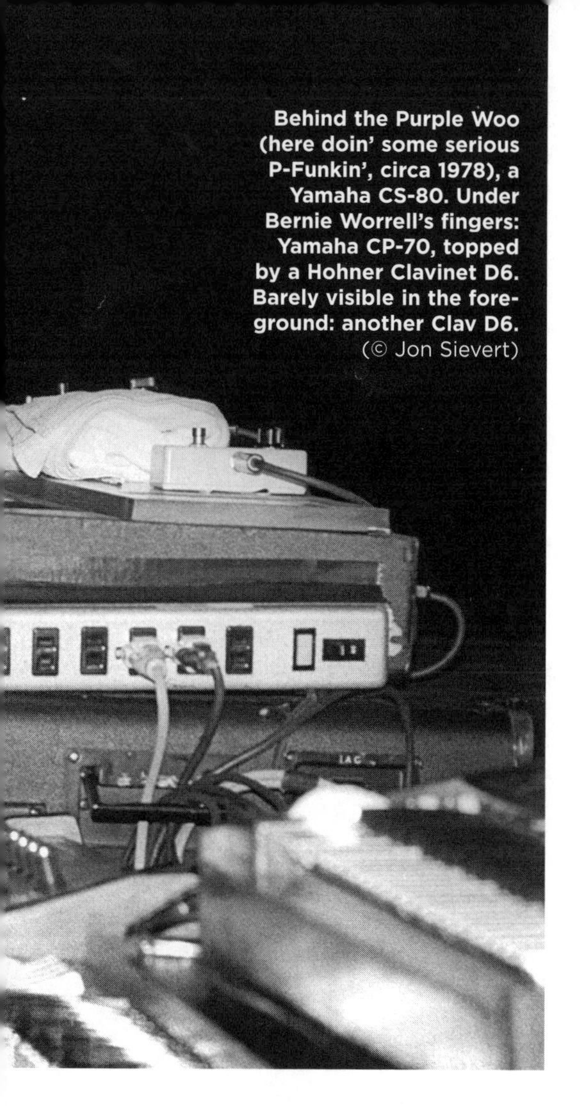

Behind the Purple Woo (here doin' some serious P-Funkin', circa 1978), a Yamaha CS-80. Under Bernie Worrell's fingers: Yamaha CP-70, topped by a Hohner Clavinet D6. Barely visible in the foreground: another Clav D6. (© Jon Sievert)

secret code as far as Parliament and its geepies and maggot brains—er, fans—are concerned. They know that in the end, it's all funkological anyway.

Anyone can listen to the music of Parliament, though, and hear the sharp, versatile multi-keyboard work of Bernie Worrell, a member of the band for the past ten years. The 35-year-old New Jerseyite has also played with Funkadelic, Bootsy and His Rubber Band, and other groups in the billowing musical family that centers around Parliament, exhibiting with each of them a combination of classically trained chops, street-bred soul, and carefully honed showmanship.

In some respects Parliament, with its boggling stage show, hip insider's lingo (a taste of which is offered above), and long hypnotic arrangements spiced with audience chants and electronic effects, is more a contemporary black music phenomenon than a band. Its roots run deep, though, reaching back 20 years to when singer/songwriter George Clinton founded a vocal group called the Parliaments that literally sang in a barbershop in Plainfield, New Jersey. Clinton later took the group to Detroit, where they affiliated themselves briefly with the Tamla/Motown label before scoring their first hit in 1967 with "(I Just Wanna) Testify," on the now defunct Revilot label.

While Clinton was convening the Parliaments, his childhood friend Worrell was busy getting his own music together. Bernie's mother had been his earliest musical inspiration. "She sang in church choirs," he remembers, "but she also took private voice lessons and learned some classical pieces, just out of her own interest. Like they say, she had a gift. She could pick out notes on the piano too, so I used to go to the keyboard every day and practice a scale she'd taught me. She observed me, and pretty soon she started wondering if maybe there was something there."

Bernie was only three-and-a-half years old when his mother took him to his first formal piano lesson. "The teacher's name was Mrs. Adelaide Waxwood," he noted, "and she is now my godmother. She kept saying, 'Oh, he's too young for lessons,' but her husband, who was principal of a grammar school, convinced her after about two or three weeks to take me as a student and try me out. So she did, and that was how I got started."

It didn't take long for Worrell to master the fundamentals of the instrument. He gave his first concert at the age of four, playing 40 pieces by John Thompson. After moving with his family from his Long Branch hometown to Plainfield four years later, Bernie continued his studies with Faye Barnaby Kent, a former pupil of the composer Edward MacDowell. Two years later the ten-year-old pianist made his orchestral debut with the National Symphony Orchestra in Washington, D.C.

"It was a child prodigy thing," Worrell explains. "I started out playing Schubert *Impromptus*, a little Bach, Beethoven sonatas, and a lot of Mozart—I liked him, but I can never remember the opus numbers. And of course there were the Hanon studies. Classical music was all I played. I knew church music, because I'd played for Baptist church teas and backed my mother up when she sang at funerals, but I had no idea what R&B or rock and roll were. I heard bits and pieces over the radio, but I was never allowed to listen to too much of it. I didn't even know who Elvis Presley was!"

Presley's music was what finally moved Worrell to broaden his own tastes. "All the kids were raving about Presley being on *The Ed Sullivan Show*," he laughs, "so I watched it, and when I finally heard him sing I went, 'Oh!' It just happened like that, and soon I started getting into different kinds of music."

Although he began listening to rock more regularly at that point, Bernie continued to pursue his classical studies as well. During his freshman year in high school he started taking private lessons once or twice a week with Olegna Fuschi, a student of Rosina Lhevinne, along with theory and harmony instruction from John Noge, a professor at the New York College of Music. Thanks to this training, Worrell was able to skip first-semester harmony and theory when he entered the New England Conservatory of Music in Boston.

Bernie never finished his studies there; his funds ran dry half a semester before graduation when his father died. But his move to Boston still had a decisive effect on his music, because it allowed him to follow his own interests more freely, without the immediate conservative influence of his family. "I went wild," he states. "Everything I'd kept inside just busted out. I stayed away from school and started hanging out. Boston was where I started playing in clubs. I got myself a job with the house band at Basin Street. You know Jim Nash, the football player with the New England Patriots? That was his club, and I backed up a lot of people there, like the Tavares, who were Chubby and the Turnpikes back then—I was with them for about two years—and [singers] Tammi Terrell, Freddie Scott, and Valerie Holiday, who is with the Three Degrees now. She didn't have any vocal training, so I helped her out and coached her. She also won the Miss Tan Boston contest; they called it 'Tan' back then," he adds with a laugh.

> "It's just too slow for me sometimes to work together with a group in cutting a record."

Thanks to this kind of experience, Worrell was able to find work soon after leaving the Conservatory. For more than three years he toured with singer Maxine Brown, a stint that came to an end when his New Jersey friend George Clinton stepped back into his life. "I was in college when 'Testify' came out," he recalls. "George's voice had changed slightly, but I finally picked up on it and recognized him on the record. Anyway, I was in Bermuda with Maxine years later when I got a long distance call; the operator said it was from George Clinton at the Apollo Theater in New York. The message was: 'Bernie, come on up. We're ready.' At that time Maxine was on her downward trend—she was just doing nightclubs—so I switched over to George and played my first gig with the group at the Apollo."

Before joining Parliament—or Funkadelic, as it was called then—Worrell had performed on only two keyboards. In addition to the piano, he had had some experience with the Hammond B-3 organ while playing in churches as a child, going back to it during his stint at Basin Street. Shortly after becoming a part of the P-Funk organization, Bernie bought a Hohner D6 Clavinet, and it remains the senior member of his keyboard family. On the road with Parliament today he carries, along with the Clavinet, an ARP String Ensemble, an ARP Pro Soloist, a Minimoog modified to have a two-voice capability, an RMI electric piano, a Yamaha CS-80 polyphonic synthesizer, and a Yamaha CP-70 electric grand piano with a stereo output. Worrell has also been known to play the melodica on occasion, using it as a portable practice keyboard on tour and to provide harmonica-like effects on "I'd Rather Be With You," from Bootsy and the Rubber Band's album *Stretchin' Out*.

"I've had most of my instruments a long time," Bernie says. "Stevie Wonder bought the first RMI in Detroit, and they say I got the second one. I still take it on the road, but it got dropped a while back and it's got to be repaired. The CS-80 takes the place of the old Hammond, which we don't lug around anymore. And when I played on [singer] Alice Cooper's Yamaha electric grand in his band's rehearsal room, I said, 'I've got to have one of these!'

A SELECTED BERNIE WORRELL DISCOGRAPHY

AS A LEADER
Improvisczario
Free Agent—A Spaced Odyssey
Blacktronic Science
Funk of Ages
All the Woo in the World

WITH FUNKADELIC
Free Your Mind and Your Ass Will Follow
America Eats Its Young
Standing on the Verge of Getting It On
Tales of Kidd Funkadelic
One Nation Under a Groove
Uncle Jam Wants You

WITH PARLIAMENT
Up for the Down Stroke
Chocolate City
Mothership Connection
The Clones of Dr. Funkenstein
Funkentelechy vs. the Placebo Syndrome
Motor Booty Affair

WITH TALKING HEADS
The Name of This Band Is Talking Heads
Speaking in Tongues
Stop Making Sense

FOR MORE INFORMATION ON BERNIE WORRELL, VISIT www.bernieworrell.com.

"The only defect with the Yamaha is that it goes terribly out of tune," he continues. "I've had trouble with its tuning on the road ever since we got it. The low octaves go way out, so we've tried to find a way of modifying it. We moved that strip of ribbon that's on the soundboard to beneath the big bass strings at the low end, but it still went out of tune whenever the temperature changed. So we have to rely on getting a piano tuner in each town, and some of them are really bad. They'll tell me they've tuned it, but since I've got perfect pitch, it still won't sound right when I come in and check it. It gets touchy, but we're doing the best we can right now."

One characteristic of Bernie's approach to the synthesizer is his use of unusual effects to complement Clinton's vocals and punctuate the insistent beat laid down by the band. On the tune "Bop Gun (Endangered Species)" [from *Funkentelechy vs. the Placebo Syndrome*], for example, he sets his Minimoog to a short attack and decay, and a low cutoff frequency, with the resonance set high, to create the blipping sound of the bop gun—which was invented, incidentally, by Dr. Funkenstein to zap Sir Nose d'Voidoffunk, purveyor of the infamous Placebo Syndrome, according to Parliament lore. Worrell's Pro Soloist spices up another catchy number, "Night of the Thumpasorus Peoples" [from *Mothership Connection*], with a subterranean growl that seems to plumb the lowest depths of musical perception.

Some of the more standard sounds frequently imitated by synthesists—such as big band parts—are actually played by Parliament's brass and reed section, the Horny Horns, in arrangements written out by Worrell, leaving him free to explore more abstract effects or to play string lines. Eventually he would like to see the latter job taken over by live string players as well. "I've been playing the strings myself," he points out, "but there's nothing like the sound of the authentic wood string instruments. I get tired of that ARP String Ensemble. You can hear that synthesized quality, and sometimes it bothers me, because how can metal sound better or richer than wood? I thought of using a Mellotron instead, but it's a fragile instrument and the tapes would just get messed up on the road. I've heard a lot of keyboard players who are down on it, so I didn't even try to get one. I'll really appreciate it when I can start doing some more string arrangements."

Despite his interest in off-beat keyboard sounds, Worrell doesn't rely heavily on effect pedals. In fact, he only uses two devices, an MXR flanger and a Morley Power-Wah, and both are employed on just one instrument, the Clavinet. "You don't need the pedals on synthesizers," he explains. "I did have an MXR phase shifter that I used on the String Ensemble one time, but I didn't like it. Your effects are already there with the Yamaha Polyphonic, the Minimoog, or whatever. I just like to keep the Yamaha grand straight, like a concert grand, so the Clavinet is the one that gets it all!"

Worrell feels that the changes he has seen Parliament go through over the years have reflected trends in popular music to some extent. "Back in the old days our music was a lot funkier than now," he observes. "It was less structured, with some heavy rock overtones. We'd just go into a chant thing and start to jam. The costumes were a little freakier then too, and George was more into what they'd call vulgar language—that was when he used to strip onstage, and he wore a freaky haircut. It was wild then, but it's changed. You can't do that now, not the way we were doing it before. We're still not a conservative band, but we've disguised it.

"I'm into the costume thing myself," Bernie laughs. "At tonight's gig I wore a gorilla mask I bought in a novelty store. It was the first time I wore a mask with the band, but I didn't dig it, because I don't like having my ears covered and not being able to see when I'm playing. At the beginning of the show I wore it for maybe ten minutes, and then I found myself tipping it up on top of my head. Our show is still evolving with us, but I'm really just concerned with the music, with keeping it together, making sure that everything is rolling smoothly, with everybody in tune, and nobody rushing ahead or falling behind me. We like to think of ourselves as a good rock and roll funk band, with tinges of jazz and classical coming through from me and now from Junior—that's Walter Morrison of the Ohio Players. He's been playing his own Minimoog and Clavinet with us on tour, and I think he's going to be joining the thing too."

The influx of fresh personnel into the Parliament family is a major reason why Worrell has stayed with the group for so long. The staleness he felt in other areas of music has been continually offset by the new faces, new bands, and new ideas that steadily flow in and out of the P-Funk community, erasing every trace of the dreaded Placebo Syndrome. "It used to bother me that we played a lot of one-chord stuff, or songs without many changes," Bernie says, "but that was true maybe three or four albums ago. The tunes now have more chords, more patterns and structures. We're cutting a lot more ballads now, because we're branching out with the other acts we have, like the Brides of Funkenstein [backup singers], so it gets more interesting at times.

"When Parliament is not on the road, the members can go out with one of our other groups and help them out, or do studio work," he continues. "There's a variety of things you can do. Lately both George and myself have been going out on the road helping Bootsy [Collins, bassist] and his band because he's having a few problems with his sound company, although I don't necessarily want to go out on the road right now myself. If I did, it would be within the confines of Parliament; my act would go on first, and then I'd change and come right back on with the group!"

Whether working on his own project or with Parliament, Bernie prefers to do his studio playing alone, without the pressures of dealing with other musicians. "It's just too slow for me sometimes to work together with a group in cutting a record," he explains. "I don't have to bother with the attitudes or the egos that way. When I record with Parliament, I go down with George, Gary [Shider, guitarist], or whoever it is, to help put the rhythm track together. Then most of the time everybody will cut out, and I'll come in and do all the overdubs to fill it in here, or help it out there. At times I'll do the rhythm track with the other guys, so it's about half and half, but I like to come in and overdub after everything else is done."

From his vantage point of commercial success with Parliament, Bernie can now look back over his career, from his early days in classical music on to the present, and be satisfied with the directions he has chosen to follow. "Your technique does go down over the years from playing rock," he admits, "and my mother is kind of disappointed that I didn't become a classical musician. I'm glad that I had that kind of training; I think everyone who plays keyboards should go through it, although not everybody is going to. I liked classical music, but I couldn't go for how they would talk about rock and roll or R&B back then. They put classical music up on a pedestal. Well, the hell with that! Music is music, and that's what it all boils down to."

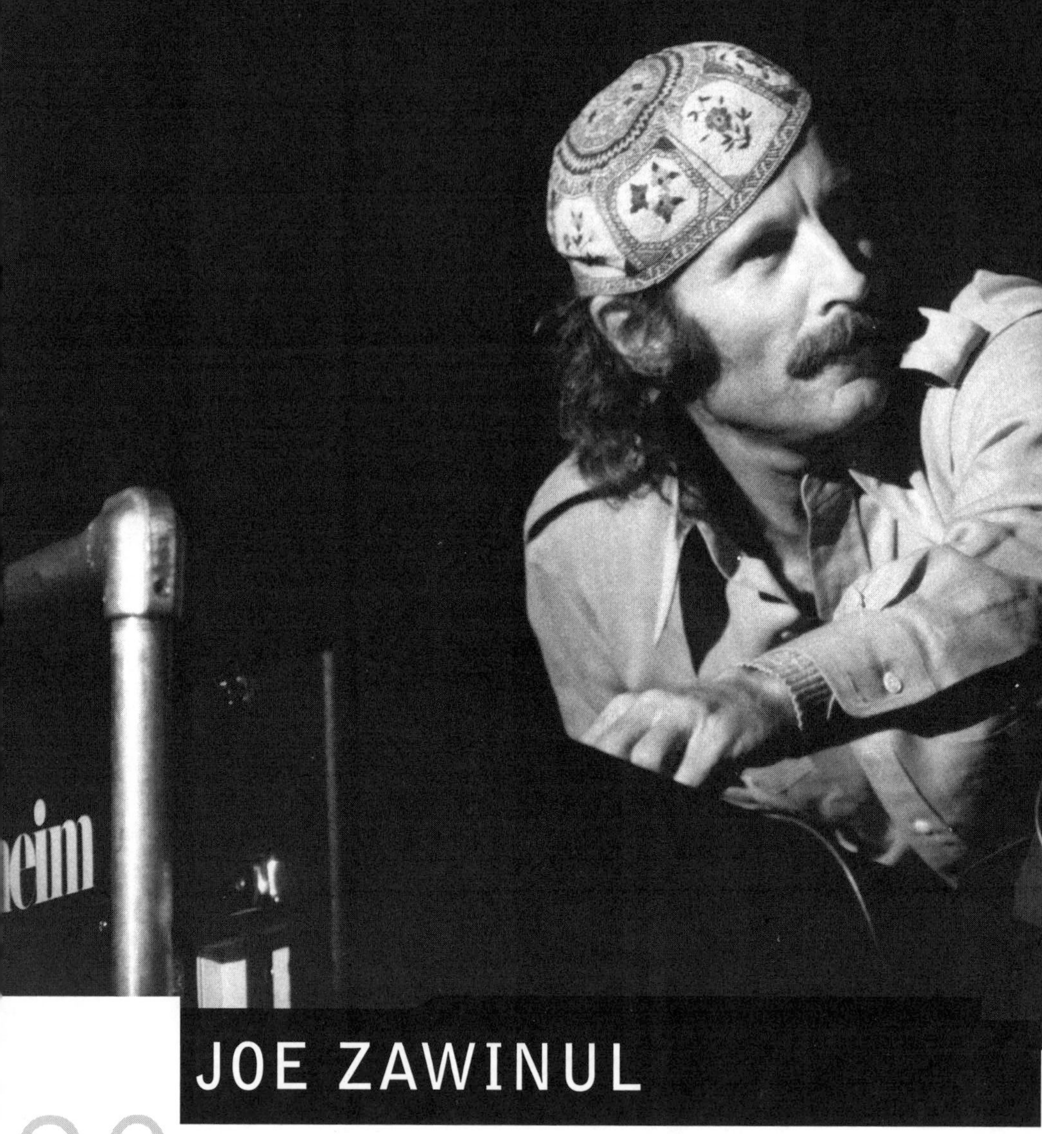

20 JOE ZAWINUL

SYNTH STORIES

by Greg Armbruster

Portions of this chapter originally appeared in the March 1984 issue of Keyboard *magazine.*

Unpredictable as the weather itself, Weather Report has been surprising and exciting audiences around the world since 1971 with their original, innovative music. More than just a band, Weather Report is a family that speaks a universal musical language. They celebrate a philosophy that embraces life—exuberant, moving,

Heavy weather indeed: Joe Zawinul makes his Oberheim 8-Voice do the talking during a mid-'70s performance by Weather Report. (Michael Ochs Archive /Getty Images)

and fun. Band members, like family members, have grown and left to seek their own musical fortunes, but founding fathers Josef Zawinul and Wayne Shorter have remained, and Weather Report continues to evolve.

Zawinul is a musician of the world, who has absorbed the cultures, played the instruments, and expressed the feelings of many countries in his music. Born in Vienna in 1932, he started his musical studies at the Vienna Conservatory when he was seven. "I had the good fortune to grow up in Vienna, where everybody plays everything," he remarks. "My parents were great folk singers, and I always played music they could sing with. I've been an accordion player most of my life, and I liked it because of the many sounds. The accordion is the original synthesizer."

During the war, Zawinul received a scholarship to continue his education. He later formed his own trio and played for Special Service clubs in France and Germany. He also achieved widespread popularity in Austria leading his own quartet on a radio series from 1954 to '58. Moving to New York in 1959, he landed a job with Maynard Ferguson's band, but his first real break came with the chance to accompany Dinah Washington. He toured with her from October '59 to March '61. Leonard Feather summed up this collaboration in his "Giants of Jazz" column: "No pianist without a thorough feeling for Afro-American music could have satisfied Dinah, but their relationship was mutually stimulating: Joe was qualified by virtue of a rare combination of intelligence, technique, sensitivity, and soul."

Julian "Cannonball" Adderley hired Zawinul in '61, and together they generated an excitement that made jazz history. Disc jockey Rodney Jones described the quintet's music in his liner notes for the album *Mercy, Mercy, Mercy*: "They played like blue smoke. They played like sweet preachin'. They played like nobody was ever going to go without honey butter again!" Zawinul's compositions, such as "Walk Tall," "74 Miles Away," "Country Preacher," and "Mercy, Mercy, Mercy," which became a jazz standard, played an important role in the success of Cannonball's band. Near the end of this association, Joe recorded several albums with Miles Davis, using electric keyboards, including *In a Silent Way*, *Bitches Brew*, and *Live-Evil*. In the liner notes on Zawinul's first solo album, *Zawinul*, Miles commented that "Joe sets up the musicians so that they have to play like they do, in order to fit the music like they do. In order to fit this music you have to be cliché-free. In order to write this type of music, you have to be free inside of yourself."

In 1971, Zawinul, saxophonist Wayne Shorter, and bassist Miroslav Vitous formed Weather Report, with drummer Alphonze Mouzon and percussionist Airto Moreira. Clive Davis, then president of Columbia Records, described their first album as, "a soundtrack for the mind, the imagination, for opening up heads and hearts. Weather Report is not only about feelings and emotions, it is also about human reality." For more than a dozen years, Weather Report has recorded and travelled the earth, bringing their rare brand of musical artistry to millions. Their sound has always been characterized by energetic rhythms, lyrical melodic lines, and fresh creativity. *Keyboard's* first interview with Josef Zawinul appeared in our September '77 issue. Since then, Weather Report's personnel, instruments, and music have changed: bassist Jaco Pastorius and drummer Peter Erskine have left the band, programmable polyphonic synthesizers and drum machines have become standard equipment, and Zawinul's compositions have evolved beyond classification. He recently sat down with us and allowed us to probe the inspirations and processes of his music.

How closely related is your compositional style to the way you play?

I would say it must be exactly the same, because I compose by playing. I could always sit down and play for a long time. Rather than playing eight-note phrases or something, I could put together a whole piece of music with a long thought. Then I might return at the end to certain things without really thinking about it. It's more of a natural construction. Concentration is what it really is. I'm not thinking of construction, or anything—I just let it move. When it is done, I write it down note for note without changing anything.

What inspires you to write a tune?

I'm inspired by sounds. When I program my instruments, I find a sound that I like and out of that sound comes a tune. I switch on the tape recorder and play. I'll jot down the tape number, the day, and maybe the program of the sound. I have maybe 2,000 cassettes full of music, much of which is usable. If I need some music, I just listen and write down what I want. Very often I could have a hipper harmony or something, but I don't do that; I let it be, the way it happened. You see, these tapes are more than sketchbooks; the only thing I do is edit them, because all the compositions are fairly long. Wayne works differently. He writes everything right from the beginning and works with the form. I'm an instinctive composer.

Don't you analyze your music after you write it down?

Yeah, that's the fun; and often I'm surprised. "Damn," I say, "There's some real thinking going on!" But it's not thinking; maybe the feeling has a certain amount of intelligence. Like I said, I'm hardly aware of the way I'm composing; it's a talent, a lucky break.

After you've written out your compositions, how do you score them for the rest of the band?

That's what I do with all these instruments. I get my sounds all ready—like I said, the sound is the inspiration—and then it's already orchestrated. All I have to do is write down what I've already played. I may want a soprano sound or a woodwind sound, so I have Wayne play it that way. He's so versatile on his instruments that he can make the soprano sax sound like an oboe or even a bassoon. But the music itself, the melody notes, will never be changed. Sometimes when we perform it, I might change a harmony here and there, but when we play it for the very first time, there will not be a note changed from the original improvisation. Also, when we first record it, there's not going to be a chord changed, or a melody, or a rhythm, but everybody is going to add a little something. We work on it during rehearsals and there are additions being made. There's got to be enough room for somebody to really express himself. Wayne has been a great contributor by playing beautiful solo lines when he is improvising; for that you need great musicians.

How would you describe your compositional style?

I can't define exactly what it is, but I know what it is not—it is not "licks." I'm a melodist, and licks I don't play. My music is linear, with many lines, and they can go up or down or whatever, but they're all lines in their own right. They're melodies—melodic melodies. The rhythm is moving and the harmony is sometimes beautiful and sometimes abstract. I guess all my music has a certain similarity. It doesn't all sound the same, but there are favorite ingredients, like introductions. I like introductions, but I don't often like a bridge. In "Young and Fine" [from *Mr. Gone*] there were three bridges after the melody. But there again, I find this out later. I don't know this while I'm composing. I'm involved with the sound and I just play.

How do you organize your material for a new album?

Before we decide to record or go on tour, Wayne comes over and I play maybe ten songs for him. He plays what he has, and slowly we work ourselves through a lot to a little. We find a common denominator: What could we use for the album to be different from the last album? It must have a certain accessibility, which has nothing to do with making concessions.

When you record, do you play as if it were a live performance rather than overdubbing all the parts?

Right; you have to have that feeling. Here and there you can overdub a solo, and that's all right. But there has to be that spontaneity—that factor has to be in there. When I play an accompaniment in the studio during a Wayne solo, I concentrate on that. This very accompaniment is giving the whole tone to a tune, the way those lines move. I'm not trying to get too busy with it; I'm just laying it down, so that in a live performance I can figure out a way of doing it again while adding something else. It's a lot of inspiration right in the studio, and the improvisations we do are done right there. Leave it like that—don't touch it! That's our recipe for success.

Then you don't use any studio "magic," like equalizers, limiters, or reverb, after you record?

You have to, sometimes. But I feel the best way to do it is to record it the way it's going to be. If you already have your echo and reverb, then it makes you play differently. If you do that, then I think it's easier to get it right on tape. But we do some fooling around in the studio, too. On "Milky Way" [from *Weather Report*] I silently held a chord down on the piano and had Wayne play an arpeggio of the same chord, blowing his saxophone right inside the piano at the soundboard. The tape recorder was started on the echo at the end of the sound, not when he was playing. We played different chords and edited them together. It was definitely not magic; it was an idea I had a long time ago. I'm going to go back to this eventually. I'm going to lay my piano on its side, put bass drum pedals in different positions on the sides, and use the acoustic piano as a soundboard; it has the greatest sound body of any instrument.

How do you create acoustic instrument sounds with your synthesizers?

That's something you either can or can't do. I don't think certain things are learnable. I think everybody plays like what they hear. I know what I want to hear, and I know I can duplicate that sound. Also, there's a certain way you have to play those sounds. I was a violin player, so I know the nature of how to play it. I have heard non-violin players try to play the string sound on my instruments, and they never get it. I have a fantastic string sound on the [Sequential Circuits] Prophet-5, unequaled by any other synthesizer. But there's a certain way of playing a violin;

with the right hand there's the gravity factor, and with the left hand you have vibrato. That's what I'm thinking about when I record a string line. Or the clarinet: how is it being played? How do you get that sound? What is the anatomy? How is the body of the viola vibrating? You can understand that scientifically, but the moment you feel in your inner ear how it's supposed to sound, then I think you are able to be a synthesist. I think there are very few synthesists; I have heard very few things on synthesizers where I have said, "Hey, this person can feel what's happening with these instruments."

> "When I program my instruments, I find a sound that I like and out of that sound comes a tune."

Which synthesists do you admire?

I like [Isao] Tomita, especially what he used to do in the beginning. That was inspiring to me. Stevie Wonder had some things I was interested in. I know Jan Hammer can play. I just heard a thing he did with Al Di Meola, but the music sounds plastic—and the guy's a hell of a musician. There are a lot of good musicians out there playing synthesizers, but there are very few, I think, who can really get the essence of the music on those instruments.

How have the changes in your instruments affected your music?

Enormously, because the imagination doesn't have any limitations, and now that the technical aspects have been improved, everything is possible. The more they get these instruments together, the easier it's going to look, even if it is difficult to play. The playing itself, the music, is always going to remain difficult, especially if you want to do it great and be relaxed every night, with all the fire in there. For me, it's like being a drummer, only playing drums with melody notes.

Tell us how your keyboard collection has changed over the years.

For a long time I hadn't had anything new except for the two ARP 2600s, but they're just too slow for today's musical demands because you had to do a lot of moving of patch cords. What I always liked about them was the way they were coupled together, so that I had six oscillators instead of three. On "Scarlet Woman" [from *Mysterious Traveller*], the melody chords would have been impossible to play without coupling the 2600s and de-tuning the oscillators. Then the same company came up with the Quadra, which had an excellent bass sound and lead voices that had touch-sensitive detuning. I also had plenty of Rhodes electric pianos. Then I got my first Prophet-5, which was modified to hold 160 programs. Then I got a second Prophet-5 with 120 programs. I had a Korg Trident, which was nice, but it broke down after a while and I quit using it. I played for years with the same instruments, and by having a lot of programs I made it sound like there were more instruments. I also had the Yamaha electric grand piano onstage for a while, plus a little kalimba and some other percussion instruments. But early in '83 I replaced the Rhodes electric piano with the [Rhodes] Chroma, which I now use for solo playing. I've got some really hip solo sounds on it, which are not guitar sounds but have the strength or the power of a rock and roll guitar, only with more possibility for flexibility in the sound itself. It's a fine instrument. I can invert the keyboard the way I did with the 2600s, but I don't have to use patch cords. The newest thing I have is the Emulator, and I think it's the greatest instrument around. They have some pretty good sounds on disk, like the French horn and the timpani. But I've recorded 30 or 40 different sounds on my own, including Wayne's sax and an acoustic piano sound that's incredible.

You mentioned earlier that the Prophet-5 had the best string sounds even better than the Emulator?

Yes, and I'll tell you why. On the Emulator I can get a solo string sound that's real good. You can record a solo sound that's going to be as total as anything you ever want to have. But the moment I play a chord and there are four or five voices moving, it loses it, and I don't know why. You don't program the Emulator; you feed it the sound and there it is, exactly what you put in there. With the Prophet-5 I can program the sound while playing chords, and then I can tweak it—that's what I like about the Prophets. I've programmed lightning and thunder on the Prophet which beats even the most expensive Synclavier; they can all pack up. I've done a few things on the Fairlight and the Yamaha GS-1, and it's all valid if you use them in a meaningful context. However, I don't think they're as flexible as I want them to be. I played the DX7 for a couple of nights in Japan and I really like it. But if I had a choice between the DX7 and the Chroma, I'd take the Chroma. I think Yamaha has some really good things, but I can't deal with all the sounds they've got—after a while, they get stale.

Doesn't that happen with any sound after a time?

Sure; all of a sudden the sound doesn't ring a bell in your eardrum anymore. It's wasted, so I put another sound in its place. I have 160 programs in one of my Prophets, and it would be very difficult for me to totally detach myself from 130 of them. They have something that I haven't gotten tired of yet. It's like going on the road somewhere and you take 20 books. You're only going to read one, but you don't know which one, so you take them all. When I go on the road I've got so many books with me that I usually don't read a single one; but if I didn't have them, I would go crazy.

Are any of your keyboards connected together?

I've hooked up the two Prophets so that I can play on the keyboard of

Prophet number one and some random note of the chord will also sound on Prophet number two, which has a different program. The random melody on Prophet number two inspires new improvisations. I also do a lot of things with different tunings, like the inverted keyboard. The *F#* and the *C* are the same, but the *B* becomes *C#*, the *A* becomes the *D#*, and so on. I came up with the melody for "Black Market" [from *Black Market*] through this kind of playing. I have a special keyboard that Jim Swanson built that controls the Oberheim Eight-Voice modules. Each oscillator is set on a different note—I just make up a scale, and each time I hit one key repeatedly, I get the next note of the scale. For example, if I hit a *C* eight times, each time it becomes another note. This allows me to do all these octave jumps with only one hand. Then, by being inspired with this setup, I get this sound in my ears and begin to do the same thing on a normal keyboard. It just opens one door after another. But when you're performing with this, you have to think fast. You've got to know exactly what you're doing; otherwise you'll run off the track somewhere.

So you have to orchestrate not only your music but your moves for each hand as well.

When I start getting the set together, it's got many, many moves. On one tune there might be 20 to 25 moves, and they all have to be done sleight-of-hand; otherwise you look like a clown up there onstage. And in the beginning years, it was like that; I had to move so much because there was no other way—I only had the two ARP 2600s. As new instruments were developed, I always tried to find shortcuts, like a foot pedal or a switch. Now, all my instruments are programmable, and I write down all the programs that I have to go through. And then, slowly, I just learn it. Sometimes the first few concerts are a little rough, but then, when it becomes a part of me, I really have fun with it—it's like having a football play all set up and you know exactly where to spot yourself when the pass comes. I know when that last note sounds and I'm already playing the next one, with another sound ready after that.

Which song requires the greatest number of moves or program changes?

For a long time, "Birdland" [from *Heavy Weather*] was a hard one. It's always been interesting, because it's one of the hardest tunes I've ever had to play as far as hand independence is concerned. When we did it in the studio, I overdubbed all the parts, even the solo; but then I realized what I had done. You don't want a record that can beat your performance or not be able to play the tune onstage. So I had to really practice "Birdland" to get everything to sound like the record, and it wasn't easy. I have to switch octaves in unison, operate the foot pedals for the Oberheim, play the entire accompaniment with the left hand while the right hand plays a different rhythm. I have to play all the counter-melodies in the solo, and for a while that was a hell of a challenge for me. Another hard tune was "Volcano for Hire" [from *Weather Report*]. My right hand has to move together with Wayne's playing and the left hand is the orchestra. The right hand is in a totally different aspect of time, so you have to somewhat divide your head.

Couldn't you learn that kind of technique just playing the piano?

I don't think so, but I'll tell you one thing: It's made me a much better piano player.

Where have you used the vocoder?

I've done a lot of things with it over the years. The whole melody on "8:30" was a vocoder melody. And, for instance, on "Procession" the didgeridoo-type sound is all done with the vocoder, as well as the "chipmunk" voices on "Two Lines" [also from *Procession*].

You've described your accompaniment style as setting a tone for the tune and not being too busy. How would you describe your soloing style?

It's definitely in the chordal framework and more or less a variation on a theme. It's a melody, like a violin solo with a symphony orchestra, but it's an instinctive thing. Originally, I play all the melodies for my tunes. Wayne is the saxophone player and he is the lead voice, so I have him play the melody. I feel he is performing the original improvisation. If we are interpreting original improvisations, then it's often not necessary to do a whole lot of re-improvising. The framework, melodies, bass lines, and main rhythms are like the original improvised versions, but in concert, everyone is free to add something. Sometimes we play a tag at the end, and during the tag I might play an improvised solo. But there are different ways

A SELECTED JOE ZAWINUL DISCOGRAPHY

AS A LEADER
My People
Stories of the Danube
Faces & Places
Di-a-lects

WITH THE ZAWINUL SYNDICATE
Vienna Nights: Live at Joe Zawinul's Birdland
Black Water

WITH WEATHER REPORT
Forecast: Tomorrow
Heavy Weather
Mysterious Traveller
Mr. Gone
8:30
Procession
Tale Spinnin'

WITH MILES DAVIS
Bitches Brew
In a Silent Way
Live-Evil

FOR MORE INFORMATION ON THE LATE JOE ZAWINUL, VISIT www.zawinulmusic.com.

to play a solo. On our new album, *Domino Theory*, I play a solo on a ballad called "Blue Sound, Note Three" where I change the programs in rhythm, rather than playing everything on the keys. For the concert finale, Wayne and I improvise a duet at the end of this song, where I use the French horn and the tuned timpani sounds on the Emulator. My left hand is playing the two Prophets through the keyboard of Prophet number one, while my right hand is playing counter-melodies with Wayne. On "Molasses Run" [from *Procession*], each Oberheim module has a different bandwidth as well as a different pitch, so the solo line is always changing timbre. This kind of thinking keeps your mind moving. I don't know what's happening when I play some of these things; I don't know what might come out, and that's the fun of it. I invert my keyboards, change the tuning, set up different scales—sometimes all these things are going on every note. I like to surprise myself; that is my guarantee to surprise others.

Do you use the pitch-bender to articulate your solo lines?

Hardly; I don't use it on the end of every phrase. It seems like most people do it when they're on the highest note, like guitar players. I don't like that too much. If you're a synthesist, you're not a guitar player. If you have a heavy background, you have to have something that stands out, like a guitar, but you have to measure this so that you have a balance, a certain taste. I feel that what a guitar player can do for me, I can do better for the band. If I want a guitar sound, I can certainly get it.

Did you play the accordion on the *Procession* album?

Yes, on "Plaza Real" I played an accordion that Jaco [Pastorius] had given to me for my 49th or 50th birthday. The melody is actually played by Jose Rossy on a little concertina that I bought in Spain. The shop was on a little side street off the Plaza Real in Barcelona. I had him try it one day, and the first time he grabbed it he could kind of play it. So I said, "Here, you got it!" He plays the melody of "Plaza Real" on it and I join him on accordion. Then Wayne comes in whistling and I play some counter lines.

You've collected quite a number of percussion instruments from around the world. Other than using these on your albums, how has travelling the world affected your music?

If you're an open person, you learn wherever you go. I'm not that much interested in other people's music, but I am interested in other people's behavior. For instance, when we went to Torino [Italy], I went to the marketplace. I walked around in the street, listening to people arguing and selling, and watching their reactions. And sometimes you hear this sound, or spectrum; you don't hear individual voices, you hear it all together and it makes something. You get the character of a people rather than the character of their music. I hardly ever listen to music of other cultures; I did this 30 years ago. But I do pay attention to people—how they walk and talk. There is a certain walk they have in Japan that is different from the walk in Yugoslavia. It is the rhythm of a people. In "Procession," you hear that walk in the bass drum; that's the human walk.

What are you doing to improve yourself musically?

I'm playing other instruments and learning more about them. I'm also learning a lot from my three kids; they play and have ideas. They bring records in; otherwise I would never listen to anybody. I've heard the Talking Heads and other bands, and I appreciate some of their music. If somebody can do good music, they should do more of it and let me enjoy it too. Everyone should play what they feel like playing. I think that's the only way it means something. I don't like it when too many people play the same way; that's not happening. When you hear somebody playing what they want to play, that is an expression of their personality. I couldn't do my music any other way. I've played music for people my entire life. If you always play for people and enjoy what you're doing, you'll learn to be an entertainer. People will see that you enjoy what you're doing and they'll enjoy it too. I don't want to sound like I'm bragging, but I do like all my music for what it is—sometimes simple, sometimes complex. Most of all, it's fun; that's what I like most about it. One cannot ask for more.